Rock Vegas

LIVE MUSIC EXPLODES
IN THE NEON DESERT

"Music gives soul to the universe,
wings to the mind, flight to
the imagination, and life to everything."
—Plato

"Music breaks down
the barriers people erect."
—Pete Townsend

"Music is escapism,
because life is so damn hard."
—Bob Lefsetz

Rock Vegas

LIVE MUSIC EXPLODES
IN THE NEON DESERT

PAT CHRISTENSON

HUNTINGTON PRESS
LAS VEGAS, NEVADA

Rock Vegas
Live Music Explodes in the Neon Desert

Published by
  Huntington Press
  3665 Procyon Street
  Las Vegas, NV 89103
  Phone (702) 252-0655
  e-mail: books@huntingtonpress.com

Copyright © 2017, Pat Christenson

ISBN: 978-1-944877-05-7
$19.95us

Production & Design: Laurie Cabot
Photo Spread: Pat Christenson, Tom Donoghue, Erik Kabik/The Joint, Gary Naseef, U2 Claw: David Ridley

DEDICATION

In memory of my mother
Catherine Christenson
1922-2017

CONTENTS

ACKNOWLEDGMENTS

Rock Vegas was written to chronicle the history of live music in Las Vegas. To do so, it was critical to do the background work, including gathering information about promoters, management, venues, ticketing, and production. I'm grateful to the characters of these stories for taking the time to share their perspective on the development of live music.

It took me three and a half years to do all the work, then write the book. Ninety percent was done at night while my wife, Vicki, patiently sat there. The last three months at night, I disappeared into my Rock Room to finish it. I'm thankful for her patience.

If it weren't for Anthony Curtis, the book would not have been published. He had the faith in a manuscript that was written by someone who had never written one before. Huntington Press editor, Deke Castleman, took a lot of information, stories, and writing and created a book.

Thank you also to the photographers who lent their fine work for the photo insert—Tom Donoghue and Erik Kabik—as well as Gary Naseef for sharing from his archives.

As Director of UNLV's venues, I had a good understanding of the live-music business. That was 16 years ago. Doing this book properly meant catching up and then learning all that's new in the industry. In addition to the people I interviewed, I supplemented a lot of information from industry media. I would like to especially thank Dave Brooks at Amp Media and *Billboard*, *Pollstar*, Promoter 101, and Recode Media (Podcasts), *Venues Today*, and Bob Lefestz' daily blog.

Also, I found some great books and videos that were critical to rounding out the coverage. I've cited them as references. Most notable were the books *Altamont—The Rolling Stones, the Hells Angels, and the Inside Story of Rock's*

Darkest Day, by Joel Selvin, and *Barefoot in Babylon—The Creation of the Woodstock Music Festival, 1969,* by Bob Spitz. To ensure these two stories were told accurately, I cited information from both books liberally.

This book includes a lot of people who were instrumental in growing the Vegas live-music scene. However, there are so many more who were, and are, even farther behind the scenes. I believe everyone in the book would give the unsung heroes the majority of the credit for their success.

And last, but certainly not least, I have to mention the hotels that have made and continue to make major investments in live music. Their vision and commitment to the live-music experience enables Las Vegas to keep growing.

INTRODUCTION

Jerry Garcia had to feel peculiar waking up in a suite at Caesars Palace.

It was 1991 and he could look out his window to the north and south and see more desert than hotel-casinos. Even so, Garcia's band, the Grateful Dead, was selling out major arenas, and here he was in a city more defined by Sinatra and Liberace than The Rolling Stones and The Who.

Las Vegas wasn't sure what it was getting into either. The casinos had yet to make a commitment to touring concerts and had decidedly mixed mindsets on the followers of the Grateful Dead. Vegas wasn't alone in its ambivalence toward these fans. The Dead were having a hard time finding venues and cities willing to tolerate the somewhat lawless and drug-oriented nature of the Deadheads. On the other hand, wherever the Dead went, the hordes who filled the stadiums—and ostensibly hotel rooms and casinos, were close behind.

Until then, no stadium tour had played Las Vegas. So, feeling strange or not, when Garcia opened his eyes to the new day at Caesars, he and the Dead were about to make history—not for the band, but for Las Vegas.

And that's saying something, given Las Vegas' storied past, much of which has been covered in books, documentaries, and movies. That morning was a mere two years after Steve Wynn had opened the Mirage, launching one of the greatest building booms in world history. Is it a coincidence that the city's meteoric rise coincided with the growth of live music in Las Vegas? Live music didn't kick off the surge, but it kept pace with the explosive growth of the new Las Vegas.

Since their inception in 1931, Las Vegas' hotel-casinos have integrated entertainment into a visitor's experience. For 60 years, however, the top acts in town were bait, attractions to get people into the casinos. So entertainment departments played it safe, hosting traditional headliners like Liberace, Wayne Newton, Frank Sinatra, Tom Jones, and Rodney Dangerfield; the most risqué they got was Buddy Hackett and Don Rickles—earning the putative Entertainment Capital of the World a reputation as an old-age home for artists.

Beyond the showrooms, there were only two concert venues in Vegas. The Rotunda at the Las Vegas Convention Center hosted a limited roster of events, primarily prizefights (that the Beatles performed two concerts there in August 1964 was an anomaly of the first order). The opening of Aladdin's Theater for the Performing Arts in 1976 brought in a few mid-level shows; Neil Diamond was the inaugural act. But it was underused for years. Major touring acts in the '70s and '80s remained leery that playing Vegas correlated with a perceived decline in their drawing power, thus steering clear of the stigma. And acts that did play achieved less-than-stellar results in venues no bigger than 7,000 seats.

Then came the Grateful Dead in the early 1990s; their annual concerts helped transform Vegas from a mid-tier touring town into one of the top five live-music markets of the early 21st century. Today, there are two stadiums, three 4,000- to 5,000-seat theaters, four festival sites, five arenas, and more than a dozen 1,500-plus-seat showrooms. Collectively, these venues sell more than three million tickets a year to live-music events.

How did we, and I, get here?

♭   ♭   ♭

As a 10-year-old in a family of nine kids, I was introduced by my two older brothers to rock 'n' roll. I regularly helped myself to their collection of 45s and albums that included the Beatles, Dylan, Leonard Cohen, and Hendrix, to name just a few.

In high school, I went to my first rock concerts. I splurged for a couple of tickets to see Deep Purple at the Milwaukee Arena; a couple of months later, I took the same girl to Alice Cooper's Billion Dollar Babies tour. It turned out the girl wasn't hooked on me, but I was hooked on the music.

Any concert fan will tell you that the front row is the ultimate in concert seating. I landed my first one early. As a college student at the

University of Wisconsin in Madison, I was invited by a group of football players to drive overnight to Detroit to serve as bouncers for a Led Zeppelin concert. We arrived at Pontiac Stadium, where I was assigned bottle-check detail. This would not do! I hadn't spent eight hours cramped in the back of a station wagon just so I could frisk fans more than three football fields from the action. I took a little initiative and made my way inside the stadium. Fortunately, the security force was so large that no one knew where anyone belonged. At least they didn't know where I belonged. And I belonged right in front of the stage behind the barricade.

Tickets for the general-admission show were $10.50. The air-conditioning engineer for Pontiac Stadium must have taken the night off. More than 75,000 sweat-drenched half-dressed kids formed a writhing, yearning, grasping mass of humanity—the show set a record as the largest audience ever for a single-act concert.

I'd purchased a disposable camera, which came in handy, considering the choice spot I had just landed. I still have close-up pictures of Page and Plant.

After the show, I wandered backstage to see the superstar foursome about to be rewarded for a job well done. The group's manager was Peter Grant, a larger-than-life professional wrestler (once billed as "His Highness Count Bruno Alassio of Milan"). Sporting an earring and a beard that flowed to his chest, he had four lit joints in his mouth. Each band member helped himself to one as they climbed into the limo.

Boy, was I hooked.

The year before, I won a NCAA wrestling title at Wisconsin and was sure my destiny lay in coaching and teaching. After graduating, I spent three years doing both in Waunakee, a small rural community just north of Madison. In 1980, I accepted a stipend to be the assistant wrestling coach at Louisiana State University, where I planned to earn my master's degree.

However, two weeks before leaving for LSU, I received a call from Dennis Finfrock, assistant athletic director and head wrestling coach at University of Nevada Las Vegas. Finfrock, a former BYU football player, sported a mustache reminiscent of Kurt Russell's Wyatt Earp in *Tombstone*. He offered me a part-time position as a wrestling coach and event coordinator for the athletic department.

I traveled from the lush green landscapes of the Midwest to the white sand and palm trees of the Mojave Desert. When I arrived in Las Vegas, I learned that my new boss Dennis Finfrock also ran a company (FINCO) that provided ushers and crowd management for casino-hotel events.

Less than a month later, Caesars Palace was assembling a 25,000-seat outdoor boxing venue in its parking lot to produce the Holmes-Ali championship fight. This was the biggest spectacle that had ever taken place in the city. I didn't have the liberty of maneuvering my way to ringside seats for some good pictures. Instead, I had real responsibilities. I supervised a crew of UNLV-athlete ushers who were as lucky as I was to be a part of this unprecedented piece of Las Vegas history.

Three years later in March 1983, my imagination ran wild as I gazed over the freshly poured cement foundation of what would become the 18,500-seat UNLV arena, Thomas and Mack Center. University boosters had managed to secure funding to build the TMC, but there was no plan to operate the facility. Finfrock, sensing a new career opportunity, convinced UNLV to give him a shot at managing the fledgling arena. Instead of looking around the country for a seasoned venue manager to assist him, he chose me.

So began a 36-year career in which I witnessed the evolution of one of the greatest cities in the world and the events that helped shape it.

I've been heavily influenced by the rock (Beatles-Stones), tech (Gates-Jobs), and hospitality (Wynn) superstars of the last 50 years. These legendary personalities had rabid imaginations and were insatiable risk takers who continuously pushed new ideas and created new paradigms. While they possessed completely different levels of emotional discipline, their obsession with creating and re-creating what we as consumers desire, whether we know it or not, has been the staple of our modern economy.

However, this book is not about the stars. Rather, it's about the people behind the scenes: the promoters, agents, venue managers and staff, and fans who carved out a live-music niche and expanded it to its current role as one of the driving economic forces of Las Vegas.

Though the characters in this book have, until now, been unsung, they've been blessed with many of the same attributes as the big names. They're the ones who created *Rock Vegas*.

CHAPTER ONE

ROCK 'N' ROLL'S ROOTS

In the late 1940s, expressions of faith and hope bellowed out of the churches in the South, as gospel was transformed into the blues. Rock 'n' roll and almost all forms of live music today were, according to Quincy Jones, "bred from Africa to the black church to gospel, which turned into blues, jazz, and country music. It cross pollinates and that's the way it ought to be."

From the energy coming out of the churches, blues artists such as Robert Johnson, Muddy Waters, and Howlin' Wolf spawned riffs that were mimicked and interpreted by generations of guitarists to come. Ray Manzarek of the Doors said, "If it hadn't been for black Americans, we'd be doing the minuet and dancing on our tippy toes."

In the mid-'40s, black artists were not only relegated to playing to their own, but getting a record published was as likely as landing a white-collar job. Their music, ragged, crude, and explicit, couldn't get anywhere near the radio. A few record companies determined everything contemporary-music lovers heard on their phonographs: Frank Sinatra, Pat Boone, Judy Garland, and the other white crooners. But then, an interconnected network of independent distributors—the Chess Brothers, Imperial, and King—began producing records by black artists. Producers such as Atlantic Records' Ahmet Ertegun, an immigrant from Turkey, heard something few others did. He signed and developed artists performing gospel and the blues from the Delta and Chicago to Texas and the West Coast.

In the early '50s, a disc jockey, Alan Freed, began playing rhythm and blues by black artists on WJW in Cleveland and popularizing the phrase "rock and roll" that he'd coined to describe the music. Freed also promoted what's considered the first-ever rock concert, which took place in Cleveland in 1952.

Early rockers like Little Richard, Bill Haley, Chuck Berry, and Jerry Lee Lewis appealed to rebellious teens, but it was Elvis Aron Presley who delivered the new genre to living rooms everywhere. His 1956 performance on Tommy and Jimmy Dorsey's "Stage Show" on TV inaugurated a new era. Four weeks later, he played to a deafening and doting crowd on "The Ed Sullivan Show." It was, as the U2's Bono has said, "the Big Bang of rock 'n' roll."

Presley's skyrocketing fame forever entrenched rock 'n' roll in America and around the world, including Las Vegas. By then, R&B singles and LPs were making their way to England and onto the record players of Keith Richards, John Lennon, Eric Clapton, Eric Burdon, and others who would be influenced by all forms of the blues.

In the early '60s, while the Quarrymen, the group formed by a teenage John Lennon, were apprenticing in seedy neon-lit Hamburg, Germany, American songwriters like Carol King and Neil Sedaka were churning out tunes in Manhattan's Tin Pan Alley for acts like the Everly Brothers and Ricky Nelson.

At the same time, Greenwich Village became the center of the folk-

---

The Two Faces of Rock

Probably no two contradictory quotes more aptly sum up the impact of Elvis and the transition from the margin to the mainstream that he and his music represented.

"Rock 'n' roll is the most brutal, ugly, degenerate, vicious form of expression, lewd, sly, in plain fact dirty—a rancid-smelling aphrodisiac and the martial music of every sideburned delinquent on the face of the Earth."

"There have been many accolades uttered about Elvis' talent and performances through the years, all of which I agree with wholeheartedly."

The first quote is from Frank Sinatra in 1956. The second is from Sinatra in 1977.

music movement, populated by musician-poets such as Tom Chapin, Pete Seeger, Woody Guthrie, and Peter, Paul and Mary who were writing and performing sociopolitical songs.

In 1961, a kid from Minnesota made the pilgrimage to Greenwich Village. With his messy hair and disheveled clothes, he fit right into the folk scene, though his singing and guitar playing didn't impress anyone, at least at first. Bob Dylan wasn't much of a guitarist or vocalist, but he could write and his fellow artists quickly took notice; Peter, Paul and Mary's version of "Blowin' in the Wind" catapulted Dylan from a footnote to a headline.

"Folk music had emotional intensity, lyrical depth, and many musical textures. Those were the things rock 'n' roll was interested in. About rock 'n' roll, folk was interested in the electricity, literally and figuratively, the sense of excitement, but most of all the access to a larger stage and a larger audience than ever would be possible for folk music by itself. That's why the marriage of folk and rock took place in the mid-'60s," explains Peter Fornatale, a pioneer of FM rock stations and author of many books on rock 'n' roll.

The Sun Came Up for Rock First in San Francisco

Greenwich Village churned out a "bohemian" subculture. In a few years, San Francisco broadened and popularized the bohemian lifestyle when it hosted the first "hippies."

Two major factors contributed to the explosion of what we now know as a "live music." In the '60s, the Vietnam War and the assassinations of John F. Kennedy, Martin Luther King, Jr., and Robert Kennedy left a hole in the heart of the youth of America. Rock and politics were suddenly colliding. If not for politics, rock might not have made it out of the '60s and if not for rock, there wouldn't have *been* a "Sixties." The seismic growth of this music was a direct result of a rebellious counterculture of Baby Boomers being introduced to an invasion of musicians who were part of an evolving system to present themselves, live, to the masses.

"There always were pockets of people in our society seeking alternative lifestyles," legendary San Francisco concert promoter Bill Graham said. "In the '60s, the funnel opened wide. People may have rejected the status quo before, but the difference this time was in sheer numbers. The vehicle was music. And millions of young people got on the bandwagon."

Live-music's seed found fertile ground in San Francisco, nurtured by Bill Graham. As a child, Graham escaped from Nazi Germany in a children's refugee program and he grew up in the Bronx with American foster parents. After earning a degree in business from City College of New York, he migrated west to San Francisco in the early '60s; a few years later, he began to manage the seminal San Francisco Mime Troupe. From there, he started organizing benefits and free concerts; his business acumen and obsession with detail led to a career in which he not only developed some of the most iconic names in rock 'n' roll, but he helped create the scene that fostered them.

On July 5, 1968, Graham opened the 1,200-seat Fillmore West Auditorium, where he broke such acts as the Grateful Dead, Jefferson Airplane, Big Brother & the Holding Company with Janis Joplin, the Eagles, Country Joe and the Fish, New Riders of the Purple Sage, Moby Grape, Santana, Frank Zappa, Steve Miller, the Mamas and the Papas, Crosby, Stills, Nash & Young, Deep Purple, Taj Mahal, and many more. In 1971, after closing the Fillmore, he moved his shows to the 5,400-seat Winterland, an old ice-skating rink. While Graham became known for the iconic acts he booked, his contribution to developing the music experience and business was just as important.

Graham controlled every aspect of the act, the venue, and the audience. In the process, his bookend Fillmore music halls (San Francisco and New York) served as the training ground, as well consistent paydays, for bands that dominated live touring for decades to come.

Graham's style was both revered and despised. He obsessed over every aspect of the live-music experience, taking detailed notes at each show. His concerts were accompanied by psychedelic light shows, strobes, spaces for uninhibited dancing, even food service (including breakfast for all-night shows). On the other hand, he wasn't above cooking the books and cheating agents when it came to ticket sales.

But the live-music train was building a head of steam that, initially at least, left Graham behind. In 1969, Woodstock was more than a pivotal event for the counterculture; it also demonstrated that fans would not only tolerate large-scale crowds, but the enormity of a concert could be part of the experience. Graham didn't see it that way.

"A couple of geniuses put on something called the Woodstock Festival. It was a tragedy. Groups recognized that they could go into larger cattle markets, play less time, and make more dollars. What they've done is to destroy the rock industry."

Woodstock was the biggest, but it was neither the first nor the best rock festival of its time. In 1967, record producer and music executive Lou Adler and John Phillips of the Mamas and the Papas created the Monterey Pop Festival. Ironically, it was anything but pop and would be the first successful commercial music festival. Acts relegated to small venues like the Fillmore could now play in front of hundreds of thousands of music lovers. Jimi Hendrix, Janis Joplin, Santana, Jefferson Airplane, The Who, and more than 50 others, including the introduction of Otis Redding, played sets that revolutionized the live-music experience—all for a mere $3.50 admission fee.

The '60s End Badly for Rock, But Kickstart the Live-Music Industry

But after Woodstock, things changed quickly. In the business, managers and agents looked for ways to get their acts regular work via a national network of promoters who, in time, created a live-touring industry. And the free-spirited hippie movement, embodied by the Summer of Love, took a dark turn with the assassinations of Martin Luther King, Jr. and Robert Kennedy, the shockingly brutal murders of Sharon Tate and four friends by Charles Manson and a small group of followers, and The Rolling Stones concert at Altamont.

On December 6, 1969, the Stones headlined a festival at Altamont Speedway in the northern California hills 60 miles east of San Francisco. The Hell's Angels were hired for crowd management, just one of the bad decisions that left an acid-addled fan stabbed to death and many injured.

While Bill Graham's business model had shifted dramatically in only a couple of years, he didn't go away. Joining the mass-concert movement, he created and put his stamp on one-of-a-kind events, such as Day on the Green in Oakland. Headliners like Led Zeppelin, The Rolling Stones, or the Eagles performed with four or five other acts in a custom concert experience on the grass at Oakland Stadium. Graham produced up to eight different "Day on the Green" events a year.

Meanwhile, a new wave of auditoriums and arenas were lining up with promoters. Using the newfound power of promotion from FM radio stations, acts were routed through over 100 cities per year. Madison Square Garden and the Los Angeles Forum hosted a sellout every month for acts like Pink Floyd, Fleetwood Mac, The Who, and many others.

And then there was Las Vegas, a live-music anomaly in the desert and hardly even an afterthought for superstar rock acts.

CHAPTER TWO

ROCK ROLLS INTO VEGAS

As early as the 1930s, Las Vegas was attracting gamblers and visitors by putting the names of top-notch entertainers on their marquees. In May 1931, the Cornero brothers retained seasoned producer Jack Laughlin to open their new hotel, the Meadows, with the *Meadows Revue* to perform for a crowd of more than 5,000. In 1945, Billboard proclaimed the Last Frontier Hotel a "big-bracket operation" after it signed Sophie Tucker and Harry Richman, viewed locally as a critical breakthrough for the city. By the mid-1950s, a dozen hotels on the Strip were vying for a limited pool of talent.

At that time, live music around the country centered on clubs, dance halls, gymnasiums, and ballrooms. In Las Vegas, deep-pocket casinos booked the top entertainers to play their showrooms and lounges. No city could match the experience for a couple making the scene, the man in a tuxedo and the lady in an evening gown, dropping ten bucks on a maître d' and being seated at a table for a cocktail or dinner show within 30 feet of Betty Hutton, Red Skelton, or Milton Berle.

As new casinos opened during the Vegas '50s' building boom, the competition for entertainers skyrocketed. In 1953, the bidding drove salaries to $30,000 a week. When the Riviera opened in 1955, its inaugural performer, Liberace, earned $50,000.

But it was Elvis Presley who introduced the heavily segregated Vegas of the time to the forerunners of rock, bringing blues and race music to a white audience and challenging social and sexual barriers. Elvis was as close as Las Vegas came to mainstream touring music. On April 23, 1956, on the heels of his first million-selling LP *Heartbreak Hotel*, the 21-year-old Presley, dressed up in a jacket and bowtie, debuted in Las Vegas in the Venus Room at the New Frontier Hotel. It was an inauspicious opening, according to Paul Lichter in his book *Elvis in Vegas*.

"The curtain rose on a very nervous Elvis. He and the band were met with quiet stares of amazement. To this audience, it appeared to be a bunch of hillbillies or some form of alien life. During the show, one high-roller sitting at a ringside table shouted, 'Goddamn shit! What is all this yelling and noise?' He got up, as did the rest of his party, and they stalked out of the showroom."

In his book *Cult Vegas*, Las Vegas entertainment writer Mike Weatherford summed up the aftermath. "Hollywood was beckoning Elvis and the Strip was happy to go back to non-rock nightclub fare."

Indeed, in 1963, Elvis became the highest-paid actor in the U.S., earning $1 million per film. That year in July, he did two weeks of location work for his film *Viva Las Vegas*, which co-starred Ann-Margret, who, according to Weatherford, "many believe might have been the one true love of his life."

But four years later, Elvis, by then 32, returned to Vegas to marry Priscilla Ann Beaulieu, 21, at a private ceremony at the Aladdin Hotel-Casino on May 1, 1967. And two years after that, Elvis began his epic run at Kirk Kerkorian's new 1,519-room International Hotel-Casino (later the Las Vegas Hilton and now the Westgate) in the 2,000-seat showroom at $15 a ticket for the dinner show, with entrées of steak, prime rib, or lobster tail.

For his performances, he assembled the best studio musicians in the world and wore a black-leather karate outfit with bright-red leg vents; a red scarf hung over his bare chest. Paul Lichter wrote about the opening. "For over an hour, he flogged himself to near exhaustion. He was like a wild man! He turned the stage into a karate exhibition: He kicked, crouched, and punched like a man laced with LSD. The audience had just witnessed a seven-minute resurrection, a rebirth, a reinvention." Elvis had borrowed a lot of those moves from Tom Jones.

Between 1969 and 1976, Elvis sold out 636 performances, a staggering number by any live-event standard. During that time, Las Vegas witnessed the slow erosion of this androgynous, lean, gyrating, black-haired idol into an overweight, prescription-drug-addicted, mail-it-in performer.

"Elvis was sinking into his own private hell. A world where the love of millions of strangers and all the rights of entitlement he had earned were not enough. He no longer considered Las Vegas a challenge; he thought it was a trap with no way out," according to Lichter.

The Beatles (Fans) Blow the Roof off the Rotunda

Five years before Elvis' run at the International, the Beatles were the leading edge of the British Invasion, on tour in the U.S.

Most major tours are routed based on the size of the market. At the time, Las Vegas' population was 200,000, while the average population for cities on the Beatles' tour was more than a million. But the Beatles were eager to play Las Vegas, which they'd heard so much about. Strangely, Las Vegas wasn't so eager for the Beatles to play. Though six months earlier in February 1964, 73 million people watched the Fab Four perform on "The Ed Sullivan Show," Las Vegas hotel entertainment directors didn't seem to know who they were. All except for Stan Irwin.

Stan Irwin was born into a show-business family that dated back to vaudeville. The rest of the Strip passed on the Beatles, but Irwin, entertainment director at the Sahara, first considered having them play in the Sahara's main venue, the Congo Room, but it only sat 600, while the Beatles were selling out arenas and stadiums. Instead, he booked them into the Rotunda at the Las Vegas Convention Center where, as Irwin related to John Romero for his book *Las Vegas, Untold Stories*, "They told me they could put 7,000 a show in the Rotunda. I said that was still too small and asked for the balcony too."

On August 20, 1964, the Beatles sold out both shows at the Convention Center with ticket prices ranging from $2.50 to $5.50. The date paid off for Irwin, generating twice what the Beatles earned. But the fans who attended got a memory that was priceless. One remembered, "It was the most exciting day of my life. I was 18 at the time. We had floor seats about two-thirds of the way back. The screaming started before the Beatles were even onstage, and when they did appear the cheering, screaming, and clapping made the loudest human noise I had ever heard or ever would. I was a little annoyed, because I really wanted to hear them sing."

For their part, the Beatles didn't get to see much of Vegas; Beatlemaniacs surrounded the Sahara, so they were confined to their room.

Irwin had a slot machine sent up to entertain them. George Harrison recalled that Liberace also visited them. But his strongest memory was of his view from the stage. "I think the first four rows of that concert were filled up by Pat Boone and his daughters. He seemed to have hundreds of daughters."

The Sound of Vegas

Ironically, the two most influential acts in music at the time had little effect on touring. While few shows had more energy than a Beatles concert, there was little artistic appreciation for the music. Their last three albums had a dramatic impact on rock, but they didn't tour in support of those great LPs. For most of the '60s, Elvis left live performing behind in favor of starring in movies and a residency at the International Hotel. Beyond his early influence, he had little effect on the evolving music industry.

In 1969, Led Zeppelin, Creedence Clearwater Revival, the Doors, Buffalo Springfield, and the Grateful Dead played Las Vegas' Ice Palace, an ice-skating rink that occasionally hosted rock concerts; it was in the Commercial Center on East Sahara Avenue, the first major shopping center in the growing city. However, Las Vegas didn't play any part in the evolution of rock 'n' roll; its live-music scene developed much differently. Entertainment was primarily a diversion for visitors and, much like rooms and restaurants, a revenue loss leader to boost the primary source of profit: gambling.

It wasn't that Vegas didn't have its fair share of great musicians. More than 500 players worked full-time, and more part-time, backing the headliners up and down the Strip. Tony Bennett, for example, had a 100-piece orchestra. The shows went on seven nights a week, but due to union rules, the musicians could play only six. Relief bands filled in on the seventh.

Rock was unheard of, and even jazz was a little too avant garde for the showrooms. However, there was a lively after-hours scene at Ferdinand's, the Tender Trap, the Speakeasy, and Black Magic. Joe Darro, a long-time Vegas pianist, remembers, "After hours, you saw Sarah Vaughan and Ella Fitzgerald. They played until dawn."

"I played with the Rat Pack, Nat Cole, Billy Epstein, Jack Benny, Ella Fitzgerald, and Sarah Vaughan," recalls Roger Hall, saxophonist. "Usually, the shows ran four weeks, so you really got a chance to nail down the music and sometimes you got to know the headliners, hanging out with them backstage."

One of Liberace's opening acts was an unknown young singer named Barbara Streisand. Even the musicians didn't know who she was. "When she opened," Ron Simone, one of those musicians, says, "You could hear a pin drop. Wow! What a voice."

"Sinatra always talked about how his Vegas musicians made it great," Daniel Falcone, trumpet player, said. "When he came to Las Vegas, he was always excited; he could perform at his top level, not having to drag the band behind him. They lifted him up and made him even better."

The musicians in that era also had to deal with race issues. "At the time, they thought black musicians couldn't read music, so nobody called them," said Woody Woods.

Black musicians, and even performers, had to come through the back door. Sammy Davis, Jr., couldn't stay at the Sands where he performed with the Rat Pack, eat in the restaurant, or bring friends with him. Frank Sinatra finally put his foot down. He said, "If Sammy can't stay here, mix with the people, and drink, I'm not going on."

Gary Naseef—Rockin' the Boat

It was Gary Naseef's first week on the job as the assistant entertainment director at Caesars Palace, which had recently opened. Naseef's boss, Dave Victorson, had challenged him to find a band to play in the typically dead time right before Christmas. Victorson was looking to do something atypical. With little experience and only what he heard on radio, Naseef recommended several acts, though he didn't believe any would show up.

"In those days, you couldn't get a rock act to play Vegas," he says. "It wasn't big enough. And it was too plastic for the hippie bands. They didn't want to be associated with the place."

Caesars' choice: Blood, Sweat & Tears.

Naseef wanted Caesars to commit to an aggressive six-night stand.

Caesars went for three. However, the shows were so successful that the band ended up playing those six shows, two per night. It was the first rock band to play in a Vegas hotel-casino. Caesars' Circus Maximus Showroom became something Las Vegas hadn't had until then—a hip venue. Naseef's stock was quickly rising.

Naseef's upbringing was far from routine. His dad, known as "Fast Eddie," owned a chain of package liquor stores and a bar that fronted for his real source of money—illegal bookmaking.

When Naseef was 13, his father was throwing a regular "party" in the basement of their home in Illinois. "There was a knock on the door. My mother talked to these people. It was the feds. They wanted to search the house. Meanwhile, my dad's downstairs throwing all the parlay cards in the furnace."

The next day, his father announced they were moving. First stop was Daytona, Florida. A short while later, they were on their way to Phoenix. But they were really headed to Las Vegas, where Fast Eddie drove a cab and continued to do what he loved most—gamble.

Ironically, Naseef had a normal life in Las Vegas. He didn't care much for high school, but he met a girl who captured his heart and whose father had a major influence on his future. Naseef explains, "I didn't know it at the time, but Sandy Carter was the daughter of a powerful Teamster boss. He didn't like boys getting too close to his daughter. So we ran off and got married unannounced."

When Bill Carter went to retrieve Sandy, the newlyweds approached his car. "I went up and said, 'Sandy, get into the car. It's your father. You should show respect.' From then on, he liked me. Not many people went near Bill Carter's car."

He and his new father-in-law became close, but Naseef wanted to join a friend who lived on the beach in L.A. Bill didn't want his daughter to leave, so he got Gary a high-paying job driving a truck on the Caesars Palace construction site. That position led to steady employment when Caesars opened. Gary trained on every job in the hotel-casino: cleaning rooms, dishwashing, cooking, catering, receiving, purchasing, sales, advertising. He finally landed the plum position of assistant entertainment director.

The successful Blood, Sweat & Tears performances not only looked good to Naseef's boss, they made a strong impression on the group. Naseef was at their beck and call throughout their stay. He formed friendships, especially with lead singer David Clayton Thomas. Appreciative of Gary's work, they wanted to repay him.

Naseef had an idea. "Do a concert for me."

Thomas said, "Sure!"

Their manager happily agreed, adding, "We get $15,000 a night."

Naseef didn't have 15 cents, much less $15,000. But it was the moment he knew he wanted to be a concert promoter.

During a brief stint at Caesars Tahoe in 1969, he met the agent of the group the Carpenters. The agent offered Naseef one of the biggest rock stars of the '60s—Janice Joplin. No female exemplified rock 'n' roll more than Joplin. With a voice like Steven Tyler and moves like Tina Turner, she quickly found her place near the top of the developing rock scene.

With no money, little experience, and his signature on a $15,000 offer, Naseef launched his new concert company, GANA, and set out to put the pieces of the Joplin concert together in Vegas. He added B.B. King, Country Joe McDonald, the Young Rascals, Jessie Colter and the Youngbloods—all these great acts, just a few months after Woodstock.

The Las Vegas Convention Center was unavailable, so he set his sights on Cashman Field, a sports venue just north of downtown on Las Vegas Boulevard. In those days, the venue had concrete bleachers, a sparse concourse, and a plain green fence. But its capacity was 30,000.

Once again, Gary's father-in-law, Bill Carter, stepped in. He helped raise the money to advertise and stage the concert and secure Cashman Field. (Though Gary and Sandy divorced after a few years of marriage, that never interfered with his relationship to his ex-father-in-law; indeed, Gary was a pallbearer at Bill Carter's funeral.)

Rock was rolling into Vegas. Or was it? Unfortunately for Naseef, its reputation preceded it. It was too new and different to sit well with a city whose performers had short hair, wore tuxes, and fronted full orchestras. Eventually, the owners of the downtown casinos, especially cowboy Benny Binion, got wind of Cashman Field "bringing all these damn hippies to town."

"Woodstock scared the hell out of them," said Naseef, who was about to experience one of his many run-ins with authority.

Ticket sales were in the tens of thousands, but a showdown loomed with a newly formed Commission on Rock Concerts after the city passed an ordinance that gave it the power to cancel the concert. Naseef lost all his investors' money.

The leadership in Las Vegas was sending Naseef and rock 'n' roll a message. But Naseef wasn't listening. He jumped right back in.

Whether it was his proficiency in promotion, the onslaught of rock, or both, he managed to put together a string of successful shows, most of them at the Convention Center.

"The Rotunda was one of the best facilities I ever produced a show in, acoustically and intimately. We sold seats all the way around the stage," Naseef reminisces.

The Rotunda had a box office, but it was really just an office—no computerized ticket system, no phone sales, no ticket sellers; just a room.

Also, unlike today's venues, the Rotunda didn't provide services to the promoter. The Convention Center rented Naseef the building, but he had to secure all the services to produce the concert. For that, he hired Tycho Brahe from Hermosa Beach, California, for sound and lights. The sound was stacked on wings on each side of the stage and the lights were suspended by a custom truss system they built. These were critical to his success, because as the promoter, Naseef was responsible for the quality of the production.

In the '70s, loading in a concert and coordinating the production of sound and lights with the band were inconsistent and challenging. Each show had three or four bands that all came from different parts of the country. "They all had their trucks, and they were all late, and they were all stoned. But I had my own guys who were good and sober," he says.

The system for scheduling concerts at the Las Vegas Convention Center was primitive at best: All the promoters' names went into a hat and someone picked them out, establishing the order in which they could rent the Rotunda. Naseef's GANA Productions came out last. With six promoters ahead of him, it looked like he and his crew wouldn't put on a show for seven months. But the first three promoters couldn't deliver. The fourth show's promoter, Bob Jasper, was pursuing the Grateful Dead, but couldn't get a commitment. Naseef approached him about co-promoting his next show—Deep Purple, Fleetwood Mac, and Rory

Gallagher. Little did Naseef know how much this show would change his life and the course of Vegas rock history.

Rock-Concert Riot

April 27, 1973, started like most of GANA's concert dates. All 7,800 tickets for the Deep Purple concert were sold. Naseef was delivering the bands' $10,000 checks when he got the first bad news from Deep Purple's manager: The lead singer, Ian Gillian, was sick; they weren't going on.

Panicked, Naseef convinced Gallagher and Fleetwood Mac to play longer sets, while he worked with Deep Purple to reschedule a free show for later in the week at the Las Vegas (now the Sam Boyd) Stadium, where the UNLV Rebels football team played. All that was left was securing the stadium, so he could announce the new date to the crowd.

The stadium date had to be approved by the chairman of the Convention and Visitors Authority, Bob Broadbent. Broadbent, however, wanted the concert cancelled and all the ticket money refunded.

Naseef told him, "We can't refund the money. There's no money in your so-called box office. It's in the bank. I can't access it till tomorrow."

Broadbent didn't understand the precariousness of having nearly 8,000 fans, lit up on various kinds of dope, disappointed. He said, "You tell those kids to exit single file."

Naseef said, "Listen, you're going to have a problem here. People are going to get hurt."

Broadbent got angry. "If you ever want to do another show in this facility again, you'll do what I say."

Naseef said to himself, if it's a riot you want, it's a riot you got.

It was after ten p.m. The crowd was fully juiced and growing impatient when Bob Jasper and Naseef walked onto the stage. Jasper announced he had some good news and bad news. The good news was Rory Gallagher and Fleetwood Mac would jam together. The bad news: Ian Gillian was sick and Deep Purple couldn't play, but a makeup date would be announced.

"Just then," Naseef recalled, "a bottle of wine came sailing over our heads, hit Mick Fleetwood's drum, and broke. Behind me, I heard Mick say, 'I'm out of here, man!' And I think he flipped off whoever threw the bottle. The audience thought he was flipping them all off, which he might have been doing. I didn't see it. But many in the crowd did.

"Well, it was the fastest teardown you ever saw in your life. The bands, the equipment, the roadies, they were out the door and gone.

"By then, chairs were flying everywhere and it became a contest to see who could throw a chair the farthest. And that was just inside the Rotunda. In the corridors, the crowd was breaking glass display cases and outside they pushed over police cars. They even tore off the metal sprinkler heads and threw them through the windows of the ticket office where we were cowering."

The riot made national news. Shortly thereafter, the county passed a stringent Rock Concert Ordinance, which still exists today, requiring promoters to secure a license to produce concerts.

Under the ordinance, a minimum number of police officers per attendee are required, along with a bond for the full refund of tickets. In 1973, while the rest of the country was adapting to rock concerts, Las Vegas took a big step backward. For the next 10 years, Las Vegas would host half the shows it did in the past.

Though that was his last concert at the Las Vegas Convention Center, Gary Naseef had paved the way. "We were setting the tone and the way it was done. In Las Vegas, we pioneered it."

CHAPTER THREE

THE SECOND GENERATION
OF LAS VEGAS LIVE

In the late '70s, the Rotunda at the Las Vegas Convention Center was off limits to Gary Naseef. It was the only Vegas venue large enough to promote the kinds of acts with whom he was involved, so he moved on. For a while, his company, GANA, was doing multiple shows across the U.S. But it wasn't long until he found his way back onto the Vegas concert scene.

In 1978, Lenny Martin, vice president of entertainment at the Sahara Hotel-Casino, Stan Irwin's old joint, was looking for something to spark the hotel. He and Naseef had a mutual friend who mentioned Gary's history of promoting concerts. It took one meeting to convince Martin that he had the right guy. But Martin had to convince risk-adverse hotel managers. Not wanting to miss the opportunity, Naseef offered to fund the entire venture: production, advertising, promotion, security, even a percentage to the Sahara. Before long, the Sahara Space Center started to rock.

The Space Center was a cavernous events hall with a low 14-foot ceiling. Naseef built the stage against the wall that fronted the kitchen. The stage was surrounded by a roped-off VIP section featuring 10-tops with table-cloths and candles; drink service to the VIP section was provided from the kitchen's bar. That section accommodated 2,000 and a maître d' showed the holders of those tickets, which cost $2 extra, to their seats. Flanking the roped-off section and filling the rest of the room was theater-style seating. It was a far more intimate and fan-friendly venue than the Rotunda.

The carpeted Space Center and its low ceiling created great acoustical possibilities. He hired Paul Gongaware (now a principal with Concerts West and AEG Live), who, with plywood and four by fours, assembled large sound wings that enabled them to hang the large Tycho Brahe sound systems.

Back then, very few venues flew the lights and sound over the band.

But Naseef did. To achieve this, Gongaware had to punch through the tile sections of the ceiling, then tie the sound wings to the room's support structure. This created a 360-degree obstruction-free sightline. The quality of the sound, the small capacity, and the low ceiling created a great-sounding room.

His first show was Sly & The Family Stone, Eric Burdon & War, and the Average White Band. That was followed by Richie Havens, Mahavishnu Orchestra, Jean Luc Ponti, the James Gang, Minnie Ripperton, Al Green, KISS, Rush, Rare Earth, Fleetwood Mac, Loggins & Messina, Linda Ronstadt, Rufus featuring Chaka Kahn, and the Ohio Players.

In 1974, the Sahara concert series garnered Naseef *Billboard* magazine's Trendsetter Award for bringing touring rock concerts to the Sahara's headliner showroom. Better yet, his success there drew attention from another hotel looking to grow its live-music business.

A Jewel in the Middle of a Mine Field—The Aladdin Theater

In 1969, wealthy Detroit widow Mae George purchased 24% of the Aladdin Hotel-Casino on the south Strip. Her business adviser was her late-husband's foster brother, James Tamer, who later earned a spot in Nevada's Black Book, a list of personae non gratae in casinos due to their criminal backgrounds.

Because of his unscrupulous past, Tamer was denied a gaming license as a key employee of the Aladdin. To get around that minor detail, the hotel gave him the title of executive show director and a salary of $15,000, the most he could make without being licensed. In that position, Tamer built the Aladdin Theater for the Performing Arts.

Naseef tried repeatedly to contact the theater, where he hoped to promote his rock concerts. But his calls were ignored. Finally, he pulled some strings and met with Tamer, who told him, "We're going to do it ourselves. We think we've got someone special coming who'll set the theme, not only for the theater, but the Aladdin itself. If we need you, we'll call you."

By then, Naseef wanted to take a break from promoting concerts. He returned to Lake Tahoe to chill in the thin mountainous air.

Promoting might seem elementary to those who haven't done it. If an act sells a lot of records, it should sell a lot of tickets. But as the Aladdin soon discovered, it wasn't that easy. Though the Aladdin Theater pulled off a dramatic opening with Neil Diamond, a two-night stand by Chicago bombed, George Benson couldn't get the piano he wanted, the bands had to rent substandard house sound at an exorbitant $15,000, and there were reports of staff demanding kickbacks.

It didn't take long for the word to get out to touring agents about the bad experience the acts were having in the venue. Suddenly, the theater couldn't book shows. At the same time, the hotel-casino was hemorrhaging money, losing $500,000 per month.

In 1976, Naseef was sitting on his porch in his secluded Lake Tahoe condo, reading the paper and drinking a cup of coffee when a big black limousine made its way down the curvy road. In the limo was Tamer, who managed to convince the reluctant promoter to return to Vegas and the business.

Naseef's strong relationships with talent agents put the Aladdin back in the concert business; he booked practically every act that toured. He got them started with Journey, then Cheech and Chong and Firefall, then a two-year run of more than 100 shows. The theater drew 50,000 people per month to its concerts and quickly turned the hotel's burdensome red ink to profitable black.

The first time I met Gary was at a ZZ Top makeup concert he promoted in 1980 at the Las Vegas Silver Bowl (formerly the Stadium and now the Sam Boyd). The concert was part of a federal-court settlement between Naseef and the Texas rockers over the band's sudden no-show at the Sahara six years earlier. I saw first-hand the grudge that the police and county authorities still carried against Naseef over the riot at the Convention Center and other run-ins. In addition, the Silver Bowl was an unfamiliar concert venue that had everyone a bit nervous—except Naseef himself, who'd earlier promoted Manassas featuring Stephen Stills and then Faces, featuring Rod Stewart, Ronnie Lane, Ron Wood, and Jeff Beck, at the stadium.

I recognized from the official ambivalence, all those years later, that Las Vegas was still undecided about being in the rock-concert business. It still had only two venues for touring concerts: the 6,700-seat Rotunda and the 7,000-seat Aladdin Theatre for the Performing Arts.

Consequently, it couldn't compete for major tours such as The Rolling Stones, Billy Joel, or Journey even if they wanted to play Vegas, which they didn't. Also, unlike venues throughout the rest of the country, a Las Vegas promoter managed every aspect of the show—reserving the venue, selling the tickets, and providing ushers, stagehands, and police. It was the only option.

An Evening Star over Las Vegas—Danny Zelisko

In 1978, Las Vegas had a population of 350,000 and a distinct shortage of experienced concert promoters. In the aftermath of the Deep Purple riot at the Convention Center, promoting concerts in Las Vegas required a license that had stringent requirements and made it burdensome on promoters from outside the city. However, a pair of promoters, originally from Phoenix and Chicago, along with one of the original rock-concert promoters, Barry Fey, were about to usher in the second generation of live music in Las Vegas.

While friends in his Chicago neighborhood were playing Little League baseball, Danny Zelisko was working in the majors. At a very tender age, Zelisko stumbled into a business that today rakes in millions for professional athletes. "When I was seven, my brother and I started writing away to baseball and football players for their autographs," Zelisko says. "Even that young, I was aware of celebrities." Within a few years, he had amassed a huge sports-card collection.

"I called players just to talk, because I was such a big fan." He got to know some of the players well. "We never paid to get into a Bears game; we walked in with the players as if we belonged."

His familiarity with players also resulted in booking them into speaking engagements for his friends' Little League teams' social events. "The first speaking engagement I arranged was for a pitcher named Johnny Klippstein. I looked him up in the phone book, called, told him I was a big fan, and asked if he'd speak to my Little League team. My parents were skeptical, but sure enough, there was a knock on the door and there he was."

Haunting the couple hundred yards between the parking lot and Wrigley Field, he and his brother befriended the likes of Ernie Banks and Ron Santo. "This was 'meet and greet' way before its time," Zelisko says. "For those two hundred yards, we had complete access to all these stars."

Working the phones for engagements and autographs drew the ire of his father. "My dad got the $12 phone bill, which was normally $8. Though Milwaukee Avenue was just across the street, it was a ten-cent long-distance call."

Over the years that he was growing up, Zelisko booked hundreds of engagements for the Chicago athletes. While many of the kids gravitated to stars like Dick Butkus and Gayle Sayers of the Chicago Bears, Danny found a special kinship with Brian Piccolo—and learned for the first time about the payoff.

"I'd booked Brian into an engagement at the Old Tree Inn, an old mob hangout, for $300," Zelisko said. Piccolo gave up a spot with the kids' dads to sit with Danny, then took him to the restroom. "Standing side by side at the urinals, he slipped me $30. I said, 'What's this?' He said, 'It's your commission. Don't Fortunato, Pettibone, or Sayers give you any money?' I said no. He said, 'Fuckers. You get *paid* for this.'"

That day, Zelisko learned how agents earned a living.

In 1962, before millions of Americans discovered them, Zelisko was listening to the Beatles. "The Beatles were a baby band to me. I discovered them as an eight-year-old listening to Top 40 radio. This was before they broke on Ed Sullivan, before rock was a term, and long before FM radio."

Every week, Zelisko rode his bike down to the local record store to sort through the Top 40 hits. His passion and ear for good music foreshadowed what was to come.

His taste and fascination with music grew just as music began to explode: the British Invasion, San Francisco Summer of Love, Hendrix, the Doors, *Circus* and *Sixteen* magazines. He amassed a huge collection of singles.

In 1970, Stevie Wonder played in Zelisko's high-school gym. Something puzzled him: Although he was a big fan, why didn't the show appeal to him or others? Something was missing. What was it? He realized there was no real buzz for the performance. This was the first hint of what was to come for Danny Zelisko the promoter.

The second hint was when news of the San Francisco music culture, led by impresario Bill Graham, hit Chicago. Zelisko left the Windy City for Berkeley so he could be in the heart of the quickly emerging music scene. He wanted to *be* Bill Graham.

His stay in San Francisco was brief; the shows he promoted didn't do well and he ran out of money. Looking for a friendlier market, Zelisko found a niche in the newly opened 3,000-seat Celebrity Theater in Phoenix. He convinced his dad to give him a stake.

"In 1974, I did my first show, Mahavishnu Orchestra," Zelisko said. "Tickets weren't selling well, so I added this up-and-coming group, Journey. Only I didn't tell anyone about the opening act. On the day of the show, Mahavishnu's manager asked me, 'Is this your first show?' 'Yes, why?' 'We don't allow opening acts. We have a three-and-a-half-hour show and there's no time for an opening act.' So the first show I ever did in Phoenix, I had to fire Journey."

Zelisko started doing shows more regularly, making a point of meeting and getting to know the agents and managers. He was hungry and he learned, but continued to struggle; ticket prices were too low to cover the upfront expenses of band, hall deposits, and advertising.

In 1976, he created Evening Star Productions. In its first year, Evening Star did 40 shows. The second year, it promoted 70. As record sales started picking up, the club acts he was booking were beginning to break. "My problem was the agencies were reluctant to sell the 'big acts' to a 24-year-old kid."

He continued to build relationships and demonstrate his promotional acumen until 1979, when he got his big break, Bob Seger, who sold out immediately. "I went out of my way to make this date special," Zelisko said. "I was there all day on roller skates. The stage and scaffolding, PA, and lights were up and the doors were ready to open.

"I heard Bob in the dressing room warming up his voice. As I passed by, he came out and asked if I was the promoter. He told me he had to cancel the show. He had problems with his voice and didn't want to threaten his big dates in L.A. Fortunately, Bob is a decent guy. He advanced all the expenses for the makeup date and a second show that I promoted."

Zelisko is five foot six, with a paunchy unintimidating frame that fits perfectly with his Bill Murray grin. Much of his success can be attributed to his passion for music and the relationships he built with the players in the business: agents, managers, venues, and acts.

Fred Ordower and Jammin'

Not far from where Zelisko grew up, another kid who would have a profound effect on the Vegas music scene was cutting his teeth in the Chicago rock culture. In 1964 at 12 years old, Fred Ordower received a gift from his dad: a shortwave radio that picked up AM and FM stations from around the world. Fred quickly found stations that played the new wave of breaking bands, including, of course, the Beatles.

He joined a band, but having the least amount of talent in the group, he found his niche in what would eventually define his career: booking. While the band terminated him as a member, it employed him to do everything else. Throughout high school, he acted as manager, agent, roadie, and promoter for several bands.

Ordower enrolled in the University of Illinois and majored in geology, but quickly gravitated back to the music business, serving on the student concert committee. In 1969, he introduced Chicago blues bands like Muddy Waters, Howlin' Wolf, and Moon Dog Taylor to the U of I students, which led to booking Chicago blues bands on campuses all over the Midwest.

Ordower became acquainted in Chicago with Arny Granat and Jerry Mickelson, two promoters who put on concerts at the university; they came to appreciate Fred's promotional skills. In 1976, Ordower left his university aspirations behind and joined Granat and Mickelson's Jam Productions.

Fred Ordower is a diligent patient communicator and orator, something like Henry Kissinger, but with the look of Henry Mitchell, Dennis the Menace's father. He was a thorough and effective negotiator with an innate ability to pinpoint an issue and calmly and analytically resolve it.

Jam Productions, forced to compete against established national promoters like Concerts West and Howard Stein, focused on smaller markets and college campuses in the heartland. In 1978, Fred met another up-and-coming promoter in Phoenix, Danny Zelisko. Together they began sponsoring shows in Phoenix, Tucson, Albuquerque, and Las Vegas.

The first show promoted by Jam, Evening Star and Michael Schivo Presents was the Stray Cats and Scorpions at the Las Vegas Convention Center. It wasn't a good start and it didn't get better for a while.

"We hated doing shows in Vegas," Zelisko said. "It wasn't a modern city—no culture, professional sports, or arena. Besides the Rotunda, the only other concert venue was the Aladdin. In Chicago and Phoenix, we had multiple concert venues—halls, ballrooms, and stadiums."

In addition, Zelisko continues, "The police were real rednecks. They were untrained and irritated by the detail, and they brought German shepherds into the audience at the Rotunda, which was really dangerous. It was a Nazi-like state." Rather than alienate acts and fans, Jam and Evening Star elected not to do any more shows at the Convention Center.

The Aladdin wasn't much better. "Ticket prices were around $10, so grosses were $60,000 or $70,000. They charged $20,000 for rent," Zelisko says. "It was a very difficult place to make any money."

Finally, in 1983, UNLV opened the 18,500-seat Thomas and Mack Center and the trio began regularly promoting shows in the Entertainment Capital.

Barry Fey the Rock Father

As a promoter, only Bill Graham had more influence in the concert touring business than Barry Fey. Fey produced more than 1,000 concerts, including the US Festival in San Bernardino in 1983. In Las Vegas, his concerts launched a new era of live music, including shows at Sam Boyd Stadium, a Bally's concert series, and the original MGM Grand Garden concerts.

While the '60s and '70s were a magical time in music and Fey was at the epicenter of it all, his life was anything but magical. According to his memoir, *Backstage Past*, the last time he'd been truly happy was when he was 11.

"That may seem odd coming from one of the biggest rock-concert promoters in history, the man who booked Led Zeppelin's first North American appearance and the Jimi Hendrix Experiences, the man who counted many of rock's royalty as personal friends and dozens of others, including political royalty, were more than just acquaintances, the man who was repeatedly honored in the business and in the community, from 'Promoter of the Year' by *Billboard* magazine three consecutive years to a videotaped message of personal thanks from President Bill Clinton. Odd coming from a guy who has heard countless times, 'I would have loved to live your life!'"

Fey was born in Manhattan in 1938, but moved to New Jersey, Pittsburgh, and Chicago before he was 13. By his senior year in high school, he was a self-described bully who "didn't get along with anyone."

That same year, Fey's father died and with no money to go to college, he enlisted in the Marine Corps.

"A week after I turned 17, I was in the Marines," Barry said. "It was 1956, we were broke, I couldn't go to college. I was 237 pounds and I felt worthless. They beat the shit out of me. It's a miracle I got through boot camp."

Fey was 19 when he got out of the Marines and received a scholarship to University of Pennsylvania.

Fey tried hard to fit in, but "The Marines ruined me for college. I got out with a huge chip on my shoulder."

In 1960, he dropped out, abandoning his scholarship, and returned to Chicago, where, without a car, he walked everywhere; he didn't even have money for bus fare.

In 1965, Barry and a roommate sponsored a dance at an American Legion Hall and brought in Baby Huey and the Baby Sitters to perform. The dance was successful. After paying everyone, he and his partner each earned $92.50, more than he made in a week at his job as a salesman, which he quickly quit to start his own concert-promoting company, Thumbs Up Productions. Word got around about his Baby Huey concert and soon, an agent called him about booking the Beau Brummels, on the charts with "Laugh Laugh," followed by the Byrds, who'd just put out the hits "Turn, Turn, Turn" and "My Tambourine," and The Kingsmen, who had the hit "Louie, Louie." Then he landed a new act, the Association, and got them gigs at Colorado colleges just before their first smash hit, "Cherish." Fey moved to Denver to be an impresario in Colorado.

One day in Denver in 1967, he noticed an ad at the bottom of the front page of *Billboard* magazine: Family Dog Productions in San Francisco was looking for original bands to start a record label. Fey knew of one original Denver-based band, Eighth Penny Matter. He called the Family Dog and told them he had a band. They asked him to fly to San Francisco to meet with Chet Helms, the founder of the company.

Barry and his wife Cindy were amazed by what they saw in the City by the Bay. They went to the Avalon Ballroom, where Chuck Berry was playing; it was the first time he'd ever seen strobe lights. In Haight-Ashbury and at Golden Gate Park, people were getting high in public, bands were playing, and groups like the Diggers were doing community-service work by feeding people. This was the height of the hippie movement and the Summer of Love.

Though way out of his element, Barry told Cindy that he had to find a way to import to Denver what he saw in San Francisco. That opportunity arrived when, after a teen club called the Bird closed, the owner of the building contacted Fey about bringing in some acts and keeping the venue going.

In Sept. 1967, the Denver Family Dog opened with Big Brother and the Holding Company and Janis Joplin.

To associate his production company with the Family Dog, he named it Feline Productions. A sales rep assumed that, since Barry's last name was Fey, someone had left out the "y." The ad announcing the new Family Dog came out as "Feyline Presents."

Fey was blessed with promoting shows at the most iconic concert venue in the world, Red Rocks Amphitheater, the 9,500-seat amphitheater cut out of the mountains 10 miles west of Denver. It has been hosting concerts since the early 20th century. *Pollstar*, the leading concert-industry magazine, awarded Red Rocks the honor of best small outdoor venue 11 straight times before removing it from the running and naming the coveted designation the "Red Rocks Award."

Fey's first show there was Jimi Hendrix, on September 1, 1968; though it had an all-time high-ticket price of $5, it sold out in a week.

Fey sponsored every act that ever toured (except the Beatles), but his history with U2 was the most special, going far beyond the promoter-artist relationship. Fey believed, not incorrectly as it turned out, that U2 would be one of the biggest bands in the world and the band repaid

Behind Every Great Man ...

Pam Moore was Barry Fey's right-hand person for 20 years. A military brat, she lived in New York, Ohio, and Alaska before settling in Hawaii. In 1972, she attended a music festival in the crater of Diamondhead volcano on Oahu. Entering through a 300-foot tunnel, fans listened to live music in a geological marvel. She was hooked. After graduating from UC-Davis, Moore returned to the islands to promote both the Crater and Sunshine rock festivals.

In 1978, Moore joined Feyline. Fey, like many in the music business, had a short fuse. Moore was petite and even-tempered, yet assertive, a good fit for Fey and the concert industry. She survived some early tempests—hurled plants and staplers barely missing her head—but managed to establish a cordial and professional relationship with Fey.

"When I started booking concerts," she said, "I quickly got acquainted with the cast of characters on the tour assembly line: manager, agent, promoter, and building.

"Before booking events, the only thing I'd ever negotiated was buying a car. I was hardly prepared for the well-oiled promoter pressure cooker. I quickly learned three lessons: Don't take anything personally, be prepared, and look at the long-term picture."

his early enthusiasm with loyalty and friendship. After their debut in Denver, he took them sightseeing; the first stop was Red Rocks Amphitheater. The band members were blown away and anxious for their shot to play there. Their chance came in 1983. Fey agreed to partner in the filming of the concert, *Under a Blood Red Sky*.

The day of the show was one of the nastiest on record—thunderstorms, sleet, hail, rain, flooding. Despite it all, the band was insistent on playing and 4,400 of the 10,000 fans who bought tickets showed up. Fey remembered the evening. "When I got there, the amphitheater was in a cloud. Literally in a fucking cloud. It was raining. It was barely above freezing. Stagehands were using squeegees to get the water off the stage and away from the wires. They were throwing ice melters onto the stage, so Bono wouldn't slip. It was so cold that you could see Bono's breath. How Edge was able to play, I don't know, because his fingers had to be freezing." *Rolling Stone* magazine called the performance one of "the 50 moments that changed the history of rock 'n' roll."

Fey's business expanded and his impact on Las Vegas cannot be overstated. Feyline started promoting shows in Las Vegas in the '70s, but ramped up its presence when the Thomas and Mack Center opened in 1983. His first concert was Willie Nelson and Waylon Jennings, which drew close to 12,000. In the first year, Feyline promoted five more shows: Elton John, Lionel Richie, Ozzy Osborne, Hall and Oates, and Kenny Rogers and Dolly Parton. U2 played Thomas and Mack Center for first time in 1987; Las Vegas and Sam Boyd Stadium have been a part of every U2 stadium tour since.

Fey forged a strong relationship with a senior vice president at Bally's, Richard Sturm. Together, they created a concert series at Bally's. When the MGM Grand opened in 1993, it included the 17,000-seat Grand Garden Arena; the Bally's concerts were largely responsible for landing Sturm his new job as MGM's entertainment director.

The Grand Garden Arena added a whole new dimension to the Las Vegas entertainment scene, formidable competition for the Aladdin Theater and Thomas and Mack Center. And it expanded the concert universe for the regional promoters like Danny Zelisko, Fred Ordower, and Barry Fey.

But one hotel was ready to step into the touring game—by itself and with a unique twist.

CHAPTER FOUR

CAESARS PALACE TAKES LIVE MUSIC UNDER THE STARS

The grand opening was fit for an emperor of Rome, an extravagant premiere that remained unsurpassed for more than 20 years. Nearly 2,000 invited guests included a who's who from show business and politics. When it debuted in 1966, Caesars Palace set a new standard for themed hotels.

The Bacchanal Room was one of the top restaurants in town, and certainly the most grandiose. The Garden of the Gods pool area was modeled after the Pompeii baths. Andy Williams opened the Circus Maximus showroom, where residencies included the top names on the Strip—Frank Sinatra, Diana Ross, Tom Jones, Tony Bennett. Others who performed there? Only Judy Garland, Liberace, Cher, Shirley MacLaine, Henny Youngman, Johnny Mathis, George Burns, Julio Iglesias, Bette Midler, Buddy Hackett, Ann-Margret, Flip Wilson, Dionne Warwick, Burt Bacharach, Natalie Cole, Harry Belafonte, Peggy Lee, Milton Berle, Woody Allen, David Copperfield, Eddie Fisher, and of course, Sammy Davis Jr.

The Circus Maximus also hosted more than 100 championship boxing matches; Roberto Duran fought there nine times, Sugar Ray Leonard nine, Marvin Hagler six, Tommy Hearns 11, and Larry Holmes 14.

In addition, it featured some of the first Broadway productions to come to Las Vegas in the late '60s and early '70s. Tony Randall performed in Neil Simon's *The Odd Couple* there for the first time, prompting his role in the hit television series.

Caesars continuously reinvented itself in order to dominate entertainment in Las Vegas. Evel Knievel made an unsuccessful and near-fatal attempt to jump his motorcycle over its iconic fountain. The hotel hosted Formula One Racing, Wrestlemania, outdoor NHL hockey, and tennis tournaments.

It's a testament to Caesars Palace's hegemony on the Las Vegas Strip that Steve Wynn had to spend $650 million, nearly $500 million more than any other Las Vegas hotel up until then, when he built the Mirage next door.

Las Vegas was now in the '80s and things were changing. From 1981 to 1984, Caesars held outdoor concerts.

Las Vegas' First Outdoor Concerts

Tom Pilkington was raised in a family with six sisters, first in Rhode Island, then in Vermont, then back in Rhode Island. He met his first wife when he was 22.

"She had two sisters and a couple of brothers who lived in Las Vegas," Pilkington says. "They were all stagehands. We went out to visit and it was the land of milk and honey. It had nothing to do with gambling. It was just the weather, the culture, how different it all was."

On the flight back, Roger told his wife, "I don't want to live in Rhode Island anymore. I don't want to work in a bank. I'd like to move out to Vegas."

He didn't know what he'd do in Nevada, but he turned in his notice, packed the car, and drove cross country. "My family thought I was cracked, that I'd completely lost my mind, going out to Sin City."

They arrived on New Year's Eve 1973. His in-laws took them under their wing and got Roger started.

"Back then, the Stagehand Union had an iron-fisted grip on all the shows in all the showrooms. I went through about a three-month 'break-in.' Today you might call it an internship. But it was simple free labor. It's illegal now, but I did it seven nights a week."

The union required a sponsor. Tom's brother in-law, ex-president of the union local, got him started at the Stardust as a spotlight operator. He moved to the Fremont, then the Desert Inn. During the day, he hustled up whatever jobs he could find.

His first long-term position was back at the Fremont with *Minsky's Burlesque.* He did that for over a year and on nights when the show was down for maintenance, he worked a Strip property where someone was sick or extra people were needed for a show that was loading in or out.

He helped open the Marina Hotel, then worked at the Sahara in the

Congo Room as a spot operator and lighting technician. He could now afford a family.

It wasn't long before he was offered a job at Caesars' Circus Maximus. The stage manager, Eddie Lynch, who opened the property was getting on in years. Lynch was a character you might see in an old black-and-white movie out of central casting as a stage manager. He was diminutive, tough, and gruff, but everyone loved him. Of Irish heritage, he wore dark horn-rimmed glasses and made his mark with Harold Minsky on the burlesque circuit in the '40s and '50s. He took a liking to Pilkington and hired him. Tom transitioned from being a union stagehand over to management, which proved to be a bit awkward for a while.

But Pilkington learned a lot from Lynch about production and how to deal with people, when to be or not to be diplomatic, particularly with performers and their entourages. In 1978, after Lynch had a minor stroke, Tom was promoted to stage manager. Year by year, thanks to his diverse skills, he picked up more responsibilities and eventually became assistant entertainment director.

In 1981, Caesars started an entertainment division, primarily to better position the company to do feature films and to upgrade its entertainment in Tahoe and Atlantic City. As part of that process, they hired Alan Bregman, who was booking venues for the Nederlander Organization, which operated a couple dozen theaters around the country, and was considered one of the top talent buyers in the United States. Caesars began to block book Tahoe, Atlantic City, and Las Vegas. "Caesars was doing residencies before anyone knew what residencies were," says Pilkington.

Bregman and Pilkington hit if off immediately. "Alan was essentially my mentor. He took me under his wing and I was a pretty eager learner. Over the next year and a half, I became directly involved with artist negotiations."

Administering contracts, Pilkington began to develop relationships with band managers and agencies like William Morris, CAA, and ICM.

Then one night they hatched a new idea. "Alan and I were having dinner at Caesars and we were talking about bringing back the Alan King tennis event, which had gone on for years, but was now in hiatus. He said, 'Well, how many people can you put out there?' I said, 'We can probably get five or six thousand if we bring in temporary bleachers.' He said, 'Well, why don't we also do concerts?' We closed the restaurant that night talking about what we'd need to do outdoor rock shows."

Pilkington did some homework. He came up with a stage, a roof design, and crowd control. Then he and Alan discussed booking acts outside the traditional Vegas headliner box. The problem was, even into the 1980s, Vegas was without a large venue. It wasn't even a secondary market for touring bands, who'd truck right through the city on their way to and from Phoenix, L.A., and San Diego. They crossed off the triple A acts and hoped for double A or even single A. Finally, they started to shake the bushes to see what artists they could attract with revenue-sharing deals.

Then they had to sell the whole idea to the bosses.

"I'll never forget sitting at an executive committee meeting and discussing our plans with a lot of old-school people who looked at me like I had three heads."

About that time, a seemingly unrelated event played into Bregman and Pilkington's hands.

Over July 4, 1980, '81, and '82, the Beach Boys and the Grass Roots performed on the National Mall in Washington, D.C. But in 1983, Ronald Reagan's controversial Secretary of the Interior James G. Watt banned Independence Day concerts on the Mall by "such groups." Watt believed these shows encouraged drug use and alcoholism and attracted the wrong element.

Watt's ban met with immediate media backlash and a national fury ensued. President Reagan reversed Watt's ban. On learning that his boss was a fan of the group, Watt issued an apology to the Beach Boys.

The media storm reignited their career. Caesars Palace took advantage. The Beach Boys became the first act to play a "Concert Under the Stars."

Tickets went on sale at nine in the morning with no online ticketing system, a small phone sales system, and some consignment. Still, the show sold out by three o'clock.

"People who live in Las Vegas know that June, July, and August are the monsoon months," said Pilkington. "At seven o'clock on the night of the concert, it got very *very* dark when a significant thunderstorm rolled through the valley with a lot of wind and rain. We were supposed to start at eight o'clock, right at dusk. We held off the show for 30 minutes. We were backstage, talking to Mike Love and Al Jardine. Mike and Al were regular folks. They were in and out of the trailer. Everyone was looking up at the sky when it stopped raining for a bit. We called the tower at McCarran to get a weather report. They told us, 'You've got about a 50-minute window.' We got the guys on stage and they opened the show with 'Help Me, Rhonda.' They hadn't gotten even halfway through the song when the skies opened. It rained for the entire two and a half hours. No one moved. No one sat down. It was a warm summer rain. It was fantastic. People still talk about it."

America. The Go-Go's. George Benson. Al Jarreau. The performers started playing Under the Stars.

Ticket distribution was 60% local and 40% out of town. The fans, consisting of 25- to 30-year-olds, weren't typical Caesars customers. The casino rolled out promotions using the ticket stubs as coupons, plus slot and bar promotions, to coax the audience into the casino.

The concert series continued in subsequent years; it took the summer of 1987 off, but came back strong in 1988 with a larger 12,000-seat capacity and a more sophisticated stage and roof system that also hosted outdoor boxing matches.

The larger venue for boxing and concerts had its advantages. Steve Winwood's concert in July 1988 was a good example.

"At the time, Winwood was one of the top touring acts and had the number-one album," Pilkington recalls. "About 45 minutes before the show started, he came out and asked to see the facility. We walked to the corner of the ground floor; we had close to 13,000 people and the place was buzzing. He turned to me and asked in that British accent, 'Is this where Marvin Hagler, Sugar Ray Leonard, and Larry Holmes fight?' I said, 'Yeah.' But I felt like, 'Oh my God! Our venue is known all over the world!'"

He walked onstage and did his first three songs. The place was rocking. He stopped and thanked everyone, as most performers do. But he went on to say how honored he was to be at Caesars Palace in a venue he'd seen on closed-circuit TV watching prizefights."

Ironically, Winwood was the last big show of the Caesars concert series. They hosted boxing, Wrestlemania, and other special events up until 1990.

"Facility wise, we had a leg up on almost everyone in town. That's how we could knock down the big barrier the music industry had for Vegas. And we had the will to spend the money to make the statement. Also, we knew that to be the best, we had to break new ground continually."

Toward that end, starting in 1985 when the big National Finals Rodeo event moved from Oklahoma City to Las Vegas, Caesars was again ahead of the times, booking Willie Nelson eight straight days before any other entertainment department was doing country music at all. Reba McEntire, Vince Gill, Clint Black, and Tim McGraw followed close on Willie's heels.

Caesars began a culture shift toward more mainstream music. More and more agents and managers started to take Las Vegas seriously as a viable place to play.

CHAPTER FIVE

BIG, BOLD, AND BRASH—
THOMAS AND MACK CENTER

The vision for a new state-of-the-art Las Vegas arena was hatched in the mid-'70s after UNLV convinced Jerry Tarkanian to leave Long Beach State to coach the Runnin' Rebels basketball team. From 1971 to 1982, the Rebels regularly sold out the 6,700-seat Rotunda at the Las Vegas Convention Center. Was Vegas ready for the "Big Show"?

In 1979, UNLV Boosters and legislators began to work feverishly to finance an arena. They, the state, and the federal government crafted a tax on slot machines earmarked for education. A small portion of that tax was earmarked to fund Thomas and Mack Center and Lawlor Events Center in Reno. Bankers Parry Thomas and Jerry Mack donated the Las Vegas land, earning the honor of having the arena named after them.

Originally, Thomas and Mack Center was designed to seat 15,000. But boosters believed the demand from Runnin' Rebel fans mandated more seats. However, UNLV was unsuccessful at increasing tax funding. Even so, construction forged ahead on an 18,500-seat facility.

As the opening of the TMC approached, there was good news and bad. UNLV was the proud owner of a new 18,500-seat arena. But financing for the additional 3,500 seats never materialized. How to pay for them?

Pavement for the 6,000 parking spots was cut. The concourse, which separated the 9,500 balcony seats from the 9,000 plaza seats, and the concession stands were as bare as Mother Hubbard's cupboard. Although the VIP suites were a first for a college venue, they were just holes in the concourse, with exposed pipes and wires.

Just as critical, the courtside seats at both ends of the arena were made of concrete, prohibiting the production of any events besides basketball, boxing, and small-capacity concerts. To further the burden, there was no operating budget to open the arena.

UNLV had a problem.

Thomas and Mack Center Inc.

Dennis Finfrock grew up in Yuma, Arizona. He played football at BYU before moving to Las Vegas to teach and coach wrestling at Chaparral High School. In 1976, UNLV hired him to start a wrestling program. Finfrock was ambitious and resourceful, with the endurance of a marathon runner. He juggled his assistant athletic director duties with his position as head wrestling coach and ran his own crowd-management company, FINCO. While he aspired to one day to be athletic director, he also saw that UNLV was struggling with the fiscal challenges of its new arena. He had an idea.

He proposed operating the arena as an enterprise, rather than a traditional state-funded university facility. The University had little choice; without additional state or university funding for operations or even to complete construction, the arena had to pay its own way. Finfrock lobbied then-Chair of the Board of Regents, Jack McBride, to run with his idea.

Las Vegas now had a venue with a capacity equal to those in the west like the L.A. Forum, Oakland and Phoenix coliseums, San Diego Sports Arena, and the Salt Palace. It sat just a mile and half east of the Las Vegas Strip on 11 acres at the entrance to McCarran International Airport. In 1983, the population of Las Vegas was just shy of 500,000. Not quite the market base of other western cities, but for promoters, it meant another venue with the capacity to host major tours.

Thomas and Mack Center eschewed the old way of doing things in a new era of live music in Las Vegas. Not only was its capacity double that of anything in the market, it greatly refined the promoter experience. It was no longer the burden of the promoter to hire ushers, security, and stagehands or manage the venue's ticket office. In addition, replicating what was learned from the L.A. Forum, Houston Summit, and New York's Madison Square Garden, a professional venue-management operation was put in place.

John Meglen of Concerts West cites its significance. "Thomas and Mack Center's opening was a big deal, because suddenly you had a new 18,500-seat university building that was operating like a professional business. There were only four or five other college venues in the country where the guys running them could be entrepreneurial."

For Fred Ordower with Jam Productions, one of TMC's first promoters, the biggest difference was that the venue actually *welcomed* live music. The Rotunda at the Convention Center was primarily in the convention business; only reluctantly did it serve as a concert venue. "Both the Convention Center and Aladdin were overstaffed with police. To the fan, it felt more like a heavy-duty lockdown. The TMC was a destination for concerts that created a professional, concert-friendly, crowd-managed environment."

A concert is an emotional experience. For some fans, it's their first. For others, it's a four-hour liberation from life. But for a few, it's a chance to misbehave.

Thomas and Mack Center was committed to safety and allowing fans the freedom to enjoy the music. Before opening TMC, a crowd-*management*, versus crowd-*control*, plan was developed based on best practices from the top arenas in the country. But a system was only half of it. The venue needed people who would buy into a service philosophy.

In June 1983, I was sitting in my TMC management office when two businessmen, who had just relocated from Michigan, walked in. "We want to get in on the ground floor of the Thomas and Mack Center," said former high-school athletic director, Ed McPeek, while his cohort, Vern West, nodded. Knowing nothing about either of them, I made them pass a couple of tests by putting them to work managing the parking-lot staff at the Silver Bowl.

The two quickly demonstrated good organizational skills and a natural ability to manage customers and employees. They went on to become heads of the usher staff at both venues, recruiting and hiring most of our team from the Clark County School District. When MGM Grand Garden opened, they were put in charge of ushers there and McPeek assisted in opening T-Mobile Arena.

TMC eased the burden for the concert promoter in another way. The Rock Concert Ordinance was created to protect the public from unscrupulous promoters. Considering TMC sold all the tickets and managed the crowd, the public was protected. As a facility with its own campus police force and an in-house crowd-management staff, we asked for and received a waiver from the Rock Concert Ordinance.

Though it was built for the basketball team, concerts were a big piece of TMC's revenue projections. Thomas and Mack's first concert, Loverboy, was promoted by New Orleans-based Beaver Concerts, which had promoted several concerts at the Aladdin and Convention Center. We established the cost for using Thomas and Mack Center—$3,500 minimum rent against 13.5% of the gross, 4% of gross for use of box office, and a 35/65 split of all tour merchandise sales. In addition, the promoter paid all expenses—ushers, ticket takers, security, and police. The promoter's profit depended on ticket sales against expenses.

I'm sure Beaver got better deals to rent arenas elsewhere in the country. However, the only way we were going to pay our bills and, in effect, ourselves, was to generate revenue from events.

To assist in training staff, we brought in Staff Pro, a well-respected crowd-management company out of southern California. We'd spent a lot of time formulating our strategy for managing the fans, visiting four arenas around the country. We were ready—or so we thought.

Loverboy Shows No Love

Though fully committed to controlling our destiny, we were green. When we opened the doors to the Loverboy fans, few on our staff had much, if any, experience. It would turn out to be a challenging night.

The evening started calmly. However, we quickly found that the 15-foot space between the stage and first row (per the fire code) and the 12-inch orange flashlights our special ushers carried weren't seasoned decisions.

To ensure crowd safety, it's critical to impose rules that fans understand: a timely and orderly bottle check, aisles clear, no standing on chairs, etc. Basic practices establish a psychology with the fans that makes them feel safe, yet uninhibited enough to enjoy themselves. But if the band doesn't understand the power it has with fans and perform responsibly, it often means trouble.

We'd heard from other venues that Loverboy's lead singer, Mike Reno, had incited crowds to ignore security and charge the stage. Even though we made it clear in our security meeting that this would not be tolerated, 45 minutes into the show, Reno took exception to the 15-foot space between him and his fans and the rigid feel of the building, and he called on the crowd to come closer.

You can have the world's most sophisticated crowd-management plan, but the act has complete control and, therefore, a duty to act responsibly. There's little a staff of 50 ushers can do to prevent a crowd of thousands from suddenly surging.

We instructed our ushers to clear the aisles and get people back to their seats. But again, Reno called the crowd forward, using some choice four-letter words to describe our staff and police. The scene in front of the stage was a mass of humanity. He was naively endangering them all.

This was the first of many rock concerts we planned to host. At stake was not only the safety of fans that evening, but a demonstration of our ability to manage a crowd. Fans attending our concerts had to know the limitations imposed by the venue.

I huddled with Cory Meredith, the owner of Staff Pro, the crowd-management company. Meredith advised us to notify the lead singer that he was liable for what he was doing and if he did it again, we would remove our staff from behind the barricade. In other words, he and the band would be on their own. Head of security gave him the message. We again cleared the aisles and ushered fans back to their seats. There were no further incidents.

Crowd management is both a science and an art. In 1971, 13 people were killed in a melee at a Who concert at Riverfront Coliseum in Cincinnati. At that time, general-admission shows were commonplace. With more than 10,000 people waiting outside, only two doors for the concert were opened. Consequently, 200 people were overrun in the stampede. Thirteen died. Systems for managing rock-concert crowds had to improve in a hurry.

On the other hand, we took Mike Reno's sentiments seriously and after the Loverboy concert, we petitioned the fire department to reduce the 15-foot space in front of the stage.

We also purchased pen flashlights to replace the menacing light batons and staggered the rows of seats, so it would be difficult for fans to move as one toward the stage. Today, crowd management has become a high-profile priority for all levels and types of events.

Las Vegas Jumps on the Touring Caravan

A second milestone for Thomas and Mack Center took place on February 2, 1984, when a Jam/Schivo/Evening Star partnership promoted their first concert, Genesis. While the arena was incomplete in many ways for rock shows, critically missing was the ability to rig from the ceiling. TMC was built for basketball. You don't need to hang lights and speakers from the ceiling for a sporting event.

It was about this time that the production for shows around the country began to grow exponentially. In the '70s, most concerts rigged all sound and lights from the stage and floor. In the early '80s, bands began to fly the sound and lights from the venue roofs. By the mid-'80s, there was an all-out rigging race for the biggest, brightest, and loudest concert production.

When Thomas and Mack Center opened, engineers rated its roof to hang a paltry 35,000 pounds. Genesis' massive show production was flying 70,000 pounds. The lighting equipment alone filled more than two of the five trucks that carried the whole setup; the special stage lights emitted 60 different color blends.

To accommodate the rigging requirements, the promoters contributed $15,000 toward a permanent truss. Six equilateral triangles were built and hung with 200 Varilites in the shape of a giant hexagon above the stage.

At the concert, Phil Collins looked around the arena and told fans, "All you who are here tonight are the center of the universe!" When the applause died down, he added, "Of course, I'll say the same thing tomorrow night in Salt Lake City." It was a memorable show.

At that time, Van Halen was at its peak and sold 15,000 tickets to its first show at TMC, then a record for the young arena. The tour production was so large, it had two sets of sound and lights that leapfrogged each other to the next city.

To accommodate the massive tour, we doubled the size of the truss donated for Genesis. Still, that was a quarter of the capacity most other venues could rig. While we understood the capacities of our rigging, our young operations staff didn't recognize all the pitfalls.

Van Halen formed in 1972, spent their first five years playing parties and small clubs, before the release of the three consecutive albums that began to establish an arena crowd. Their *1984* breakout album coincided with their concert date at Thomas and Mack Center. More than 4,000 fans camped out overnight for the first-come first-served tickets. It was the biggest show to date, both in attendance and production—15,000 tickets and 90,000 pounds.

The morning of the show, creative solutions needed to be found for the weak rating of the TMC roof. At issue was how much of their sound and lights could be flown safely from our grid. It was correctly weighed, counted, and hung. Or was it?

The show was a huge success. Van Halen hummed along like a super-charged Ferrari hitting on all 12 cylinders. However, what we discovered after the show was alarming: a badly damaged truss. To accommodate the band and deliver on the quality of sound and light show, safety was compromised. "We simply didn't know how much sound they were using until we saw them load it out," says TMC Operations Director Jeff Hightower.

It was apparent TMC needed a safer solution to manage this trend of heavier tour sound and lights. Through creative bridling (reducing weight by tying two cables together) and hanging points from the ceiling, TMC continually had the rating of its roof increased. Today, it can hang close to a million pounds.

While Vegas might have been the Entertainment Capital of the World, locals often found themselves traveling to L.A. or Phoenix to see the top touring acts. No longer. In its first full year Thomas and Mack Center hosted 24 concerts, including Van Halen, Rush, Elton John, and Ozzy, twice the number of concerts Vegas had hosted in any year prior to that. With music from every genre, the new venue introduced many locals to their first live music. There was a lot of excitement for the new venue. However, there were still challenges.

By the end of September, Las Vegas usually gets a little relief from the heat. But for the September 29, 1984, concert with Lionel Richie, whose career was at its peak, it was unseasonably warm. We'd sold a record 16,000 tickets. The trip for the production trucks from Oakland to Vegas, where they'd sold out the night before, should have landed them at our load-in dock at eight a.m.; typically, a show loaded in between six and eight a.m. Lionel's equipment didn't arrive until noon. Excuses varied from weather to breakdown, but as I learned later, the real reason was a stop at one of Nevada's famous cathouses. The noon arrival resulted in two problems that had repercussions far after this night.

When concert fans started arriving, the production wasn't set and the tour manager wouldn't allow us to open the doors. Even though the line wrapped around the arena, we were forced to keep our 15,000 guests sweating and getting angry out in the heat for 90 minutes. So much for a good first impression. Our problems didn't end there.

Also thanks to the condensed load-in, there was no sound check. The sound check took place *during* the show. For Richie's first six songs, none of the words he was singing could be distinguished; during the seventh song, the check was completed. It also didn't help that the interior of the arena was skinned with a very cold steel, concrete, and glass finish—not an ideal acoustical setting.

Starting the night of the Richie concert, it took the TMC 15 years to recover from the reputation of a poor-sounding concert venue.

Brooks and Bono

Despite the acoustical weaknesses, the lack of real competition allowed TMC to average 15 concerts a year for the next decade; it took that long, and longer, for the Strip to fully grasp the impact of live music.

We weren't, by any means, sitting on our laurels. We still had to pay our own way. Typically, arenas and stadiums subcontract some or all of their services, but to insure control over the customer experience and maximize the bottom line, we did everything in-house. To keep quality and pricing in line, we operated our own food service. We created usher, crowd-management, ticket, merchandise, cleaning, and maintenance divisions. We were running a big business and we attracted the biggest stars in various genres.

Billy Joel, Whitney Houston, Rod Stewart, Stevie Wonder, and Fleetwood Mac highlighted shows for the MOR (middle of the road) concert fan. AC/DC, Metallica, KISS, Scorpions, Def Leppard, and Mötley Crüe satisfied the heavy-metal appetites. N' Sync, New Edition, Boyz to Men, Run DMC, New Kids on the Block, Spice Girls, and Bobby Brown all played Thomas and Mack Center.

And then there was Garth Brooks.

Brooks' first album was released in 1989 and peaked at number two on the country album charts. He quickly earned a reputation as a country showman with no peer. At the beginning of the summer of 1993, we were approached to host a Garth Brooks concert. At the time, Brooks was managed by his brother Kelly and promoted by his cousin Patrick Dial. As a family affair, the negotiations for the show were more focused on the fan experience than financial terms. All of this was a precursor of what was to come.

We spent a couple of weeks developing a detailed ticket-sales plan. The goal was: Every fan who wanted a ticket got one. The day of the sale, we monitored our own ticket office and the ticket outlets as, one by one, three shows sold out—upwards of 50,000 tickets at $18 apiece. The third show, though, didn't sell out until a few days later, so few fans were left out.

Brooks had a reputation of showing up for load-in. My attitude was, if an artist of his stature was going to be there at 6:30 in the morning, the building manager could do the same. When the trucks pulled up, I introduced myself. Brooks watched the work for a while, then pulled a football from his vehicle. For the next half-hour, I ran routes for what turned out to be a country rocker with a pretty accurate arm.

Flames thrashed the stage on the set opener, "Standing Outside the Fire," as Brooks walked through the inferno to get to its center. Crowd favorites "Shameless" and "The Thunder Rolls" were accompanied by lightning, booming cloud claps, and rainfall. But the highlight of the show was Brooks flying over the audience during the first encore. Strapped into an almost invisible harness and guide wires, Brooks took flight singing "Ain't Going Down." The crowd response shook the roof.

For me, the most exciting part of the three-day stand came after the last song. Finishing a second encore, Brooks expressed his sincere appreciation to the fans. They wouldn't let him go. What he blurted out next, I'm sure was never uttered by any artist before or since. "You've been such a great crowd. When I return, the price will be the same as tonight. Eighteen dollars." In 1998, he did return to the Thomas and Mack Center, selling out four shows at, yes, $18.

U2 could be considered the Irish equivalent of Garth Brooks when it comes to a deep and abiding respect for the fans. U2 formed in 1976. By combining an original sound with honest lyrics and a challenging social message, this band earned the respect of peers and critics and an almost fanatical following of fans around the world. The keys to U2's permanency are their respect for one another and their fans, the knack for continuously reinventing themselves, and powerful music with a social message.

U2 hit Vegas a day before one of their concerts. They saw Sugar Ray Leonard beat Marvin Hagler in a controversial split decision at Caesars Palace. Later, they got Barry Fey to score them VIP tickets (normally $25,000 a table) to a Frank Sinatra midnight fundraiser show at the Golden Nugget. Warming up the crowd, Don Rickles brought them to the attention of ol' Blue Eyes himself. "Hey, Frank, before you start, there are some people in the audience you really should meet. It's a band called U2. They're going to be very very big." Rickles gestured for the spotlight to shine on the Irish quartet as they stood up and waved.

Sinatra took one look at them, turned to Rickles, and said, "They may be getting big, but they haven't spent a dime on clothes."

Later, when asked about the night, Bono told BBC Radio, "We got to meet Frank afterward and an ongoing relationship started with him. He and [drummer] Larry hit it off, because Larry was talking to him about Buddy Rich. Oddly, I don't think many people talked to Sinatra about music."

After the concert, U2 shot a music video. Pretending to be buskers walking downtown's Fremont Street, they lip-synced the song on their *Joshua Tree* album, "Still Haven't Found What I'm Looking For." According to *Rolling Stone*, this video elevated the band's stature "from heroes

Phishing Expeditions

Another band that fell in love with Las Vegas was Grateful Dead-influenced Phish. Formed at the University of Vermont in 1983, Phish is renowned for their extended jams, improvisation, and amalgamation of genres, including progressive and funk rock, folk, country, blues, bluegrass, and jazz. *Rolling Stone* credited Phish with "spawning a new wave of bands oriented around group improvisation and super extended grooves."

Like the Grateful Dead, they've steadily built their following by word of mouth and developed a fanatical fan base that follows them from city to city. In Las Vegas, they've sold out 11 shows, nine of them at Thomas and Mack.

to superstars." Done on a shoestring budget, it was nominated for five MTV Music Video Awards.

U2 bucked the trend of major acts at the time. They loved Las Vegas and returned many many times to perform in Sin City.

During Thomas and Mack Center's first eight years of operation, we established a steady roster of concerts and special events that not only covered all of our overhead, but also financed the completion of $10 million of construction.

From 1983 to 1991, we booked every event available—concerts, the National Finals Rodeo, Pro Bull Riders World Finals, motorsports, family shows, corporate shows, major sporting events, and a Runnin' Rebel basketball team that went on a nine-year tear. In addition, the continuing lack of competition gave us a monopoly on the Triple A events of the time.

Direct revenue from all the events combined, however, wasn't enough to cover expenses and improvements. But thanks to the success of the events and the Runnin' Rebels, the value of TMC's 30 suites and advertising signage helped defray the operating costs.

But the only constant is change—and in 1992, billionaire casino mogul Kirk Kerkorian announced a new 5,000-room hotel and 15,000-seat arena. It would alter the course of my life, and the city's.

TMC Today

In 2016, UNLV finished the third overhaul of Thomas and Mack Center. It was long overdue; the mechanical, air, and electrical systems had been ignored for 10 years. Fortunately, the slot tax that originally funded the arena in 1983 continued to grow. UNLV tapped it for most of the improvements and the Thomas and Mack families also stepped up. In all, $75 million worth of improvements were made. Today, the venue is both physically and operationally one of the finest arenas in the country.

CHAPTER SIX

THE GRATEFUL DEAD

On September 14, 1968, the Division II Nevada Southern College Rebel football team played its first game at Cashman Field, beating the St. Mary's Gaels 27-20. Shortly thereafter, the school's name changed to University of Nevada at Las Vegas. UNLV boosters quickly took on the cause of advancing the school's football team. Part of that plan included a new stadium.

In 1970, coyotes, snakes, and rabbits roamed freely over the desert east of Boulder Highway on the east side of the valley. County Commissioners and big UNLV Rebel boosters Tom Weisner and Bob Broadbent hatched a plan to turn the barren land between Russell Road and Tropicana into the new home of the new university's football team. They convinced the Las Vegas Visitors and Convention Authority to invest $3.5 million in building a stadium.

On October 25, 1971, Las Vegas Stadium opened with 15,000 seats. As the football team experienced exceptional early success, the boosters weren't content with remaining in Division II. They again lobbied the LVCVA, which added another 15,000 seats and changed the name to the Las Vegas Silver Bowl.

The LVCVA, owners of the stadium, didn't actively pursue booking other events there. One of its few non-university uses took place in 1977 when the North American Soccer League's Las Vegas Quicksilvers played for one season; soccer legend Pelé appeared when the Quicksilvers went up against Pelé's team, the New York Cosmos. The stadium averaged an attendance of 7,000 for the soccer games.

In early 1983, the Convention and Visitors Authority offered to deed the stadium to UNLV for one dollar. Dennis Finfrock and I, two novice operators, were already strapped with the challenge of running an unfinished underfunded arena and we should have been hesitant to take on a stadium with one event to its credit. But Finfrock jumped at it.

It almost cost us our jobs.

From Tragic to Magic

Our challenge at Las Vegas Silver Bowl, like at Thomas and Mack, was to generate revenue. In the summer of 1984, we booked a half-dozen motorsports events. To ensure the protection of the AstroTurf, we required the promoter to put down two layers of four-by-eight sheets of quarter-inch rubber padding. Unfortunately, when the promoters loaded in the dirt, our operations director wasn't there.

The schedule of first-time motorsports events at the stadium included truck and tractor pulls, mud bogs, monster trucks, and motorcross. That summer we sold more than 125,000 tickets and generated $500,000 in revenue. But then came the load-out.

In early August, after we'd finished patting ourselves on the back, I got a 5:30 a.m. wakeup call from the boss. An hour later, Finfrock and I were looking at 40% of the dirt removed and about that much of our turf torn up.

The promoter, it turned out, hadn't installed the two layers of rubber matting; he hadn't put down even one. He just dumped his dirt on our turf; the only thing between them was a single layer of visqueen, slightly thicker than saran wrap. The front-end loaders did such a half-ass job of removing the dirt that they made our field look like Frankenstein's face.

It was less than a month until the Rebel football season. Our first summer on the job, we'd managed to damage the field surface beyond repair. Unless we came up with a solution, our careers at UNLV would be over.

Wiping the dirt, mud, and shredded AstroTurf off our shoes, though not out of our memories, we formed a plan. In a week, Monsanto had a crew repairing the field. We held our breath as we prepared for the players and fans to file into the stadium for the Rebels' first game of the season.

Team members who played in the Silver Bowl between '80 and '84 all experienced turf burns and lacerations. The field consisted of the original turf, now more than 10 years old and baked as hard in the unforgiving Vegas sun as the parking-lot pavement. Even after the repair job, it had a 16-inch crown that made it impossible to see the corners or hit a soccer ball straight. If it were a pool table, you would have had to aim at the middle of the table to make a side-pocket shot.

Our summer of events proved the Silver Bowl could generate sizable revenue. However, we weren't willing to put our jobs on the line every time we booked an event. Thus, our interest was piqued by a new Monsanto product dubbed the "Magic Carpet."

There was one problem. It cost $1.2 million.

Dennis Finfrock was an industrious problem solver. He used to say, "Measure a man by the size of his Rolodex." I'd never seen a Rolodex bigger than his first one. Then he filled a second one—amassing the names and numbers of hundreds of influential people. In 1981 and '82 as event coordinator and assistant wrestling coach, I watched him make the rounds at Rebel basketball games, collecting donations so that the wrestling team could travel to a match the next weekend. This time he made a big call ... to Sam Boyd.

At the time, the Boyd Group owned a downtown Vegas hotel-casino, the California, and Sam's Town, less than two miles up Boulder Highway from the Silver Bowl.

Understanding the dilemma, the Boyd family ponied up the $1.2 million to purchase the turf. In exchange? Yes, the venue was renamed Sam Boyd Silver Bowl (later shortened to Sam Boyd Stadium).

On a Magic Carpet Ride

You can't help but hear Jeff Chalfant pull up to work. He drives a monster truck. Maybe not as elaborate as Grave Digger or Big Foot, but I'd be a bit nervous if he pulled up behind me at a stop light.

The mild-mannered 30-year Sam Boyd Stadium employee started as a part-time gardener when we took over the stadium in 1984. Our slim budget afforded us two employees and there was little money for equipment.

"I cut all the grass, did electrical work, and whatever needed to be done," Chalfant enumerates. "We had a couple of little old feed-up mowers and two people to manage the whole stadium. Before I got there when the LVCVA managed the place, the county was doing the maintenance—seven or eight guys, all they did was play cards all day. Dennis Finfrock ran them out."

Chalfant was there when the trucks pulled up to install the Monsanto Magic Carpet. "Twelve ducts were installed in the ground that blew air up. Giant spools of AstroTurf were delivered and installed on the east side of the stadium."

Sturdy ropes tied to the spools were hooked to motors on the west side of the field. The air ducts starting pumping air and the ropes started tugging. As the turf made its way east, it created up to 10-foot waves.

Chalfant picks up the tale. "We had 10-foot-wide hand-operated drum rollers. We used them to iron the air out from under the turf, pushing it to the sides. It took two hours to get it installed and we could roll it back up in fifteen minutes."

A magic carpet indeed!

We now had the best of both worlds: a turf that rolled up in the summer to maintain its condition and no turf to cover for events.

We did many events in the stadium, but we could not get a stadium concert tour's attention. Not until 1991.

Truckin', Got My Chips Cashed In ...

In May 1991, traveling down Russell Road, crossing Boulder Highway, it hit me: This is happening!

The scene ahead was Sunrise Mountain, providing a backdrop for the very first rock concert at Sam Boyd Silver Bowl. As I approached the stadium, hundreds of colorful cars, vans, and buses were already lined up for entry into the parking lots. It was game on.

I didn't have a lot of Grateful Dead albums or CDs, but there was no event I was more anxious to manage. I imagined the scenes I'd witnessed in San Francisco and L.A. playing out in Las Vegas. Even then, I couldn't have possibly foreseen how this eclectic, psychedelic, space-rock band would spawn a new era of live music in the Entertainment Capital.

Starting in 1965, the Grateful Dead flourished, mixing rock, blues, bluegrass, and country, continuously pushing creative barriers. The

The Grateful What?

The Grateful Dead were originally called the Warlocks. However, that name was taken. The group met to consider the options.

Bill Kreutzman, one of the Dead's two drummers who played with the band from beginning to end, spoke about that afternoon. "Garcia sat on the couch with a giant dictionary and he came across the words 'grateful dead.' The words jumped off the page. Everybody said 'What?' We'd just been smoking DMT and those words stuck out. They were so incongruous. How could you be grateful and dead?"

They soon learned the beautiful story behind those two words. It came from a folk tale in which a traveler happens on a burial scene. The villagers are refusing to bury the body of a man who hadn't paid off his debts. In a tremendous act of goodwill, the traveler pays the debt for the deceased (some versions claim with his last dollar) and continues on his way. And then, along comes a spirit who says, "I am the grateful dead and I would like to reward you for your good deed."

fusion of this music with the Haight-Asbury counterculture created one of the most progressive and beloved bands of its time. In 1971, they played the Ice Palace in Las Vegas and thereafter many times at the Aladdin, before they grew big enough to fill Sam Boyd Stadium.

New bands in the '60s had abundant influences. The Rolling Stones were heavily influenced by Delta blues, Bob Dylan by beatniks like Woodie Guthrie, the Beatles by "Big Tiny Little" (a name John Lennon made up to answer the inevitable press-conference questions about the band's influences). The Dead, however, carved out its own niche—uncompromised improvisation. It didn't matter if they were jamming in Jerry Garcia's living room, rehearsing in their studio, or playing to a crowd of 10,000; they were never anything but themselves, just playing in the band.

Mikal Gilmore wrote in *Rolling Stone*, "The Grateful Dead enjoyed a union with its audience that was unrivaled and unshakable. Indeed, the Dead and their followers formed the only self-sustained, ongoing fellowship that pop music has ever produced."

A Seven-Foot Deadhead

Bill Walton was part of that fellowship.

In the early 1970s, six-eleven (some say seven-foot) Bill Walton won three successive College Player of the Year awards while leading the UCLA Bruins to two NCAA championships. Subsequently, he had a stellar career in the NBA where he was MVP with the Oregon Trailblazers, which won two championships during his reign.

He was also a free spirit who marched to his own drummer and loved rock 'n' roll. He went to countless concerts and festivals, but no band affected him more than the Grateful Dead.

He started attending Dead shows in 1967 when he was 15. If there's a record for most Grateful Dead concerts attended, Walton would be in the top three, having logged 880 shows that he recalls—not counting the first 10-12 years.

"In those days," he explains, "no one had any money, but Pacific Southwest Airlines sold $20 weekend passes that allowed you to fly anywhere. There was no business travel on the weekend, so they had these promotions where they gave the tickets away. They served free drinks and never checked ID. We just flew around to see the Dead."

Walton meshed well with the band, whom he got to know well, traveling with them to Egypt in 1978. "The Dead were fantastic in creating their own world. They said, 'Let's go, Bill. Come on with us.'"

In 1990, Walton happened to be in Vegas for a book convention. Coincidentally, so was Mickey Hart, one of the Dead drummers who had a book out.

Bill Walton relates, "Hart had his own private party in a hotel meeting room. He spoke and played, then totally spontaneously, he passed out drums to everyone and started a big conga line. We got to a door that said 'Do Not Enter.' We pushed through the door and were in the casino—hundreds and hundreds of people on this conga line snaking through the slots. We went out another door and we were on the Strip. The line kept growing and growing.

"It was a culture. My first Grateful Dead concerts, I just couldn't believe how happy everybody was and how friendly, joyous, and helpful they were. One of the things that I love about the Grateful Dead is that it's a world of curiosity, a world of exploration, a world of experimentation. It's fun, it's exciting, and it's always different."

And the Dead, and the Deadheads, never turned their noses up at Vegas.

Doing the Dead

I first met Bob Barsotti in 1986 at a Grateful Dead show at the Aladdin Theater for the Performing Arts. The Dead had found a small home (7,000 seats) in Vegas that seemed to fit their penchant for the arbitrary. On that day, I got my first taste of the Dead and the Deadheads.

Barsotti, who produced the Grateful Dead shows for Bill Graham, wore his long black hair in a ponytail with a full beard. He had a calm and confident demeanor and listened patiently to my pitch for a bigger venue for the band and fans.

Barsotti grew up in Berkeley, one of five boys, including his brother Peter who also worked for Bill Graham. Growing up in the Bay Area during the '60s wasn't as exhilarating as it might sound. Barotti's school was on the other side of town. In between was the University of California. "I was on my way home from high school riding my bike, school books and backpack in tow, when around the corner comes a jeep spewing tear gas. It was the National Guard of our country. That set the tone for my fairly radical beliefs about government."

On the other hand, Barsotti was in close proximity to Bay Area music festivals, where he developed his taste for the blues, jazz, and folk by seeing Lightning Hopkins, Muddy Waters, John Coltrane, and Joan Baez.

When Bill Graham started producing shows in Berkeley Community Theater, Barsotti signed up for the student stage crew. After graduating from high school, he started hanging around the front door of Winterland, Graham's new San Francisco venue. Eventually, they put him to work.

He performed every job at the theater for four years before becoming its manager. When Winterland closed, Barsotti began doing shows at a variety of venues with Bill Graham Presents (BGP). Later, Barsotti reflected on his tenure. "I considered those six years my undergraduate and graduate education. When I finished, I could do any show in any building under any circumstance."

Barsotti also spoke about Graham's attention to detail.

"He himself had done every job in the venue. He'd follow you around while you did your job. He was famous for his introduction of upcoming acts, which I eventually started doing. Afterwards, he appeared, three-by-five card in hand, with his critique of how I did. 'You said this too fast. You didn't wait long enough for the audience response.' He critiqued me every night for a year."

While Graham was the face of BGP, Jerry Pompelli was Barsotti's mentor. "Jerry started with Bill when he opened the Fillmore East and traveled with him to open Fillmore West. He was a one-man business department. He did the advertising and bookings, ran the shows, and made the bank deposits."

In the late '70s, the Dead's following began to grow.

"As we did more Dead shows, we started noticing the same 20-30 people in the front of the line." In those days, all the Dead shows were general admission, no reserved seats. The earlier you were in line, the closer you were to the stage. "I mentioned it to Bill and he said, 'Maybe we should put a porta-potty outside.' The lines kept getting longer, so we arranged to have the parking lots open overnight. It turned into this camping thing, then "Touch of Grey" hit, and everything just took off."

Inside the venues, there was no other concert experience like the Grateful Dead. Graham put it best. "They're not the best at what they do. They're the only ones at what they do."

They jammed all night long, playing till five in the morning. They let people record their shows. When the shows sold out and people couldn't get in, BGP put speakers outside so they could hear the shows. At some of their appearances, more people were outside than inside.

The Deadheads were a liberal and liberated mix of America, made up of hippies and freaks, doctors and lawyers, hard-core bikers, university professors, tie-dye and candle makers, even suburban preppies, every-one looking to follow the scene.

From the early '70s, their two-set show changed nightly. In the '80s, the second set always featured what they called "Drumz," the prolonged drum solo, followed by an extended improvisational "space jam" with the rest of the band. For multiple-night gigs, the varied set list allowed the band to rotate songs every three to four shows.

The rotation created two phenomena. The desire of Deadheads to hear their favorite songs led many fans to follow them on tour and the large number of traveling fans enabled the band to perform multiple shows, knowing they'd all be sold out, often filled by the same people attending all of them.

In 1986, the Dead had been playing the Aladdin for five years. Barsotti described the first year they performed. After the shows, the fans made a beeline for the casino table games: "It was a sea of tie-dyed Deadheads." The next year when the shows ended, the fans were shown directly to the parking lots. It became the policy for all rock shows at the Aladdin.

My trips to the Aladdin became annual events in which I asked Bob Barsotti the same question: "Are the Dead ready to graduate to the biggest building in the market, Thomas and Mack Center?" They were very particular about the venues they played, usually choosing to underplay the market. Still, considering their popularity, we believed TMC would be the next logical step. Unfortunately, they found it cavernous and sterile.

But then, in the late '80s, the Dead were having a hard time finding venues to play in Los Angeles. Many of the band's problems were caused by Deadheads overrunning commercial sites near the venues. They camped on private property, relieved themselves in the open, littered, set fires, and created traffic jams.

That gave us the idea to pitch the Sam Boyd Stadium. Bill Graham was skeptical, but he sent a production crew to check it out. They were immediately entranced by the contrast of the mountainous terrain surrounding the venue. In addition, the location, eight miles east of the Strip, separated the Deadhead scene from the city.

The most tickets the Dead had ever sold for a show in Vegas was 7,000, for one night at the Aladdin. For the Sam Boyd shows to make financial sense, they'd need to sell out two 30,000-seat performances, nearly 10 times the previous sales. Unfortunately, Vegas' overall concert track record wasn't much of an endorsement: The biggest concert up until that time had sold 15,000 tickets. But Bob Barsotti had a good feeling about the stadium. He just had to convince Graham and the band.

He suggested the shows be first on the tour and announced before any other dates on the West Coast; no shows in L.A. or San Francisco were scheduled until months afterwards, so Barsotti believed the fans would travel. He also cited the lure of Las Vegas and the propensity of Deadheads to flock to unique destinations.

Both Graham and the band thought he was nuts. The Dead weren't willing to take the risk. They did, however, offer a compromise: The guarantee had to be 50% higher than normal.

Graham had a lot of confidence in Barsotti's instincts, but for a 50% increase in the guarantee, he wanted a partner.

Enter Danny Zelisko.

Zelisko was a big fan of Bill Graham and confident the shows would do well. In December 1990, six months earlier, he'd promoted two Grateful Dead afternoon shows in Phoenix, selling a total of 70,000 tickets.

That same year, Zelisko co-promoted two Lynyrd Skynyrd shows with Bill Graham. At the time, Graham was the manager of the band. The shows tanked.

Traditionally, a promoter who loses money on a show will ask, and usually receive, relief from the manager. In this case, however, Bill Graham was both the manager and co-promoter. He told Zelisko he was sorry, but he had a deal with Lynyrd Skynyrd that disallowed any refunds. But don't worry, he said; he'd make it up to him. And the Dead shows at Sam Boyd gave Graham the opportunity. Zelisko got his piece of that action.

The shows would definitely attract the Deadheads. But how many? Traditionally, the Dead didn't have opening acts. A bit nervous, Barsotti convinced Graham and Zelisko to add Santana. The day the 60,000 tickets, at $23.50 apiece, went on sale, they were gone by noon.

Now the focus shifted and we had to consider many issues in connection with our remote site.

Our first trip was to Oakland Coliseum where the Dead played three sold-out shows. Our traveling party included the lieutenant of the campus police force. The trip clearly demonstrated that while there were challenges, the Deadheads weren't a crowd-management problem. Instead, the challenges were drugs, vendors, and gatecrashers, along with vagrants perverting the scene both in the parking lots and the city.

Coincidentally, Barsotti had had an interaction with a Metro police official at a rally he'd attended a few years earlier at the entrance to the Nevada Test Site, 60 miles north of Las Vegas, protesting nuclear-weapons proliferation.

"We were holding a peaceful demonstration outside the Test Site and I could tell by the posture of the police that something was going to happen. I strolled over to the lieutenant and asked why they looked so nervous. 'We're really concerned about your dogs running free and want to let you know that if any of them approaches us, we'll have to shoot them.' I reassured him. I said, 'We don't mean any harm. We're all pacifists.' We tied up our dogs and the whole situation was diffused."

Barsotti continues, "At our first meeting to organize the crowd management of the shows, I was staring at this Metro police officer before I figured out where we'd met before. I must have made him uncomfortable, because afterwards he came over and said, 'Do I know you?' I asked him if he remembered me—the Test Site? He said, 'Oh yeah, the dogs.' Then he thanked me for having them tied up. He liked the way I handled the situation and we got along great the whole time the Dead played Vegas."

Armed with past successful Dead concert-management plans, we met with Campus Police, Metro, Highway Patrol, and the Grateful Dead production crew. We all agreed that crowd management and safety were the overarching objectives; minor drug use (pot) would be tolerated, but it was critical to stop the nitrous oxide (laughing gas), which caused the predominant medical issues. LSD and the other psychedelics were also a concern. Local hospitals weren't experienced at treating "complications" from acid trips. The Dead's representatives told us that a couple of hip doctors in San Francisco would man an onsite treatment center called Rock Med, which was critical to Dead shows. Barsotti told the police, "If you see a crazy naked guy running down the street, don't arrest him. Just bring him to Rock Med."

Camping around the stadium was prohibited, which made for an interesting fusion of Deadheads with the Strip and the surrounding parks, especially Lake Mead.

The whole long history of the build-up to these two shows crossed my mind as I drove into the Sam Boyd Silver Bowl parking lot—and my heart was pounding with excitement.

Not Such a Strange Trip After All

April 27, 1991, was a beautiful mid-70s-degree day. A $23.50 ticket got 60,000 fans in to see Santana open with a 75-minute set. Then the Dead launched into one of the most memorable sets in Deadhead lore. One fan said, "This night was the sort of gig that, later in the evening at your hotel or out in the lot, echoes in your head. The sight of the sun setting over the mountains, the red skyline, and the crowd reaction to the band seemed to be a fire on the mountain during 'Fire on the Mountain.'"

The shows weren't only an artistic success, but a financial one as well. Two incidents, however, put a slight damper on the party. Toward the end of the second show, a fan fell 40 feet off the top of the stadium. Remarkably, she sustained only minor injuries. According to the Rock Med doctor, the depressants in her body relaxed her, preventing a much more serious outcome.

A little less serious situation involved a county commissioner who still had a '60s view of rock 'n' roll. As the crowd was exiting the parking lot, he was traveling on Boulder Highway in his vintage Porsche. While waiting at a traffic light, an excitable fan jumped on his roof, causing a minor dent.

At the next meeting of the commission, Paul Christensen (no relation to this book's author) pushed for a ban on the Grateful Dead playing Las Vegas. A couple of conservative hoteliers also weighed in, complaining about the swarms of Deadheads on the Strip, some of them refreshing themselves in their water fountains and sneaking into the pools. The question, should Las Vegas host a band like the Grateful Dead, created some interesting hypocrisy, hit squarely on the nose in the *Las Vegas Review-Journal* by iconoclastic columnist John L. Smith, who took exception to the unctuousness of banning a group like the Grateful Dead from a city built on the edge of moral boundaries.

The column, titled, "Leaders Give New Meaning to Term 'Deadhead,'" started out by referring to the city fathers as "blockheads." Smith went on to write, "Thousands of members of the tie-dye fraternity made the long strange trip to Las Vegas for Grateful Dead concerts and set an attendance record at the Sam Boyd Silver Bowl. The fans generated $2.7 million in ticket sales, $910,000 in state sales taxes, and $26 million in countywide revenue.

"They also incurred the wrath of Circus Circus President Mike Sloan and Clark County Commissioner Paul Christensen for failing to display the respect due Las Vegas. Sources insist these fellows aren't tripping on bad acid; they've merely overdosed on Vegas rhetoric.

"It seems those shaggy rock fans didn't gamble enough. They also dressed funny. The former is mortal sin. The latter is no mean feat here in leisure-suit land.

"Sloan called the fans, known for their open drug use and scandalous free-form dancing, a 'slovenly horde.' He also questioned the Deadheads' morals.

"Sloan is a casino boss, political mechanic, and corporate attorney. Clearly, morality is his strong suit.

"'The people I've talked to say they sleep ten to a room,' Christensen said. 'They don't appear to be the type to be employed. I wouldn't hire any of them.' And, 'There was no way to control the drug use. They bring a group in here to promote the illegal use of illicit drugs and just wink at it."

"Carl Sagan couldn't explain what goes on in the space between Christensen's ears on some days.

"Police made only a few arrests in three days. Laughing-gas sales ranked high among the transgressions. Another big violation was misdemeanor ticket scalping, which is offered as a minor at UNLV."

Smith summed it up with, "When the dust settled, the Dead persevered and the planning for next year's show began."

And indeed, the first year's sellout gave everyone the confidence to keep growing it. In the second year, a third date was added and the capacity increased to 32,500. Again, all tickets sold out by noon. Steve Miller opened for the Dead. The desert wind blew the clouds away to reveal a night sky when Garcia played the first chords to "Attics of My Life." Long after the shows, people were still dancing on the stadium floor and out in the parking lots.

The third year in 1993, Sting opened and all three shows had continuous lightning all around the stadium, but little rain and no lightning directly over the fans.

Even more bizarre, I witnessed one fan's obsession with the Dead during Sting's set.

While Sting was singing "Heavy Clouds No Rain," a fan was sitting on a car just outside the stadium when the car was hit by lightning, throwing him 10 feet in the air and on to the blacktop. Paramedics tried to place him in an ambulance, but he refused; he had a ticket only for that day. Barsotti assured him that if he went to the hospital, he'd have a ticket for the last show. The fan not only received the ticket, but a backstage pass where he met the band.

Another story was of an even more mystical nature, common to the Dead experience. At one point, Mike Enoch, the stadium's operations manager, was standing on the top of the press box with Bob Barsotti when a double rainbow synced perfectly on drummer Mickey Hart's eyes. Barsotti turned to Enoch and said, "Bill did that."

Bill Graham had been killed a year earlier at age 60 in a helicopter crash in northern California; he'd been on a mission to promote a benefit concert for the victims of the 1991 Oakland Hills firestorm.

Year four, with ticket prices up a few bucks to $30, was complicated by routing, which forced the dates into mid-June and the shows to start around dusk. To make matters worse, the high temperature each day reached 111 degrees, a couple degrees off the record high. The early-evening winds kicking up in the parking lots made the searing heat even more debilitating. Of course, the heat stifled, but didn't ruin, the party, as four huge onstage fans (the rotary-blade, not the tie-dyed, kind) cooled the members of the Dead, and Traffic, which opened the show.

The scene in the parking lots continued to grow. An estimated 20,000 fans without tickets created crowd-management issues for police, especially after the show when they were trying to empty the lots.

After the 1994 shows, Jerry Garcia took in *Siegfried and Roy* at the Mirage and met the two magicians. Garcia was impressed that fans of the illusionists came to them; they didn't have to tour. Well-known for his drug addiction and failing health, Jerry found the idea of a residency attractive. He tried to convince the band to buy the Orpheum Theater in San Francisco so that the fans, not the band, had to travel. The band wasn't supportive.

In 1995, the dates moved back to May 19-21 where the high temperature was 20 degrees lower than the year before. More than 45,000 tickets were sold for each show. Dave Matthews Band was the first jam band to open for the Dead in Las Vegas. They were just breaking across the country and treated the 45,000 attendees to a different set each night.

Some fans in the crowd saw intimations of the end of the era—"bad vibes everywhere," according to one. But the crowds continued the fun inside, at one point starting the "wave," with a normally unflappable Garcia encouraging them and later, tortillas and marshmallows were flying everywhere.

While the true Deadheads, the ticket buyers, were cooperative and friendly, we also had to plan for the close to 25,000 others who were now gathering early and staying late. The parking-lot scene was spiraling out of control with people who had little or nothing to do with the event. While most of the scene was harmless—vendors selling jewelry, clothing, T-shirts, sandwiches, and water—there was also an element that spawned bigger problems.

Sam Boyd Silver Bowl's outer fence worked well as a first line of defense against gatecrashers. At the same time, the parking lots required as much security as inside the show. In fact, the unruly scene outside the stadium in 1995, the fifth year of the series, probably would have forced the Dead and city officials to reexamine the crowd management of the shows or discontinue them altogether.

But Jerry Garcia died in 1995, eight days after his 53rd birthday, having suffered a heart attack in his room in a rehab hospital. The Grateful Dead shows in Las Vegas, and everywhere else, were over.

In the end, the Dead had a huge impact on the city. They brought hordes of people to Las Vegas, almost like New Year's Eve in the spring. And for the most part, Vegas could handle the Deadheads, all the unreconstructed-hippie hangers-on, and the crowd followers. But the most significant outcome was the way in which the concerts accelerated the pace of large touring acts playing Vegas. The success of the Grateful

Dead gave Sam Boyd Silver Bowl credibility. We wasted no time promoting its newfound drawing power.

The aerial photographs of a sold-out stadium abutted against Sunrise Mountain was a great story to tell the live-music industry. We had a hook.

CHAPTER SEVEN

SAM BOYD STADIUM—
VEGAS BECOMES BIG ENOUGH

The first to take the stadium bait wasn't a surprise.

U2's 1987 debut tour in Las Vegas was less than stellar. But in the five years since, U2 had blown up. The band loved Las Vegas and had the confidence they could draw fans like the Grateful Dead. On our part, we had Barry Fey. Fey's long and close relationship with the band sealed the deal.

In contrast to U2's austere stage setups from previous tours, the 1992 Zoo TV Tour was an elaborately staged multimedia event. The tour's concept was inspired by disparate influences: morning talk radio, television programming, and the desensitizing effect of mass media. It satirized media oversaturation by sensory-overloading the audience. The stage featured dozens of large video screens that broadcast visual effects, video clips, and flashing text phrases. Live satellite link-ups, channel surfing, prank calls, and video confessionals were incorporated into the elaborate set.

Though Las Vegas was growing (now a population of 850,000) and that year more than 21 million people visited, Zoo Tour in Las Vegas sold less than 30,000 tickets, of which a disappointing 5,000 were from out of market. We still weren't a player on the live-music scene. But U2 loved playing Las Vegas.

Having notched five sold-out Grateful Dead shows and U2, we continued to pitch the venue. And in April 1993 in another first for Vegas, a Beatle finally came back to play. Paul McCartney performed in Las Vegas for the first time to kick off his New World Tour at the Silver Bowl.

This Ever-Changing World in which We're Living

Alex Kochan has been a promoter, agent, talent buyer, college professor, and basketball fan. In 1992, he was Paul McCartney's agent. When one of his acts, Guns N' Roses, played Thomas and Mack Center, we took full advantage of his presence.

Guns N' Roses sold out in advance, so all the business was settled early. We were awaiting an opportunity to get Kochan's ear about McCartney. There was lots of time. As anyone who's been to a GNR show knows, they don't get around to performing until after midnight. We had a great talk about McCartney, of course showing him the sold-out Grateful Dead aerial pictures, then presented him with a basketball fully autographed by every player on the 1990 Runnin' Rebels team. A week later, we got a call.

Kochan invited us and, we learned later, all the stadium managers and promoters for McCartney's upcoming New World Tour, to New York. McCartney was filming an HBO special, "Up Close," at the Ed Sullivan Theater as he celebrated his 50th birthday. (It was the last time the venue was used before it was turned into the David Letterman Theater.) Venue managers weren't used to getting this type of treatment.

Before the show, we all met in Kochan's suite for a reception where he unveiled his proposal. He wanted all the venues to accept 25% of the merchandise sales, whereas the typical range is 30%-40%. The flaw in Kochan's plan was bringing us all together to demand the lower rate.

After Kochan's pitch, we were buying our own drinks in the bar downstairs and agreed none of us would drop that low. Then we took the limo to the show where my neck was cocked at 45 degrees, my elbow supporting my weight against the stage, as I watched Sir Paul McCartney "Up Close" with 500 friends.

On April 14, 1993, close to 30,000 fans were on hand as McCartney ripped through 32 songs at Sam Boyd Stadium, including three encores. The production was a stark contrast to the unadorned set of the Grateful Dead. "Live and Let Die" had a Super Bowl production quality that peaked with fireworks rivaling the Strip rooftop pyro on New Year's Eve.

The show grossed about the same as U2, but this time more than 10,000 fans traveled from outside Las Vegas. Half of those tickets were sold in advance to the casinos for their VIPs and valued players.

We were on a roll. Production managers loved the ease of loading in on our new pavement versus AstroTurf. The venue was non-union, drastically reducing the cost of stagehands. And there was no entertainment tax.

The next target was the Eagles. This one wouldn't be easy. Down the street we could see the MGM Grand, the big green monster, growing bigger every day—and along with it, the 15,000-seat Grand Garden Arena.

Hell Freezes Over

The Eagles formed in 1971. With five number-one singles, six number-one albums, and six Grammies, they were one of the most successful acts of the '70s. But egos, drugs, and life on the road took their toll. On July 31, 1980, in Long Beach, California, tempers boiled over into what has been described as the "Long Night at Wrong Beach."

The Eagles were playing a benefit at Long Beach Arena to help California Senator Alan Cranston get re-elected; it had been arranged by Eagles singer-songwriter Glenn Frey. Lead guitarist Don Felder, especially, wasn't happy about mixing business with politics and, after years of squabbling over everything the band did, Frey and Felder spent the entire show threatening to kick the other's ass. A few days later, the band called it quits, announcing that hell would freeze over before they recorded or toured together again.

Fourteen years later in February 1994, I started negotiating for the Hell Freezes Over tour.

There was a new wrinkle. MGM's Grand Garden Arena was now open and had already hosted two sold-out Barbara Streisand concerts, the highest grossing shows in concert history. (The show commanded a new industry-record ticket price of $1,000; MGM paid her a $5 million guarantee.) I didn't realize it at the time, but that worked in our favor. The Eagles, it turned out, didn't want to play a venue where Streisand appeared. Now MGM was fighting the battle in which we at Thomas and Mack had been engaged for the past 10 years: the perception that Vegas was a retirement home for entertainers.

The three-week negotiation for the Eagles was the last time we beat out MGM and the Grand Garden. On June 14, 1994, the Eagles played a two-and-a-half-hour set that included 28 songs and three encores.

Azoff—A Small Guy Gets Big Results

Irving Azoff began promoting and booking bands while a high-school student in Danville, Illinois, then continued at the University of Illinois-Champaign-Urbana. He moved to Los Angeles in 1970 with his first client, Dan Fogelberg.

Azoff's initial contact with the Eagles happened because of a mix-up by a staffer at Lookout Management, a partnership between David Geffen and Elliot Roberts that managed the Eagles at the time. Azoff jumped in and straightened out a little problem with the band, which put him in their good graces.

A few years later, Glenn Frey and Don Henley sought out Azoff in order to vent their frustrations about their record label and the sound of their albums. They found their man, but first they had to part ways with Lookout Management.

Azoff exploited a major conflict of interest Lookout had, as the company managed and promoted the Eagles. Rather than fight a prolonged legal and PR battle, Lookout allowed the band to leave for Azoff and his company, Frontline.

Azoff was one of a handful of managers who continued what Led Zeppelin's manager, Peter Grant, had started—fighting for and winning better record and touring deals for his acts. Azoff's in-your-face persona became legendary, as described by Don Henley. "He's Satan, but he's our Satan."

Barry Fey put it a little differently. "If you bow when you meet David Geffen, you duck when you meet Irving Azoff."

Fey and Azoff first met when Azoff was a small-time agent in Illinois. Fey had a good relationship with everyone: Azoff and the Eagles, the MGM due to his long association with Entertainment Director Richard Sturm, and us, thanks to the success of his Thomas and Mack shows, plus U2 at the Silver Bowl. We quickly found ourselves in a position that became all too familiar from then on—in a dog fight with the Grand Garden Arena over a show that was playing stadiums everywhere else in the world.

There was disagreement within the Eagles as well. Frey liked the MGM, but Henley wanted to play the bigger venue in order to accommodate the locals and play for the most fans. In the end, Barry Fey delivered the show to the Silver Bowl, but it was Henley's decision.

The Eagles' return after a 14-year hiatus—Glenn Frey, Joe Walsh, and Don Felder on guitars, Don Henley on drums, Timothy B. Schmit on bass, and four backup musicians—was greeted with reverence by an audience of Baby Boomers and young fans in tattoos and grungewear. In more than two and a half hours, the band played half of their hit singles, four new songs, and a lot of material from band members' solo albums.

A major part of the city's propulsion into the live-music big time can be traced to this summer, 1994, and what was happening at Sam Boyd Stadium and MGM Grand Garden Arena.

For our part, we set all-time revenue records, selling close to 200,000 concert tickets for the Grateful Dead, Eagles, Metallica, and the Lollapalooza festival; the stadium also hosted six Canadian Football League games, where the Las Vegas Posse sold close to 75,000 tickets. That summer also set temperature records: The average temperature for each of these events was 105 degrees. It was a hot summer in more ways than one!

But MGM was a sharp thorn in our sides. A new paradigm was developing. MGM was talking to *all* tours, the ones that played arenas, as well as those that appeared in stadiums—Rolling Stones, Neil Diamond, Billy Joel, everyone. Most believed that these concerts were loss leaders. However, the sexiness of a 15,000-seat venue attached to a new hotel on the Strip allowed promoters to command ticket prices that rivaled stadium grosses. They made money on the shows.

We knew the green monster would be an ever-increasing challenge. But for time being, we kept rolling. And rocking.

Metallica and Lollapalooza Scorch a Parched Stadium

The '94 summer heat peaked at Metallica and Lollapalooza, two huge concerts that took place a couple of weeks from each other. Promoters had to be asking themselves why they chose summer in the desert to schedule these shows. Geoff Carter, writing in the *Las Vegas Sun*, called it "the living breathing equivalent of a solar hot dog cooker."

Lollapalooza was conceived and created in 1991 by the lead singer of Jane's Addiction, Perry Farrell, as a farewell tour for his band. The "farewell" ran for six years and kept growing bigger band-wise, but kept shrinking ticket-sales-wise, until Farrell was forced to transform Lollapalooza into a destination festival. In 2010 he launched the festival in Chicago's Grant Park. Today, Lollapalooza draws close to 500,000 to Chicago; Farrell also puts it on in Santiago, Sao Paulo, Berlin, and Paris.

The tour stopped in Las Vegas on July 6, 1994, on a day temperatures approached 125 degrees. It was no wonder attendance didn't top 11,000. Mist tents gave a little relief, but the Revival Tent, featuring poets and philosophers, was the only place where the temperature dropped below 90.

The festival featured some powerful performances by George Clinton's P-Funk All-Stars, the Beastie Boys, and a strong finale by the Smashing Pumpkins. A second stage hosted a couple dozen acts, such as the Flaming Lips, the Verve, the Boo Radleys, the Frogs, Guided by Voices, Lambchop, Girls Against Boys, and the Black Crowes before they got famous.

On the heels of Lollapalooza, heavy metal clanged and clanked into the Silver Bowl, embodied as it's always been by Metallica.

Heavy metal has always been a part of rock 'n' roll. In the sixties, Cream, Iron Butterfly, and Hendrix defined the new genre. Growing up in the '70s, my heavy metal bands were Deep Purple and Led Zeppelin. Alice Cooper and Black Sabbath represented the dark side. In the mid-'70s KISS, Queen, and David Bowie introduced glam-metal, donning flamboyant costumes and makeup and mixing them with bizarre theatrics and ripping guitars. Canadian band Rush produced metal concept albums and AC/DC became arguably the most reliable metal band.

As heavy metal continued to evolve, bands like Van Halen, Def Leppard, and the Scorpions found a more mainstream audience. By the late '80s, Mötley Crüe and then Guns N' Roses held the coveted metal crown.

But the metal band that broke in the late '80s and is still at the top of the heap today is Metallica.

In 1991, Metallica released its breakout eponymous album, also known as "The Black Album," which featured chart-topping songs like "Enter Sandman" and "Nothing Else Matters" (30-plus years later, the group's self-titled album has sold more than 16 million in the U.S. alone).

After three tours, Metallica played Las Vegas and Thomas and Mack Center for the first-time September 9, 1989. The Damaged Justice tour played to less than 6,000 fans. Five years later, on July 30, 1994, the band played Sam Boyd Stadium on the Shit Hits the Shed tour to a crowd of 15,000.

An original opener on the tour, Alice in Chains, didn't make the Vegas engagement. Suicidal Tendencies, Candlebox, and Danzig opened for what was billed as a one-day heavy-metal festival. Candlebox's softer rock show didn't go over well with too many of the head-bangers who came to hear loud and louder music. And Metallica took close to an hour to get to the stage, but when they did, it was party on. Plumes of weed smoke formed across the field. Everyone was fiercely sweating, pumping fists, singing along, pushing, punching, and kicking. The mosh pits kicked into gear, forming a human hurricane where anything was allowed.

Mosh pits became commonplace at heavy-metal shows in the '90s. At first sight, you can't believe anyone would join in this intense, testosterone-fueled, body-checking ordeal. After all, the object is perpetual 360-degree motion and, more to the point, knocking your concert neighbors onto their asses. But it was all in a boys-will-be-boys spirit; often, I saw a guy helping up the guy he just decked, sometimes catching him before he even hit the ground.

Metallica continuously pushed the fan experience, allowing 100 fans a spot to record the shows and creating a snake pit in the middle of the stage for another 100 special fans.

It was quite a day.

U2 Two

U2's second stadium show in Las Vegas took place on April 25, 1997. The band spent a full week rehearsing at Sam Boyd Stadium for the Pop Mart Tour, which encompassed five legs and 93 shows that sold close to 4 million tickets, 33,000 in Las Vegas for the opening of the tour.

The stars came out: Cameron Diaz, David Schwimmer, Christian Slater, Trent Reznor, Pete Sampras, Michael Stipe, Quincy Jones, Tim Burton, Dr. Dre, and Michael Keaton, to name just a few.

Instead of a dramatic entry, U2 walked through the sold-out crowd like plain folk. Bono, fully decked out in a black boxing warmup, shadowboxed until he hit the stage, which can only be described as stunning, with state-of-the-art audio and a 170-foot-wide LED screen enveloping the band.

Several bursts of showmanship included a UFO's on-screen landing. At the end of the main set before the first encore, a 40-foot motorized lemon moved to the middle of the stage under a huge disco ball that lit up the stadium in spinning lights while Paul Oakenfeld's PerfectoMix of U2's song "Lemon" played. The band closed the two-hour and 22-song show with "One" as cartoons whirled behind Bono.

U2's successfully launched tour was another milestone for Las Vegas and Sam Boyd Stadium. The opening shows of the tour drew more than 500 media outlets from all over the country and the world. The growing roster of top-name touring acts appearing at the stadium, as well as MGM's arena, were drawing a lot of attention, not just from the live-music industry, but also the hotel-casinos that started looking to jump onto the literal and figurative bandwagon.

George Strait and Friends

One of our most versatile employees, Daren Libonati, had forged a good relationship with George Strait's tour manager, Doug Clouse. About George Strait's Country Music Festival, Libonati told me, "I'm a hundred percent sure I can get this date." And he did.

We were in the middle of a $20 million renovation, but it would be done by then. Or would it? We negotiated a decent deal, but Strait's management wanted more. We pitched the LVCVA on the potential of the tour to bring visitors. They contributed $100,000, which got the date confirmed.

The improvements to Sam Boyd Stadium were significant, including electrical and plumbing, replacing the Monsanto Magic Carpet (the football coach at the time believed the team would do better on grass; the Rebels went 13-44 before that coach was fired). The size of the concourse and the number of restrooms and concessions were doubled and a new video board was being installed. A tower that included a press area, 500 club seats, and 16 suites was constructed on the west side and five acres of new pavement were added. The construction started right after the football season and was expected to be completed for the Strait festival in the spring. It wasn't. There was no other way but to face this head on. We flew in the promoter.

The thing about working with established promoters is, they've seen it all. However, this situation was about what he *wasn't* seeing: power, lights, restrooms, and concession stands. We did have 30,000 seats and a floor that held another 10,000. So our pitch was to design a temporary set-up like a festival built from scratch.

Libonati, exhibiting his stellar event-mapping skills, laid out festival grounds that surrounded the stadium complete with porta-potties, beer stands, 20 food trucks, a variety of vendors, and lifestyle exhibits. There was also Straitland, which included the Jack Daniels Lynchburg Live Stage featuring some of the country music's fastest-rising stars.

On May 8, 1999, the gates opened at 1 p.m. for the festival. In addition to Strait, the 40,000 fans saw Tim McGraw, Dixie Chicks, Kenny Chesney, Jo Dee Messina, and Mark Wills. It was a great day with the sell-out crowd sucking up the sun, suds, and songs. We still didn't have electricity, so the stadium was completely powered by generators. It's ironic, but in retrospect, the footprint we built was better than a traditional stadium concert—the alternative setup provided a one-of-a-kind experience.

From Improv to Pop

The Dave Matthews Band formed in Charlottesville, Virginia, in 1991. Their introduction to Las Vegas took place in the summer of 1995 when they opened three shows for the Grateful Dead at Sam Boyd Stadium. They steadily increased their repertoire and fan base with every subsequent album and tour. However, what makes a Dave Matthews Band concert unique is how they perform their songs live.

Before a song even makes a Dave Matthews Band studio album, it might be featured in 100 live performances. "Two Step" is a great example. First making its studio debut on *Crash* in 1996, the song was featured in 1995 on their third night at Sam Boyd Stadium. Like the Dead before them, DMB allows people to record their shows, even letting them plug into the mix console. Due to fan recordings, "Two Step" tracked heavily before MP3, YouTube, or music on the Internet.

The DMB concert experience is also unique because of how the songs are transformed. Often, intros and outros, transitions, and reprises are performed differently each night. This gives the band a broad live catalog featuring different renditions of songs they've been performing for years. A unique tradition of theirs is called a "fake." They begin the first bar of one of their songs, but quickly transition into another track. It keeps the fans, who often know every bar and lyric, on their toes.

Las Vegas dates, May 26-27, 2001, were part of a 15-city stadium tour. More than 40,000 fans enjoyed shows that continued for two hours, featuring lengthy improvisational renditions of their songs, accompanied by elaborate video and lighting.

Two months after the Dave Matthews Band's two-night stand, Sam Boyd Stadium fired it up again for the reigning kings of pop, N'Sync. They were back in Vegas on the 35-city PopOdyssey tour 18 months after their New Year's Day 1999 debut at Thomas and Mack Center (that tour grossed $90 million).

The setup, with 75 trucks of sound, lights, and effects, took four days to build. The stage was five stories high with three video screens and five mini-stages. It looked like a lavish amusement park and arcade. The Las Vegas stop on the tour began with the boys emerging from a glass pyramid, singing their hit single "Pop." While making their way down the runway, they shook the hands of some of the 30,000 fans. Almost every song came with its own extravagantly filmed introduction and high-tech effects.

The show included fireworks, comedic videos of the group on a giant screen above them, numerous dazzling costume changes, and gimmicks such as the boys flying above the audience and riding mechanical bulls.

All night long, blinking lasers, blazing pyrotechnics, elaborate stage props, radio-friendly tunes, and frenzied exercise-video choreography created a wild concoction. The stage jutted into the crowd, literally close enough to touch the audience. The ear-splitting shrieks of tens of thousands of glow-stick-wagging pre-teen and teenage girls punctuated each song.

U2 Too

But as elaborate as the N'Sync production might've been, it was outscaled, appropriately enough, but U2's 360-Degree tour, named for the stage configuration that allowed fans to see from all sides.

Concert producers rarely design tours in the round in arenas. It's too expensive to move all the rigging from one end of the room, where the stages are almost always located. In stadiums? Never. But the band's designers, who'd built the stages for every U2 tour since 1982, were up to a task of this scale. Bono said that the design was intended to overcome the staid traditional appearance of outdoor concerts. "We have some magic, and we've got some beautiful objects we're going to take around the world, and we're inside that object. We're hanging from that object, and it frees up those seats behind the stage. They may be the best seats."

To accommodate fans viewing from all around the stage, a massive four-legged structure, dubbed "the Claw," was built above the stage; 165 feet tall, it was reportedly the largest concert stage ever constructed. The video screen, as well, was 360 degrees, shaped like a cylinder and hung above the stage from the Claw. A circular ramp surrounded the stage, connected by rotating bridges. Fans were both outside the ramp and between the ramp and stage. Those who purchased general-admission tickets made it closest to the stage on a first-come first-served basis.

For more than two hours, U2 blew through three decades of hits, starting with "All That You Can't Leave Behind." Bono bantered with the crowd several times during the night. After "Beautiful Day," he introduced the band, giving them each a Vegas lounge act's name. "I'm Wayne Newton," he said. Later, he said the band was proud to play in the hometown of the Killers. Then he made some lucky kid's night when he helped him climb onto the stage. Together, they ran around the stage, then Bono gave the kid his trademark sunglasses. He finished with this:

"All performers, sometimes we end up on our knees, but we all come to Las Vegas."

The Las Vegas concert drew more than 40,000 to Sam Boyd Stadium. The tour had three legs and 110 shows that ran from June 30, 2009, until July 30, 2011. Afterwards, it was announced that the tour grossed $736 million with a total attendance of 7.2 million—both of which set records that, as far as I know, have yet to be broken.

CHAPTER EIGHT

MGM GRAND GARDEN ARENA—
A GREEN GIANT THAT KEPT GROWING

Up until 1992, the 100-plus acres surrounding the Marina, a 700-room hotel-casino that opened on the south Las Vegas Strip in 1975, were occupied by the Tropicana Country Club and Golf Course. Mega-casino developer Kirk Kerkorian acquired the Marina and country club and proceeded to build the 5,000-room MGM Grand, which, when it opened in 1993, was the largest hotel in the world. The casino, at 171,000 square feet, was also the world's largest. And the 15,000-seat MGM Grand Garden Arena was second in size in the city; only Thomas and Mack Center was larger.

For its arena, MGM initially envisioned concerts, corporate events, possibly some hockey and basketball games, and, of course, boxing. The arena managers were hoping that fight promoters would forget about the outdoor portable setup at Caesars Palace and establish MGM as the preeminent hotel for prizefights. As the arena hosted successful event after successful event, the diversity and impact of the events grew and grew.

Someone caught up in the exhilaration of attending arena and stadium events might believe that *working* in an entertainment venue is exciting, perhaps even glamorous. In the 18 years I managed Thomas and Mack Center and Sam Boyd Stadium, we hosted more than 2,000 events. I can say that the star allure quickly fades and in its place is the challenge of filling empty dates, selling tickets, servicing event producers, and satisfying fans.

Venues operate 14-16 hours a day. Days are spent maintaining the building, planning and preparing for events, and marketing. The nights are usually devoted to parking cars and securing, guiding, and feeding guests, who number anywhere from 5,000 to 40,000.

In Mark Prows first few jobs, he did every odd task he was given at the

University of Wyoming and the Cow Palace in San Francisco. But Vegas and Thomas and Mack Center were his ultimate destinations.

In March 1983, Dennis Finfrock, Mike Enoch (our Operations Director), and I made a trip to tour the Cow Palace, at the time the preeminent live-music venue in San Francisco. Taking time to show us the operation, Prows struck us as a young and ambitious event coordinator. We left with the distinct feeling he wanted to work elsewhere. That opportunity materialized soon thereafter, when we created a job selling ad signage.

Advertising signage—displaying company logos around the venue—drives a lot of revenue for event centers. Today, Thomas and Mack generates more than $8 million annually selling signage. Before opening the arena, a deal was struck with a company to sell the signage. Four years into the contract, no more than five packages had been sold, netting the building less than $250,000 annually. While this was the traditional way of selling signage, it wasn't working for us.

It wasn't the first time we'd dealt with a vendor that failed to deliver. The food-and-beverage company that won the original bid for TMC didn't even make it to the opening, defaulting on several contractual commitments made before selling a single hot dog.

We bought the advertising company out of its contract and started looking for someone to do it in-house.

The job announcement detailed our expectations for both Thomas and Mack Center and Sam Boyd Silver Bowl. Mark Prows applied for the job. "As I went through the interview, I had a sense that I had no idea how to do this job. It really wasn't in my wheelhouse, but somehow I was confident I could do it," he admits. Both were true. He was the least qualified on paper, but the most impressive in person. Prows was offered and accepted the job. In his first year, he doubled our signage revenue.

While the job was satisfying, Prows was looking to move up the management ladder. When he was offered the assistant director job at the Tacoma Dome, he jumped at it. For two years, he further groomed his venue-management skills.

In September 1993 at the Arena Management Conference in Las Vegas, a chance encounter with Dennis Finfrock altered Prows' career and life forever. In December of that year, Finfrock was poised to open the new MGM Grand Garden, having been hired away from Thomas and

Mack by the green monster. While they were well on their way to booking the venue, the operation wasn't shored up. When he caught Finfrock between meetings, Prows kidded him. "I'm surprised you never called me to come back to Vegas." Finfrock took the hint.

A week later, Prows was on a plane to Las Vegas for an interview. Barely a month after that, he and his wife packed and left the land of 325 days of clouds for the land of 325 days of sun.

Prows' first title at the Grand Garden was director of event services. Just as he'd done in his other jobs, he became the go-to guy for just about everything that had to do with opening and operating the arena.

Hearing Prows' description of the early months of the Grand Garden reminded me of the early days of Thomas and Mack ... mayhem and chaos. On top of all the construction and operational challenges, a new system, One Stop Ticketing, was installed to allow customers to book hotel rooms and buy tickets for the arena, the showrooms, and the amusement park (which opened with the hotel and closed in 2002), making the customer's experience seamless.

Prows and the arena staff also had their hands full with the commitments made to Barbara Streisand to open the arena. Streisand hadn't performed in an arena in 23 years and had two non-negotiable deal points: She had to have two uninterrupted days to rehearse in the arena and she had the right to cancel the date, up to the day of the show, if it didn't feel right.

When Prows started work December 4, 1993, no seats were installed; nothing but raw concrete was visible. Streisand had to be in a finished arena in 12 days. While Prows was used to sleeping in the building, he had no idea of the looming challenges.

In the last few weeks of construction, an arena can look like it's a year away from opening. But on December 16, the arena was ready for Streisand's first rehearsal. The staff was sitting on pins and needles in anticipation of her initial impressions of the place. Prows and Finfrock were standing with VP of Entertainment Richard Sturm when Streisand took the stage for the first song of her rehearsal. Looking at her manager, Marty Ehrlickman, she exclaimed, "Marty, this place is amazing!" Prows and Finfrock almost cried. The staff had a reprieve. Or did they?

The plan to pay Streisand's enormous guarantee was hatched

through the template used for boxing pricing, where the best tickets are extremely expensive (when bouts are held in Vegas, the best tickets are a strong lure to high rollers). The $1,000 price for Streisand's highest ticket, where the previous highest price up till that time had been $300 for the Eagles, raised eyebrows all the way up to the CEO of Ticketmaster. Fred Rosen said, "Marty Ehrlickman called and said they wanted to do a thousand-dollar ticket. Everyone was nervous about it, but those tickets all sold out first."

Fans flew in from all over the world: from South Africa to Germany, from Great Britain to Australia. The concert was delayed an hour because fans were funneled through a single entrance, an issue MGM improved, but never fully corrected. The audience greeted Streisand with a 10-minute standing ovation before the two-hour show. Backed by a 64-piece orchestra conducted by Marvin Hamlisch, Streisand intertwined more than two dozen songs, from hits such as "People" and "The Way We Were" through a scripted show aided by TelePrompTers. The evening's big surprise was when Streisand was joined on stage by Mike Myers, the "Saturday Night Live" comedian playing the alter-ego Linda Richman, an obsessed Streisand fan.

The price and gross of the show both set industry records and lay the foundation for a rising ceiling on ticket prices. The average gross for a 12,000- to 18,000-seat arena sellout in 1993 was about $700,000. By extreme contrast, the first show sold out with a $12 million gross, more than twice any previous concert, including stadium shows that sold up to 100,000 tickets.

The challenge of opening a 5,000-room hotel-casino, amusement park, and arena were demanding enough. But it was complicated by a vacuum of leadership, which put a tremendous amount of additional stress on the different divisions of the property. To begin with, there was no master plan for how the entire operation would organize and integrate the events, showroom, and park for guests.

That was exacerbated by the sheer numbers of people showing up for the grand opening of the Grand, the grandest new hotel in the world. The Strip was gridlocked. The speed bumps under the porte cochère were too high for limos. Hefty security officers, valet attendants, even Mark Prows became human tire jacks, lifting each limo over each bump. A sea of people were locked out of their rooms. MGM had installed a new cellular technology in each door, which saved a significant amount of money by not having to hard-wire them. Problem was, it didn't work and it took hours to open the thousands of rooms.

And every department—eight restaurants and a big food court, five lounges and bars, three showrooms and the arena, two dozen retail shops, 158,000 square feet of meeting space, a 6,000-space parking garage, spa and pro shop, huge sandy-beach pool and tennis courts, midway, video arcade, and youth center (this was at the height of Las Vegas' family-friendly period), plus the amusement park with seven major rides, four theater presentations, nine food and beverage outlets, and 12 retail shops by itself—had its own start-up headaches.

Dennis Finfrock had plenty of experience with another difficult start-up when he was UNLV's assistant athletic director, wrestling coach, and first manager of the fledgling Thomas and Mack Center. He took the initiative in his department, entertainment. One of Finfrock's first hires was an old hand at Thomas and Mack.

Event Edison

At age 12, Daren Libonati started racing dirt bikes and quickly became competitive. In ninth grade in a big race, he spun head over heels. Thirteen hours later, he woke up in the hospital, fortunate to have survived a crash that could have paralyzed or killed him.

The mishap wasn't his first head injury. At seven years old, he was racing when the front handlebars and forks of his BMX bike snapped, tumbling him over face first on his chin, wrenching his head into the bumper of a car. The doctor contemplated putting a plate in his skull, but settled for a preventive option; for six months, he was relegated to wearing a helmet in everything he played. The kids weren't easy on him. Another boy might have withdrawn, but Daren developed an I'll-show-them attitude, which formed a big part of his personality: Obstacles only provoke him.

Three months after the dirt-bike crash, disregarding orders from his doctor (and mom), he showed up at the high-school junior-varsity football-team's first practice. It didn't take long—the first play—to be seal his fate. Running off tackle, he went head to head with a six-foot 200-pound linebacker. Again, he woke up in a hospital, but this time he had to face reality. His career as a football player was over. Or was it?

The last thing Libonati thought he would be was a kicker. Considering his condition, it was the only option. However, Libonati was determined to become the best kicker in high school history. In his junior year, he kicked eight field goals in eight attempts, with one 48-yard bomb.

After being cut as a kicker from Cal Lutheran, a southern California college, Libonati snuck a peak at Cal Lutheran's schedule and found a nearby junior college, where he immediately walked on as the kicker. He exacted his revenge when his 51-yard field goal won the game against Cal Lutheran. But instead of heading to his sideline, he paraded along Cal's sideline taunting the coach who cut him, earning him two or three flags and a good scolding by his own coach. It was a brashness that, throughout his career, he continued to refine.

While attending junior college in L.A., a student with no money, he also learned the tricks of the "free-ticket" trade, sneaking into concerts at the Forum.

UNLV recruited him for the Rebels, but didn't offer a scholarship, which Tulane did. Las Vegas kept an eye on him in New Orleans; after one season, he got his full scholarship and moved to Las Vegas.

UNLV's football practice field is directly behind the university's physical-education complex. While kicking at practice, Libonati sailed one over the fence. Retrieving his ball, he had a chance meeting with Greg Haugen, who was on his way up the ranks of middleweight college boxers. The two struck up a friendship that took Libonati into the gym for three years where he learned boxing technique, who was who in the fight world, and how the sport worked. But as he always did and does, he was making other connections.

"As I learned more about boxing, I also learned to think strategically," he says.

With a limited bank account, he rented a room in a garage from Ron Drake, an event and marketing coordinator at Thomas and Mack and former center on the UNLV football team. That led, in 1987, into talking his way into a part-time job by convincing Dennis Finfrock that he knew all the holes in our security, would make new money for us in our parking lot, and bring boxing to the Thomas and Mack. He eventually delivered on all three.

He started out working in the trenches, parking, ushering, and odd jobs. "My first task at TMC was to dress up as Cookie Monster for a Sesame Street promotion," Libonati recalls. "But I was fortunate to be taken under Ron Drake's wing where I could think about and contribute to how to make the operation better." Libonati's career started to take shape.

While the management team at TMC was young, the philosophy became the culture. People were encouraged to challenge the status quo, redefine the venue business, and create memorable experiences for clients and guests. There were plenty of systems to improve: parking, training for part-time employees, food service, ticketing, and booking, to name just a few. Daren demonstrated early and throughout his career that this was an atmosphere he flourished in.

He moved quickly up the organizational chart. In only six months, he'd earned a full-time position. He had an insatiable appetite for negotiating, an unbridled energy and curiosity, and when fueled by either caffeine or alcohol, could be both enlightening and comical. Telling him "you can't" only galvanized him into action, whereupon he came up with revenue sources that no one else had seen, cutting-edge systems that came to define our operation, and budget cuts that improved the bottom line.

Thomas and Mack was destined to host fights—because of its size, its experience with events, the fact that the Las Vegas Hilton was tiring of the cost of holding them in their convention center, and of course, Daren Libonati. Through his gym connections, Libonati met with boxing promoter Bob Arum, who referred him to Tom Willer, vice president of marketing at the Hilton. Working with Willer and Don King, Libonati developed a comprehensive fight plan and launched the first-ever fight at TMC, George Foreman vs. Alex Stewart. That fight's success spurred more interest. Soon there was a deal for a much bigger fight—Hector Camacho vs. Julio César Chavez.

The negotiations for this fight were simple, except for the merchandise deal. I was in Los Angeles when Don King called, wanting to nail down the percentage on the merchandise. It was Libonati's first week on the job as my new booking coordinator. He begged me to let him do the deal with King and I did. He made a great deal that day.

The building's normal share for merchandise at that time was 35% of sales. On the other hand, boxing promoters traditionally shared in the profit-loss with the sponsoring hotel-casino. But because King had more than 100 different items for sale, I believed we'd do better with points. Libonati negotiated a split that lowered our percentage to 25% of sales, but eliminated any risk of sharing in a loss.

Chavez-Camacho set many records that night: Nevada attendance, gate gross, food and beverage (mostly beer), merchandise, and decibels. The Runnin' Rebels in their heyday topped out at 106-108 on the in-house decibel meter. The nearly 20,000 fans, most of them there for wildly popular Chavez who won the fight, achieved a new record for noise—118 decibels.

The 1992 fight was the most profitable event in TMC's nearly 10-year history. TMC's share of the merchandise was $80,000. At the same time, considering the tremendous number of items Don King had to sell, his profit was only $40,000. It didn't take long for King to connect those two numbers. It's well-known that it's not very often Don King gets the short end of any stick. Worse still, he'd made the deal with a green kid in his first negotiation!

The MGM Differential

When Dennis Finfrock was hired away from TMC by MGM Grand Garden, he took Daren Libonati with him to develop boxing cards and book concerts.

"Immediately, I was on the phone with the same network of promoters and agents I worked with at Thomas and Mack Center," he said. "My initial perception was that their shows were loss leaders, with the casino subsidizing each event. I soon learned differently. Three elements made the concerts profitable—the cachet of being the new hotel and arena on the Strip, which commanded higher ticket prices; the new deal I could strike with promoters; and being affiliated with a huge casino.

"In the Grand Garden Arena, the rent we charged might net out as high as $75,000. At Thomas and Mack, it was only half that and we had to share half of the half with the promoter. At MGM, even sharing half with promoter, we made double.

"Also, my number-one ticket buyer was casino marketing, so 2,000 of the most expensive tickets were purchased right off the top."

The deal was profitable for everyone. The arena made the same rent, the promoter did much better, and the acts were grossing 30% more than Thomas and Mack.

But Libonati's real introduction to the job occurred on his second day working at MGM, well before the arena even opened. After working all night, he was driving home as the sun was coming up. An hour later, his phone rang. It was Dennis Finfrock.

"I hope you don't have plans for today. You and I are traveling."

"Where are we going?"

"We're going to L.A. The Stones are playing the Forum."

"You couldn't have mentioned it last night?"

"Why? We're going today."

In 1994, Grand Garden hosted 18 concerts, but none bigger than the October 14-15 Rolling Stones shows. The Voodoo Lounge tour set a record, grossing $320 million, playing 60 shows in 37 stadiums—and one arena, MGM Grand Garden.

Rockin' All the Way to the Bank

The Rolling Stones formed in 1962, highly influenced by blues artists Muddy Waters, Chuck Berry, Little Richard, Howlin' Wolf, and Bo Diddley. Unlike the Beatles and many other British bands, they played to a rebellious counterculture. Today, they're the most resilient band in rock 'n' roll history. While the Beatles played to the pop masses, their legacy spanned only 10 years. But fully 55 years later, the Stones are still rocking and rolling (in dough).

In 1989, Concert Production International (CPI), a small promotion company out of Toronto, changed the paradigm of concert promotion. CPI made The Rolling Stones an offer they couldn't refuse: They'd promote the entire tour.

Up until that time, even if a tour was coordinated by one promoter, regional promoters were also involved. CPI proposed to cut out the middleman and include merchandise in the guarantee, thereby delivering a more lucrative bottom-line to the band. The band accepted and that's the way it's been ever since.

While the national touring business was starting to contract and centralize, it was still about relationships. Barry Fey had an established relationship with all three principals—CPI, the Stones, and MGM (thanks to his concert series at Bally's with Richard Sturm, who was now at MGM). Fey bartered a deal for the band to play the Grand Garden. It wouldn't have happened at Thomas and Mack, but if not for Fey, it might've happened at Sam Boyd Stadium. As such, the show was another significant milestone in the city's rise to the top of the concert tour ladder.

The two shows sold out with an average ticket price of $193 for a gross of $4,184,425. In fact, the two shows were the only arena dates on the tour and still managed to gross more than all but six cities, whose stadiums' average ticket was $47. The results of the shows were some consolation to me. Grand Garden didn't just outperform what Sam Boyd Stadium might have generated. The Vegas arena outsold *85% of the stadiums in the country.*

The next time the Stones played Las Vegas was November 22, 1997, as part of the Bridges to Babylon tour. The single show sold out, grossing close to $3 million. The 36-city tour was predominantly hosted in stadiums (six arenas) and again Grand Garden's average ticket price at $229 outpaced its closest competitor, New York, by more than $100.

Subsequently, the Stones continued to cash in at Grand Garden. In 1999, the No Security Tour played 28 cities. MGM's $2,780,000 gross, with an average ticket price of $221, was more than double any other city.

Keith Richards put it all into perspective in an interview with *Rolling Stone* magazine. "We're the only band to take it this far, and if we trip and fall, you'll know that's how far it can be taken. If there's someone out there doing it better than us, they can have the gig. But I ain't heard it so far."

Wastin' Away Again in Vegas

By 1996, MGM Grand Garden was dominating the Vegas concert scene. The Strip location, 5,000 rooms, and 15,000 seats were advantages the nearest competition, Thomas and Mack Center, could not overcome. Grand Garden events were commanding 30% more for their tickets and selling them all.

Concerts were flourishing—AC/DC, Bette Midler, Phil Collins, to name just a few. And Jimmy Buffett.

Jimmy Buffett started his musical career as a country artist in Nashville in the late '60s. In 1971, country star Jerry Jeff Walker took him to Key West on a busking expedition, playing on the street for donations. Buffett quickly took to the blend of tropical air, fishing, bars, and laid-back style of the Keys. He not only moved there and adopted the life, but he's spent the rest of his career writing and singing about the Caribbean way of living. Buffett's fans run the gamut, from late teens to followers from the '70s. It's a gathering of generations.

Buffett has toured every year since 1976, yet he made only two stops in Las Vegas before his historic runs at MGM's Grand Garden Arena. The first was for Caesars' Under the Stars outdoor concert series, the second at the Thomas and Mack in 1993. He didn't do well at TMC and didn't return for four years. This time he filled the Grand Garden and the shows became a regular stop for Buffet, who has sold out 32 shows in the 20 years since.

The Jimmy Buffett concert experience has evolved from an alcohol-laced Caribbean blowout to a gathering of Parrotheads. In 1985 at one of his concerts, Buffett commented about everyone wearing Hawaiian shirts and how he kept seeing the same people at his shows, just like Deadheads. Timothy B. Schmit, then a member of Buffett's Corral Reefer Band during the Eagles' 14-year hiatus from performing, coined the term "Parrothead" to describe those fans.

The costumes became more creative—leis, grass skirts, coconut bras, and parrot hats, the men as prone to wearing this stuff as the women—and the party extended to tailgating as much as eight hours before each show.

Buffett always brings his ultimate beach party to Las Vegas. In his earlier Vegas appearances, portions of MGM's amusement park were used for the pre-party. There's nothing quite like singing, dancing, and beach-balling with 20,000 of your closest friends. The concert starts early and no one ever sits down.

Fight for the Right to the Fight

In addition to concerts, the Grand Garden booked all types of events, including arena football and indoor soccer. However, this venue was built on boxing. The plan wasn't just to get into boxing, but to dominate it.

Before MGM, the standard for hotels was to erect temporary outdoor boxing facilities that were, naturally, dependent on the weather. Grand Garden, by contrast, was climate-controlled and attached to the casino; once inside the property, fight fans never had to step foot outside.

Dennis Finfrock had his own ideas about how to manage the Grand Garden. In addition to trying to isolate it from the rest of the property's management, he wanted to change how boxing was promoted, by bucking the traditional promoter-venue relationship. Rather than just booking the fights and collecting rent, Finfrock wanted to own and develop boxers. Fight promoters Bob Arum and Don King weren't impressed.

This wasn't the first time a hotel had attempted to get into the boxing business. After the Mirage opened, Steve Wynn grew tired of getting shaken down by King and Arum and attempted to cut out the middlemen. By fronting expenses, making guarantees to boxers, and contracting directly with HBO and Showtime for broadcast rights, Wynn went heads-up against the promoters. Even as formidable a competitor as Steve Wynn found that the fight-promotion business was fraught with peril.

Dennis Finfrock was about to learn the same lesson. Against Bob Arum's counsel (Arum, after all, was now a competitor), Finfrock signed Jorge Gonzalez. Gonzalez was a six-foot-six 250-pound physical marvel. Unfortunately, he couldn't box. Still, after a couple of softie fights, Finfrock went all in, promoting a fight with the reigning heavyweight champion Riddick Bowe.

Daren Libonati, working with Finfrock at MGM, knew enough about boxing to recognize that their fighter was lazy, didn't know how to prepare for a fight of this magnitude, or both. "I told Dennis that he needed to deal with Gonzalez and his camp on their training intensity. Dennis was too trusting."

In the first round, Bowe began to toy with Gonzalez. By the fourth round, he was done toying with him. He'd punched his face into the shape of a basketball.

Finfrock was out.

Grand Garden Kick-Starts Ticket Price Surge

Daren Libonati was offered the arena-director position, but turned it down; he didn't want Finfrock's dismissal to accrue to his own advantage. Mark Prows was asked to take on the job, on the condition the Grand Garden was fully integrated into the hotel. Prows looks back at that time. "Dennis managed the Grand Garden as he knew how. Thomas and Mack Center was his only point of reference. He had complete autonomy at UNLV. The venue wasn't fully integrated into the campus. Not everyone can be successful in a large corporate environment like we had at MGM Grand."

Prows learned exactly what "fully integrating the arena in the hotel" meant: more input from the casino on events. It was no longer about quality, but quantity. "It was like booking shit by committee. As soon as it opened up, MGM employees were calling right and left, giving us their wish lists and who they wanted to see next. All I could do was collate the input and take it to Richard Sturm."

After a three-year stint at Bally's as vice president of marketing where he and Barry Fey developed a successful concert series, Richard Sturm was tabbed to develop MGM's content and brand. Sturm has spent 30 years working on high-profile entertainment projects in Las Vegas, as well as redefining the MGM Grand as the City of Entertainment. With MGM since 1995, Sturm has a stellar track record.

Prows explains why. "Richard Sturm has this innate ability to remain calm in the face of adversity and find inordinate solutions under difficult circumstances." This disposition helped Sturm forge enduring relationships in the live-touring industry.

Sturm impelled the MGM to push the envelope on ticket pricing. The industry was highly skeptical of the final numbers for Barbara Streisand's two sold-out shows that opened the arena. But the Grand Garden's subsequent concert and event grosses also remained the highest in the country.

"The artists wanted to keep their ticket prices fair for the fans," says John Meglen of Concerts West. "They had this perception that tickets were going to people who could afford them. Vegas became the safest market to begin increasing prices without people realizing what was happening. We were always explaining that the casino was buying the highest-priced tickets, but this new trend started dynamic concert pricing and suddenly woke up the entire entertainment industry. 'Wow! I can get paid two to three times my normal fee from casinos that want these people on the property."

With each event, MGM honed its special-event marketing strategies to a sharp edge. The casino purchases a percentage of the expensive seats to hand out as complimentaries to its best players. In addition, they built a database that evolved into MGM's rewards program, M life, which has dramatically refined the criteria by which the best customers are measured for comps. Today, Grand Garden sells 60%-80% of its tickets outside of Las Vegas.

The success of MGM's arena turned the city into a lightning rod for proposed arenas and stadiums. Much more so than Thomas and Mack Center on the university campus, it demonstrated the viability of live music for the gambler and hotel visitor. Circus Circus Enterprises, for one, was paying attention. Five and half years after MGM Grand Garden opened, another arena came online in conjunction with the opening of Mandalay Bay Hotel and Casino.

CHAPTER NINE

THREE NEW VEGAS ARENAS

Mandalay Bay Events Center—Three Should Be Enough

MGM Grand wasn't the only hotel-casino to open in 1993. The 5000-room green monster, the 2,500-room pyramid-shaped Luxor, and the 2,700-room Treasure Island all debuted within six weeks of one another, completing what at the time was called "the Great Race." Las Vegas, with 33.4 million visitors and 1.3 million residents, was in the early stages of a massive building boom the likes of which the world had never before seen.

In 1995, Circus Circus bought the 39-year-old Hacienda Hotel at the far south end of the Strip. It was imploded on New Year's Eve 1996 and in its place was built the $950 million 3,300-room Mandalay Bay, which opened on March 2, 1999. Connected to the hotel-casino were a million-square-foot convention center and the 12,000-seat Events Center. Unlike Grand Garden, the arena had a bright concourse with marble floor covering and plenty of nearby restrooms and concession stands.

The Mandalay team went after every event: boxing, award shows, concerts, corporate, sporting, and more. Like the smaller Grand Garden did to Thomas and Mack, the Event Center, smaller than the Grand Garden, put a dent in MGM's calendar and brought new events to the city.

HC Rowe had worked at the Aladdin Theater for the Performing Arts, then did a short stint at the Rio before Joel Fishman, a friendly rival at Bally's, offered him the opportunity to open the newest arena on the Strip. The job not only included the venue itself, but also the pool-complex's concert stage. The Events Center's capacity was a head-scratcher. "I would have preferred something closer to 16,000 seats. I was a competitor with MGM for several years with a smaller seating capacity. I wanted to compete on that level. But the decision was already made."

Mandalay Bay Events Center started out with more of a whimper than a bang, opening on May 8, 1999, with REO selling 3,000 tickets, 25% of capacity. Something of a bang did occur, however, a few months later.

It all started when rock bad boys Mötley Crüe performed the final concert at the Aladdin Theater before it was closed in November 1997 for the hotel to be imploded (the theater was spared). The band provoked fans by telling them to tear the place down. Some obliged, trashing the seats, tearing payphones out of the walls, and vandalizing bathrooms, among other things. Police and security had to stop the concert for 10 minutes. Four people were injured, but no one was arrested.

On August 8, 1999, Mötley Crüe were back in Vegas at Mandalay Bay. Metro police had a little talk with them before the show. Lt. Rick Alba said, "We told them they can't conduct themselves this way, that it's against the law, and it won't be tolerated." Nevertheless, halfway through the show, Nikki Six announced, "Fuck the cops!" And he urged the crowd to "flip over cop cars." Nothing bad happened with the crowd. However, when the show ended, the band came off the stage to be greeted by a line of Metro officers and a paddy wagon. After an altercation, Nikki Six and four roadies were arrested.

The rest of that year, the Events Center hosted 15 shows, the biggest being Vincente Fernandez, the Mexican "King of Ranchera Music," who sold 7,500-plus tickets. The arena heated up in 2000, hosting 21 concerts, including Barry Manilow and the Broadway play *Annie* and highlighted by the Three Tenors, who sold out 11,321 seats and grossed $6.5 million.

In 2001, the arena hit its stride, hosting 31 concerts, as the bigger acts were starting to find their way to the smaller and more intimate venue. Andrea Bocelli sold out and grossed $2.3 million. Tim McGraw, Reba McIntyre, and Destiny's Child all sold out. The next year was the arena's most successful, peaking at 38 concerts, the biggest being Britney Spears' two sold-out shows that grossed $1.4 million.

Many promoters produced concerts in the arena, but Danny Zelisko of Evening Star was its "regular guy."

Y2K in LV—Learning a Hard Lesson in Yield Management

New Year's Eve 1999 was the most anticipated holiday in Las Vegas history. Throughout the 1990s, the price of rooms and entertainment had steadily risen, as did concert guarantees. And at no time was this truer than the week between December 25, 1999, and January 1, 2000.

The new-millennium craze started in 1998, as everyone was starting to gear up for the New Year's weekend (New Year's Eve was on a Friday that year). Danny Zelisko said, "I put out an initial very high offer for Tina Turner. Caesars came back with a very *very* high offer that had to include Elton John. I passed and Caesars ended up doing the concert at Thomas and Mack Center."

Barbara Streisand was booked at MGM at a similarly exorbitant guarantee and ticket price. Zelisko was offered two Eagles and two Bette Midler dates at Mandalay Bay. But they came with "colossal" guarantees, larger than anything he'd ever done.

"I thought anybody that was anyone would want to be in Vegas between Christmas and New Years for the new millennium," he said. "But suddenly, the hotels started to impose four- and five-night minimum stays, along with exceedingly high room prices."

An ugly side of Veganomics started to materialize.

The cost of four or five nights in a Strip hotel rose to $2,000 minimum. The concert tickets ranged from $150 to $2,500. And that was before the flight, local transportation, meals, and gambling for the 350,000 visitors expected for the biggest New Year's Eve in several lifetimes.

"It wasn't until the end of October that the hotels started to adjust, but by that time, it was too late. It was a giant money grab—by the acts, agents, hotels, and promoters—and I was one of those. Everyone lost their minds over that week." And it got worse for Zelisko.

Promoters receive daily ticket counts from hotel ticket offices. In addition to gauging the amount of additional promotion a show might need, the counts are critical to negotiating a buyout should a show sell badly. Closer to the shows, Zelisko's ticket report showed a negative 500 tickets per show, meaning 500 tickets that he thought had been bought by the hotel, but weren't. "The hotel held thousands of tickets for their high rollers, putting them in the sold column, not the held column," says Zelisko. In two days, millions of dollars of tickets were returned when the hotel finally admitted reservations from its major players and guests were less than anticipated.

"I pleaded with the acts. Their response was, 'It's too bad you didn't know that your partner hadn't sold those tickets.'"

To make matters worse, Streisand sold out her show at MGM and added a second. That show was taped for HBO and they papered the house for the second show to make sure it looked full.

All four of Zelisko's shows lost money. The tickets held and returned by Mandalay Bay represented his breakeven. He lost more than a million dollars.

Zelisko hammered out a deal with Mandalay Bay to work off the losses with future shows he promoted at the Events Center. "It took a while, but I paid back every dollar. In fact, I had a killer year in 2000. But it could have been so different. If I'd had accurate counts, I would have convinced the acts to do one show." The experience so soured him that the following year, he sold Evening Star to SFX, which was consolidating the concert business by buying up promoters. Zelisko was one of the last holdouts.

The venue stayed hot over the next three years, thanks in part to 10 Latin shows that grossed more than $1 million each.

In 2004, MGM-Mirage acquired Mandalay Bay Resorts (the renamed Circus Circus Enterprises) and with it the Events Center. Now owning two arenas, it took a couple years for MGM to sort out the situation, during which concerts at Mandalay Bay slowed to 10 per year, highlighted by Kenny Chesney and Toby Keith selling out two shows each. Starting in 2006, however, the venue picked up speed again, averaging 23 concerts a year, including double sellouts by Justin Timberlake, Spice Girls, Tim McGraw/Faith Hill, Britney Spears, Vincente Fernandez, and Mana. Other notable concerts included Shakira, Nickelback, Black Eyed Peas, Van Morrison, Christina Aguilar, Rush, Janet Jackson, Taylor Swift, Metallica, Muse, Usher, Katy Perry, Rhianna, Bob Seger, and Jennifer Lopez.

Since then, though the number of concerts has fluctuated, the Events Center is a critical piece of Mandalay Bay that includes conventions, conferences, and events.

The Orleans Arena—Four Should Be Enough

Thomas and Mack Center was a training ground for many people who now make up the Las Vegas live-music industry. In addition to Mark Prows and Darin Libonati, Chris Baldizan is senior vice president of entertainment at MGM, Damian Costa is vice president of entertainment at Caesars, and Dale Eeles is vice president of event development at Las Vegas Events, where he works with me. Three Thomas and Mack alum also played on one of UNLV's only winning football teams, going 11-2 in 1984. Ron Drake, now director of Caesars' sales, was the center; Daren Libonati was the kicker; and Steve Stallworth, general manager of South Point Events Center, was the backup quarterback to Randall Cunningham (in 1986 and 1987, he was the starting quarterback for both winning seasons). Stallworth opened the Orleans Arena.

Michael Gaughn is one of the most respected hotel operators in Las Vegas, for good reason. His formula of quality in the gaming, room, dining, and entertainment products, attention to customer details, and a fair price have resulted in a map of Las Vegas that's dotted with former successful hotels he developed: Barbary Coast (now the Cromwell, a Caesars property) Gold Coast, Orleans, and Suncoast (now Boyd Gaming properties), and South Point, which he owns and operates. When he opened the Orleans, he wanted something unique—an arena at a locals casino.

Gaughan is a one-man board of directors and his attention to detail rivals Steve Wynn's. What started as a moderately designed 5,500-seat arena grew into one of the best venues of its size in the country. Each seat is 20 inches and theater-padded (TMC's are 18-19 inches), the concourse is double-wide with granite tile and more food-and-beverage points of sale and restrooms than any arena of its size. Backstage, the dressing rooms rival NBA arenas'. There are 16 super-sized suites and club seats for 440, plus plenty of free parking. For live-music production, the Orleans Arena can load six trucks at once, the venue was acoustically treated, and it can hang 200,000 pounds of sound and lights.

Steve Stallworth started working in radio sales before replacing Mark Prows, selling advertising signage at Thomas and Mack Center. In the next four years, he switched to managing three different professional sports teams, the Posse in the Canadian Football League, the Dustdevils of Indoor Soccer, and the Sting Arena Football team—all of them joined the graveyard of over 20 minor league teams that tried and failed in Las Vegas. Then he returned to Thomas and Mack to manage a UNLV sports marketing department we created. In the three years he managed sports marketing, UNLV went 0-11 in one of the football seasons and basketball didn't make the NCAA Tournament, yet in the last year he managed it, he increased revenue by $2 million.

In 2001, when I left UNLV, two people were ready to run arenas. Daren Libonati got the job with UNLV and Steve Stallworth went to work for Michael Gaughan at the Orleans Arena.

"When the talk started about another arena, I said to myself, 'We need another arena like we need a hole in the head,'" recalls Stallworth. "But Gaughan's vision was very clear. He wanted to own the locals market. He wanted minor league hockey, soccer, football, Disney on Ice, circuses, *and live music.*" But live music now had a half-dozen major competing venues and as nice as the arena was, it wasn't on the Strip.

After Stallworth and Gaughan wrapped up a deal with the ECHL to host a hockey team, Stallworth wasted no time looking for a promoter to embrace the venue. His first call was Danny Zelisko. Stallworth recalls their meeting.

"Danny says, 'Okay. Here's my deal. We'll be 50/50 partners on everything on the up and the down. But if we lose, you pay the loss and you pay me 20 grand.' And I say, 'Whoa, whoa, whoa, Danny. What kind of a 50/50 deal is that?'" Stallworth passed.

His next idea was putting together three industry stalwarts, all in transition.

"Steve Hauser was getting tired of the agency business," Stallworth recalls. "Gary Becker was ready to get back in the game. And Louie Messina was considering his options." Messina and Becker were part of Pace concerts, which was sold to SFX. "This would have been a dream team," says Stallworth.

But it remained a dream. Messina went to work for AEG where he now promotes the most successful country tours on the road—Taylor Swift, Kenny Chesney, George Strait, and more. Hauser went back to work in the agencies.

Becker, however, hung with the Orleans. They started small. "We became the venue for the up-and-coming artists. We did Fall Out Boys and Panic at the Disco, before getting an offer to do Van Halen six weeks after they played Mandalay Bay. Gary Becker called and said, 'Hey, we've got a chance to do Van Halen,' and I said, 'Gary, you've lost your mind. Are you kidding me?' It was a million-dollar guarantee. The average ticket price was $125. I went to Michael and he said, 'Do it.' We ended up selling out a Van Halen shows six weeks after it sold out Mandalay Bay."

Orleans Arena opened with the Brooks and Dunn's Neon Circus, which included Brad Paisley and Rascal Flatts. In its first three years, the arena averaged 16 concerts per, including Peter, Paul and Mary, Jane's Addiction, Joe Cocker, String Cheese Incident (as part of Vegoose), the Black-Eyed Peas, and My Chemical Romance with Rise Against. It had its best year in 2007, hosting 24 concerts, including Larry the Cable Guy, Charlie Daniel's Volunteer Jam, and ZZ Top. The arena also became home to Latin fans, hosting a couple dozen concerts.

In 2008, Stallworth followed Michael Gaughan to South Point, divesting of most of his agents and promoters and donning cowboy boots and a Stetson. However, until three years ago, Orleans Arena averaged 10 concerts a year.

T-Mobile Arena—A Desert Diamond

Since 1993, MGM has managed to stay ahead of the entertainment curve.

"I remember getting a call in 2001 from Jim Murren [president of MGM Resorts at the time, now Chairman and CEO] asking me, 'What do you think about hockey?" Mark Prows recalls. "I didn't think the market was ready then."

In 2005, Caesars worked with AEG and the state of Nevada to see if they could get public funding for a new arena. The crashing economy a couple years later shattered that idea. But MGM leadership never let go of the idea. "We didn't want to cede our position in entertainment," says Prows. "Five years ago, Murren called again to say, 'You know, we need to build another arena.'

Prows was confident in his ability to operate the arena, but he had an abiding respect for the way AEG responsibly designed and built venues, along with its solid sponsorship and premium seating staff. MGM and AEG announced their joint-venture arena plan on March 1, 2013.

T-Mobile Arena, completed in March 2016, sits between New York-New York and Monte Carlo, connected to the Strip by a $100 million pedestrian shopping area, park, plaza with art, and restaurants. It's surrounded by three parking structures and 25,000 hotel rooms within easy walking distance.

With the desert and Spring Mountains directly to the west and pulsating Las Vegas Boulevard to the east, the arena design includes an expansive glass façade with an LED overlay, sweeping balconies along Park Avenue (formerly Rue de Monte Carlo), an outdoor stage, and a sleek exterior that's as bold as it is sophisticated, creating an iconic focal point for the city's bustling entertainment market. Two dramatic sponsor towers provide unique vantage points and showcase the glamour, energy, and see-and-be-seen nature of the city, creating a premium experience that, even only after a year in operation, is already a bold statement for Las Vegas.

The arena's interior design is a perfect compromise between premium seating, which generates sizable revenue, and sightlines for the regular fan. Its concourse is massive, with plenty of food and beverage options and restrooms. Arenas in larger markets like New York, Chicago, and L.A. have bigger footprints, but T-Mobile's 50 suites and 2,000 club and loge seats cater to casino and pro-sports VIPs.

Even then, to have a truly great building, the production and backstage experiences also have to rock and T-Mobile does them like no other arena. "Promoters, producers, managers, agents are saying pretty much the same thing in different vernaculars," says Prows. "They believe that it's literally the best building in the country, if not the world."

In June 2016, with deposits for 16,000 season tickets in his pocket, Bill Foley was awarded Las Vegas' first professional sports franchise by the NHL. In November, he announced the name of the team, the Golden Knights. In addition to hockey, the arena has already hosted UFC fights, USA Basketball, NBA exhibition games, and the biggest touring acts.

Indeed, T-Mobile didn't waste any time rolling rock into its venue and taking over where Grand Garden left off. It opened with a sellout by hometown heroes the Killers. Three-quarters through its first year, it has hosted more than 40 concerts, selling close to a half-million tickets. The Rolling Stones were the top-grossing concert with over $7 million in sales. George Strait sold out eight shows and 140,000 tickets, grossing $23 million. Garth Brooks sold out six shows. Guns N' Roses sold out two shows, grossing $6.3 million, while Barbara Streisand's return to Vegas grossed $3.6 million.

Prows says, "This market still has the ability to deliver the highest prices and the biggest events."

Big, Bad, and Black

In March 2017, it became official: The NFL's Oakland Raiders will relocate to Las Vegas in 2018. That was the biggest news for local sports fans ever. But plans for a new stadium are instructive in terms of local economics.

In 2016, Las Vegas attracted 3 million live-music fans. However, it didn't have the opportunity to host Beyoncé or the return of the reconstituted Grateful Dead, who only play the largest stadiums. Why not? Because it couldn't compete venue-wise.

In addition, a study commissioned by the Southern Nevada Tourism Infrastructure Committee (SNTIC) showed another 15 events that Las Vegas can't attract, among them international soccer and rugby, neutral-site college football and national collegiate football championships, NCAA Final Four, bowl games, UFC, and boxing.

Many economists have a problem with publicly funded stadiums. For example, Neil deMause, co-author of the book *Field of Schemes: How the Great Stadium Swindle Turns Public Money into Private Profit*, insists that the private deal made to finance the new stadium "was a really really bad job of negotiating. The people doing the negotiating weren't the people who'd be paying the costs. They don't have a huge incentive to cut a better deal, because they're playing with somebody else's money," he said.

However, in this case, it's not public money footing the bill. Other than a .88% increase in the hotel-room tax, the new stadium will be built with private money. The NFL and the Raiders are investing $500 million and Bank of America is ponying up $650 million more in loan money.

For the stadium to realize a profit, tickets for the Raiders and *as many other large events as possible* will have to be sold to locals and visitors.

For more than 20 years, Las Vegas resisted the temptation to fund a stadium. Why? Because hotel operators would have had to pay for it. Nevada is a conservatively taxed market with no state income tax and low property taxes. The decision-makers for the funding for the "Raiders" stadium comprised an 11-person advisory board, six of whom represented the casinos. The stadium was approved, but not entirely for the football team. It was also approved for the visitors and the impact they'll have on Las Vegas' bottom line.

Economists have targeted stadium subsidies as "corporate welfare." Are the Raiders getting a subsidy? Yes: 88 cents per room night. But what does Las Vegas get for its $750 million commitment? A $1.9 billion stadium estimated to bring somewhere between 500,000-850,000 new visitors. And the $750 million will be paid by visitors. The SNTIC has estimated that the stadium will attract 451,000 visitors annually; the direct impact annually will be $366 million, the indirect impact $114 million, and the induced impact $138 million.

It will also generate substantial tax revenue, all paid by visitors—the hotel tax, plus taxes on cab rides, restaurant meals, gambling, rental cars, and entertainment. Local economist Jeremy Aguero says, "There's almost nothing a visitor does that isn't subject to some form of tax. This could generate $35 million per year. With principal and interest, the debt on $750 million is $35 million, not including payroll or commerce taxes, which could raise another $10 million, all of which goes back to the state's general fund."

By 2020, Las Vegas will have 11 music-specific theaters as large as 17,000 seats, plus five arenas, three festival sites, and three stadiums, one of which is a Tiger Woods' drive from the Strip. In the past, my pitch to compete for events against cities with modernized arenas and stadiums was, "If you go there, you play in a great arena/stadium, but you don't have Vegas." Now, we have it both—the venues and everything Las Vegas has to offer surrounding them.

CHAPTER TEN

THE LIVE-MUSIC EXPERIENCE

Paul Davis grew up in Henderson, Nevada, when it was a distant suburb of Las Vegas, not completely contiguous like it is today. Paul's oldest brother was a music hound and a quintessential music fan who camped out overnight to get second-row tickets to see Ted Nugent. In the '70s, he went to every show—Boston, Queen, Frampton, Aerosmith, Steve Miller, to name just a few. He brought home albums, so he and Paul could lie on the floor, put on the headphones, pull the sleeve out of the record, read the lyrics, and look at the pictures of the band while listening to the album. "I immersed myself, doing a deep dive into every album."

Paul's brother took him to his first rock concert, Blue Oyster Cult at the Aladdin, when he was 12. "I got bit by the rock bug—music that was ten years older than me."

His brother had a routine for concert night. "He had a black van with blue velvet inside and black lights hanging from the ceiling." The first stop was a liquor store. "I wasn't drinking. I was twelve and never did drugs. But his friends, let's just say they wanted to have the full concert experience. There was always a three-hour ramp-up. I wanted to get there early to see the opening act, but the ramp-up took precedence. At intermission, a joint made its way down the row to 30 strangers, then back, followed by the beer, because everyone had dry mouth."

Also at 12, his mom bought him his first guitar, a red Court Flying V that he tricked out with stripes. "I was big a Judas Priest fan. KK Downing played that Red Flying V."

He took two years of lessons and in the mid-'80s at 15, he put together a glam metal band called Seduction. "Our outfits were legwarmers and pink jackets and we were terrible. But we were good enough to play Moby Grape."

His obsession with rock continued into high school, though now he was old enough to drive and his brother's ticketing service was no longer available. "In high school, we usually had bad seats, but I went to Journey with Loverboy, Judas Priest, Blue Oyster Cult, Heart, Night Ranger, Metallica opening for Ozzy, Scorpions, Guns N' Roses with Soundgarden, Rush, Genesis, AC/DC, REO—literally all the rock shows."

Davis enrolled at UNLV to pursue an accounting degree, but kept on rocking. "Through college, I played in a band just for fun. It was my way of chasing girls and hanging out with my buddies."

After graduating in 1991, he went to work for JC Penney, but had no idea what he wanted to do until he signed on to do retail accounting at the newly opened MGM Grand. This agreed with him. "I was working concerts like the Stones and Billy Joel, staying until two in the morning to settle with the tour-merchandise manager. And I was like, holy shit. These are my heroes. I'm getting paid to do this!"

MGM kept him busy working retail at the arena and amusement park. Then he was offered a position as entertainment business manager at the soon-to-open Mandalay Bay Events Center. This was closer to what he was looking for. "I didn't want to leave the MGM Grand, but I wanted to be a full-time entertainment guy."

Again, he was starting from scratch, but he was working with industry pro HC Rowe. "HC taught me everything, especially settling events."

Halfway through a typical event, the ticket office closes and a manifest verifies total ticket sales. Then a tour accountant, the promoter, and a venue representative meet to "settle" the show. All expenses are put on the table and discussed. Depending on the personalities in the room, it can be long or short, contentious or peaceful. Davis had an unusual take on one of the settlements. "I got yelled at by Bob Hurwitz, the Eagles' tour accountant. I was pissed off, but oh, what an honor! To get yelled at by the *Eagles'* tour accountant!"

Mysterious or Conspicuous?

Was the live music experience better in the '60s or '70s than it is today? It depends on how old you are!

When rock was new, kids formed a bond with bands via the radio and live shows let them experience the real thing. You couldn't get to Odyssey quick enough to spend that extra $25 you had in your pocket on the latest vinyl LPs. The record store was an immersive experience, with posters promoting concerts, alluring album-cover art, and Bose speakers playing that new Led Zeppelin or Alice Cooper album.

Music was life.

There was no MTV, YouTube, concert DVD, or social media. You knew very little about the members of the bands. Considering the lifestyle of rock stars, that was the way they wanted it.

The concert was the first time you saw the band. The focus wasn't a staged show—no video screens, pyro, or lasers. It was the band and only the band, playing music. The goal wasn't perfection. It was to use energy to burst through boundaries and leave it all out there. The bands had off-nights and you knew it (perhaps none more than the Grateful Dead). A concert was a chance to let loose via any legal or illegal substance with like-spirited individuals. It was an ear-thumping, frenzied, and thrilling experience.

Today, the mystery is gone. There's little fans don't know about the music. The concert isn't new; 100 million people saw Lady Gaga perform at half-time at the Super Bowl.

But the experience is better. There are options: the intimate setting of a theater or the value and social aspects of a festival. But the dominant number of tickets for the most popular acts are sold for the venues in which the artist can generate the biggest payday—arenas, stadiums, and large amphitheaters.

Either way, unknown or familiar, live is the most engaging way to experience music and it creates the strongest bond between artist and fan. Fans become more emotionally and financially invested in the artists they experience live, bringing more value to the industry—and the artists who make it run.

Shake, Rattle and Roll—How Rock Concerts Developed

In the late '50s, rock 'n' roll was peeking in the door of what was a fairly benign music scene. Artists like Frank Sinatra, Nat King Cole, and Peggy Lee topped the pop charts, while Johnny Cash, Hank Williams, and Patsy Cline were country's chart-busters. The music matched the ultra-conservative nature of the times. The real live experiences were in the black nightclubs, where acts like Howlin' Wolf, Buddy Guy, and Muddy Waters were belting out the blues.

In 1955, Carl Perkins employed blues-based rhythms to knock at the door with his huge hit "Blue Suede Shoes."

But it was Elvis Presley who blew the door down with his performance of the same song on the "Milton Berle Show." Two weeks later, he shocked the conservative sensibilities of 80 million on the "Ed Sullivan Show." His sheer flash and lusty innuendo provided the defining moment for live music. The floodgates swept open and were never dammed again.

With permission to exhibit unbridled emotion (through dance) and bolstered by new TV programming like the "Dick Clark Show," kids were letting loose. Songs like Hank Ballard's "The Twist" (popularized by Chubby Checker) and Jerry Lee Lewis' "Great Balls of Fire" broadened the appeal when white audiences, restricted from the floor, would jump from the balcony to be part of the action.

The Beatles invasion of the United States demonstrated the frenzy a live concert could generate. But other than witnessing the spectacle, the shrieking drowned out practically all experience of the music. It took another few years for the live-music experience to take form.

In the mid-'60s, the youngest audiences for rock 'n' roll saw acts in bowling alleys, college and high-school gyms, and dance halls around the country. At the same time, audiences were growing in clubs like the Troubadour and Whiskey a Go Go in L.A., where fans could rub elbows with acts like Linda Ronstadt, the Eagles Jackson Browne, and Elton John, who didn't only perform, but also hung out. These clubs catered to the burgeoning neighborhood of musicians in Laurel Canyon.

"The Troubadour was one of the most unique and respected places to play," recalls Jackson Browne. "There were Cadillacs and Porsches outside in the parking lot and inside it was a wild party. People were doing drugs and trying to get picked up, while young talent was being revealed on stage."

The clubs and coffeehouses of Greenwich Village developed a much different scene, but it was just as important to the evolution of the live-music experience. There was an explosion of creativity, politics and music, poetry and literature. Pete Seeger, Woodie Guthrie, and eventually Bob Dylan promoted social reform. And the artists took their craft seriously. They weren't competing; they appreciated one another and everyone went to everyone's shows. The residents of the Village were laid back, unconventional, like-minded musically and socio-politically. Sundays on Washington Square became mini-festivals of musicians playing blues, bluegrass, doo-wop—a social scene with music as its heart and soul.

Bill Graham—Painting the Rock Experience on a Blank Canvas

As the live-music experience evolved, bigger venues, like Bill Graham's Fillmore East and West and Winterland, flourished. They cultivated a more eclectic experience, served up for the counterculture with the hippies' "three food groups": sex, drugs, and rock 'n' roll. None of the bands booked were charting a hit; no one outside of San Francisco knew who they were. But 3,000 people nightly packed the venues.

Bill Graham had an innate ability to organize events, creating comfortable and safe atmospheres without stifling the creative energy. Maintaining high aesthetic standards and calling on limitless personal energy, he developed a live-music experience that became the foundation of what's now the "live-music touring business."

At the Fillmores and Winterland, Graham took artistic risks. The concert experience was more than just music. He wrapped sound, lights, and special effects around each performance. It was a community coming together for "something completely different" every night.

For example, at the Fillmore East, Graham hired Joshua White to create an immersive sound and light show. The Joshua Light Group was an ensemble of six visual artists, performing visual music on an ad hoc and adlib basis. Three sets, two shows a night.

The stage was small and low. The light show enveloped the end of the hall and the stage was at the bottom center. Flashing pulsing colors filled the room and it didn't hurt that pot and LSD intensified the experience.

"Everyone was tripping and you needed something to look at and we weren't real pretty and there were no real lights on the stage," explains Mickey Hart of the Grateful Dead. "No one even knew what we looked like."

"There was the direct projection of images. There were mirrored effects in which images were broken up and put back together with mirrors," Joshua White says. "There were traditional films and slides. There was a lot of color and everything changed all the time. Once Graham wanted something special for the Airplane and we suggested building a giant cutout of an airplane that takes off behind the drum set and splits in half when it goes over the balcony. One half goes to one side of the balcony while the other goes to the back of the orchestra accompanied by bright headlights and giant sound effects. Bill loved the idea."

The Fillmore developed freestyle dancing. Not the Twist, the Mashed Potato, or the Swim, but any way you wanted! The experience at Fillmore was not so much about who was playing, but about being a part of an into-the-morning scene choreographed with a liquid light show and punctuated by long improvised songs and sets.

Also demonstrating his foresight with live music, Graham called for the record industry to stop producing hit singles and instead focus on the band's entire repertoire to create real music. This would come to pass with the LP.

It didn't take long for "the movement" to spread throughout the nation. Regional promoters started using the Fillmore as blueprints for their own versions. In Boston, Don Law opened the Boston Tea Party. In Chicago, it was Aaron Russo and the Kinetic Playhouse. A young deejay, Larry Magid, launched the Electric Ballroom in Philadelphia and George Papadopoulos developed the Psychedelic Supermarket in New York.

Then the music moved outdoors and attracted crowds that were unimaginable even to promoters. The three-day Monterey Pop Festival drew close to 90,000. Two years later, Woodstock drew five times that. Six months after Woodstock, at the hastily and poorly produced Altamont Speedway festival, nearly 40 people were injured and one fatally stabbed.

Following Altamont, at the tail end of the '60s, the free-for-all atmosphere of that decade's festivals demanded a more refined and safer experience. The arena, eventually, proved the type of venue that could provide that for fans.

Houses of Rock

One of the reasons live music has improved is the quality of the venue. In a theater, arena, or stadium, the level of commitment to quality and safety, first in designing and building the venue and then in the systems to deliver on a promise, all have a tremendous impact on a concert-fan's experience—ingress-egress, parking, information, entering (with security search), food and beverage, acoustics, ticketing, seating, crowd management, and today, wifi and cellular service.

In the '60s, any place that would host rock concerts did. But then the first wave of new arenas started opening. The one old arena was the Cow Palace in San Francisco (1941), but around the west were the Arizona Coliseum (1965), Oakland Coliseum (1966), Los Angeles Forum (1967), and Salt Palace (1969). The concert touring business grew around these and the 50 other venues popping up around the country.

As crowds and demands for space grew, college and professional sports stadiums found that concert tours could be accommodated for another revenue stream.

Predominantly public venues, the event services (ticketing, security, stagehands, staging equipment, and ushers) were mostly provided by promoters. In the early '80s as the concert business matured, these venues began to control and provide their own services, reimbursed by the promoter, which significantly improved service and security.

In the '90s, rapid growth of the NBA and NHL spurred a second wave of arena construction. Live music wasn't the main money-maker, but it definitely contributed. Among those in the west were Salt Lake City's Delta Center (1992, now Vivint Smart Home), Phoenix's America West Arena (1992, now Talking Stick), Denver's Pepsi Center (1999), Oracle Arena (1997, major renovation of Oakland Coliseum), and L.A.'s Staples Center (1999).

These new venues were filled with modernized customer amenities, including wider padded seats, more and bigger concourses, and upgraded food service. In ticket offices, the latest computerized systems were integrated with pro-team databases. Club seats, which gave owners guaranteed seats, VIP suites, parking, catering, and signage became major revenue generators. Backstage, double and triple loading docks were built to allow more efficient loading in and out. Ceiling capacities increased to fulfill concerts' demands for more extravagant and weighty productions. Lavish dressing rooms replaced the sweat and stench, especially in hockey arenas.

Concert promoters, who for decades coveted a piece of the ancillary revenues (ticketing, food and beverage, parking, merchandise, and ticketing), finally determined to build their own venues. Arenas or stadiums weren't practical or cost-effective, so they built amphitheaters. These outdoor venues condensed a lot of touring into the summer months.

Because of Los Angeles' great weather and burgeoning music scene, the 6,000-seat Greek Theater, built in 1929, had already been established, same as the Hollywood Bowl, which opened in 1922. In 1981, Irvine Meadows in Orange County was added to the L.A. outdoor list. The 8,600-capacity Greek Theater at Berkeley, built in 1903, was the only amphitheater in the Bay Area until Bill Graham built the 22,000-capacity Shoreline Amphitheater in 1986. Red Rocks outside of Denver had and still has no peer; its 9,500 seats sit in a natural rock formation. Even so, in 1988, Fiddler's Green Amphitheater was built in Denver with 18,000 seats. The heat didn't deter Phoenix from building Desert Sky (now Ak-Chin) Pavilion in 1990 with a 20,000-seat capacity.

While Las Vegas has several temporary outdoor-concert venues, the heavy bookings from current theaters and arenas make a permanent amphitheater prohibitive. An exception is the Henderson Pavilion six miles southeast of the Strip across from Green Valley Ranch Hotel and Casino. It has 2,444 fixed seats and room for another 4,143 on the lawn. LeAnn Rimes, Buddy Guy, Kenny "Babyface" Edmonds, Diamond Rio, Belinda Carlisle, Drake Bell, "Weird Al" Yankovic, Paramore, *Beehive The Musical*, and Moscow Ballet have all played the Henderson Pavilion.

In the 21st century, billions of dollars have been invested around the country for new multi-purpose venues. The fan experience continues to improve, including video, backstage production, and digital telecommunications such as Distributed Antenna Systems (DAS) that allow fans' social-media experiences to continue inside the venue. The advent of e-mail, CAD drawings, and networking greatly improved the production of concerts.

The NFL and MLB have also worked with respective cities to build new and modern stadiums with the same blueprint used in arenas. In the west, San Francisco built AT&T Park for MLB in 2000 and Santa Clara built Levi's Stadium for the NFL in 2014. Phoenix built Chase Field for MLB with a retractable roof in 1998 and University of Phoenix Stadium for the NFL in 2006. Denver built Coors Field for MLB in 1995 and Sports Authority Field for the NFL in 2001. San Diego built Petco Park for MLB in 2004. Ironically, Los Angeles waited many years to build a new stadium for the NFL, but when completed in 2019 for an estimated $2.6 billion, it will be the most expensive stadium ever built.

While Sam Boyd Stadium's capacity has made it difficult to secure concerts, the ticket-revenue power of MGM Grand Garden and now T-Mobile Arena ensures that Vegas doesn't miss out on many concert tours. In 2020, if all goes according to plan, Las Vegas will have its own state-of-the-art stadium.

Ticketing—From Stubs to StubHub

Four pieces of the live-music business are critical to the experience— ticketing, crowd management, production, and social media.

Ticketing for live music took shape in the '60s when promoters printed tickets through a local printing company and distributed them via outlets they set up throughout the market.

"Tickets took two months to get printed and delivered and it was all cash at the ticket office," Bob Beatty says. "When the tickets arrived, we counted them by hand, rubber-banded them, and bundled them."

Bob Beatty is a third-generation box-office manager in New York. "My father was a treasurer at a Broadway theater in the forties and my grandfather worked in a box office on Broadway in the twenties," says Beatty. Bob's first job at 18 was at the Forest Hills Tennis Stadium, which hosts the U.S. Tennis Open and started a summer concert series in 1968. "It was strictly hard tickets. No outlets, no record stores, and no computerization." Forest Hills promoted acts like Simon and Garfunkel, Sly and the Family Stone, and Janis Joplin.

In 1969, he took a job in the box office at Madison Square Garden, which had opened a year earlier. Few concerts were hosted in the Garden's arena in the late '60s and early '70s—the Temptations, Sly and the Family Stone, Grand Funk Railroad. It was a new venue with unproven stages and sound and light systems. Instead, smaller shows were held in the Felt Forum (now the Theater at Madison Square Garden), a 2,000-plus-seat venue that hosted the Doors, the Dead, Alice Cooper, Junior Walker and the All-Stars, the Association, and the Byrds.

Things changed in the mid-'70s when rock went mainstream and New York became the epicenter of it all. Computerized ticketing started with Ticketron getting a small allotment of 1,000 tickets to sell at its outlets, mostly at suburban malls. Concert fans started to camp overnight at the outlets, which wasn't optimal for the malls. Promoters tried mail-order and phone services, but they were too labor-intensive.

Ticketron created a service for box offices, but it charged venues for the service and little was passed on to the consumer. Fred Rosen changed that.

In 1981 and 1982, Rosen was special counsel for several companies, including Ticketmaster. He became Ticketmaster's CEO in October 1982.

He questioned the practice of charging the same convenience fee on differently priced tickets. "'Why do you have a dollar service charge on a $40 ticket?' I asked. They said, 'Because we also sell $5 tickets.' And I said, 'Well, why don't you have a $2 service charge on a $40 ticket and a $1 service charge on a $5 ticket?' They said, 'We can't.' And I said, 'Why not? Is that on one of the tablets that Moses dropped?' Every question I asked, I was told either I didn't understand or that's the way it was. That made no sense to me."

This conversation continued as Rosen took over the management of Ticketmaster and began to create a new paradigm for ticketing.

Ticketing was becoming automated, but it wasn't convenient; up to 80% of the tickets were sold at the box office. Rosen envisioned a distribution system open seven days a week at convenient outlets and by phone. But that greatly increased overhead—staffing, computer terminals and phone systems, credit-card fees, processing and delivery charges, and rebates to outlets and venues. Initially, Ticketmaster charged a nominal fee of $3 per ticket on phones with a handling charge and $2 at the outlets.

As the concert business evolved, the service fee steadily increased to fund venues that used the fee rebate from Ticketmaster to replace revenue from demands put on them by acts to reduce expenses and compensate promoters whose profit margins were thinning out.

Ticketing service charges were and are hated by fans, but they rescued concert profits. Rosen used a simple formula to grow: doubling, then tripling, convenience fees. Rosen's tactics started out as unpopular with the public, but favored by his clients, the venue operators and promoters; as service charges grew and access to acquiring tickets dwindled, the anger snowballed.

"I realized early on that I had to create a persona of being the toughest guy in the room," says Rosen. "I set myself up to wear the black hat, but people never got the joke. At the beginning, nobody cared when we raised service charges."

Rosen wasn't nearly as concerned about his public persona as he was about the satisfaction of his clients. The ticket now had a component that gave venue managers a new income stream, along with incentives to pass through to promoters. Venues took this a step further by charging a facility fee on top of the ticket price and a service charge that went directly to them.

In the mid-'90s, technology, specifically Internet speed, was improving rapidly. Before then, the dial-up connection was not only slow, but it frequently disconnected. Also, credit-card use wasn't prevalent, even at the box office. In the '90s, with faster Internet speed and credit-card transactions becoming more commonplace, Ticketmaster could now sell out shows even quicker, enabling artists to roll over to multiple shows. "We brought real accounting, real disciplines, and real speed to ticketing," says Rosen.

Rosen has been variously described as combative and charming, profane and brilliant, funny, controlling, and intimidating. However, his impact on ticketing is indisputable. When Rosen joined Ticketmaster, the company had about 25 employees and annual ticket sales of less than $1 million. When he left in 1998, it had 5,000 employees and sales of $2.4 billion. Technology enabled faster and faster transaction handling, which led to quicker sellouts and multiple dates at venues. It also provided a highly accurate accounting system for settlements with artists. In 2010, the combined Live Nation-Ticketmaster had 6,500 employees and sold $7.2 billion in tickets; it's now the dominant promoter and ticketing company in the world.

At the beginning of the new century, technology allowed venues a new option: They could forgo the rebate from Ticketmaster in favor of building their own ticketing network. The highly versatile Daren Libonati, while managing UNLV's Thomas and Mack Center and Sam Boyd Stadium, helped pioneer this program when he created UNLVTickets.

Daren "Edison" Libonati Rides Again

In 1995, MGM went through a leadership change. One of the victims of the shakeout was Dennis Finfrock, who was ousted. Libonati was offered the top spot at the arena. He didn't feel good about benefitting from the loss of his boss, mentor, and friend. Fortunately, he was offered another challenge—the 6,500-seat arena out at Buffalo Bill's in Primm, Nevada.

In the 1920s, Pete MacIntyre owned a gas station on the Nevada side of the state line on old US 91, which became Interstate 15. On the side, Pete was a bootlegger. History remembers him as "Whiskey Pete." When he died in 1933, legend has it that he wanted to be buried standing up straight with a bottle of booze in his hands, so he could watch over the area.

In 1977, Ernest Primm opened a casino on the site of McIntyre's gas station to waylay travelers driving to Vegas from southern California; he named it Whiskey Pete's. In 1990, his son Gary built and opened the Primadonna Resort across I-15 from Whiskey Pete's at what was now called Primm. In May 1994, he opened another hotel-casino, Buffalo Bill's, which included a 6,500-seat arena. In all, he had 2,500 rooms on both sides of 1-15 connected by a small monorail. What he didn't have was any idea of how to book or operate the arena. The timing was good for both him and Daren Libonati.

Libonati started working the phones.

"Every place I ever worked, the phone didn't ring. I had to make it ring. I had to do the calling. I had to have call sheets. I had to have ways to attack and chase, because nobody was calling us."

Still, he had little success. He wasn't calling from the Las Vegas Strip's MGM Grand, the largest hotel in the world, but this unknown spot 45 minutes southwest of Vegas. Also, he was trying to compete with the Grand Garden, Thomas and Mack Center, and a new competitor, the ultra-hip 2,000-seat The Joint theater at the Hard Rock Hotel.

Libonati also had to teach his hotel-casino and marketing colleagues about concert touring. Once they were all-in, he started making aggressive offers to acts that traditionally didn't play Las Vegas—at that time, country. The first to bite was Alan Jackson, who sold out. Then Tim McGraw, Reba, and Brooks and Dunn. In all, Libonati promoted 15 country shows and another 10 rock concerts. At the time, Las Vegas was not a priority for country. Libonati shook the trees and now country bears bushels of fruit for the city. Then it all changed again and Libonati was forced to resign.

However, his two years at Primm might have been the most important in his career. "Working in a place like Primm meant reaching beyond what I knew how to do and that no one, including myself, expected," he reflects.

He needed work, so he joined back up with Dennis Finfrock at a startup ticket company, ETM, where he got a crash course in ticketing. It was short, because an opportune golf outing brought him back to UNLV.

On a hot summer day in 1998, he and I were on the golf course, talking business (of course). I mentioned that we were in a war with Grand Garden for the Spice Girls. He asked, "Do you want the Spice Girls?"

We took a break and he called Danny Zelisko. Within 15 minutes, he had a confirmation.

On the spot, I made him an offer to return to our venues.

A couple of months later, as we were walking to a meeting, I could feel my energy diminishing for the big job that the director of Thomas and Mack and Sam Boyd had become. I said to Daren, "I think I have three years left in me."

Since 1983, I'd been responsible for an average of 150 events per year, including upwards of 500 arena and stadium concerts ranging from hip hop to country, classical to rock, jazz to jam, R&B to rap—a full generation of live music. But I was tired. I was only halfway through my working years, but I was ready for a change.

And it came to pass that exactly three years from when I hired Libonati, I resigned, leaving UNLV, Thomas and Mack, and Sam Boyd Stadium for Las Vegas Events, a company that secures events by connecting promoters, hotel-casinos, and sponsors and provides all levels of support—venue selection, marketing, operations, and overall coordination—

UNLV Athletics ...

When Brad Rothermel arrived in 1981 as UNLV's new athletic director, the renegade department was bleeding red ink. Rothermel instilled structure and integrity and, thanks to Thomas and Mack's 12,000 more seats than the Convention Center's Rotunda and the incredible winning streak the basketball team was about to go on, he turned red ink to black and started to build the non-revenue sports programs.

Rothermel was content to have Dennis Finfrock take responsibility for paying the event venue's bills. He wanted nothing to do with the potential debt and 100-plus annual events.

After the 1989-90 basketball season, in which UNLV won its first NCAA title, Rothermel got caught in the crossfire in the epic feud between UNLV President Robert Maxson and Runnin' Rebels basketball coach Jerry Tarkanian and was forced to resign.

Michael Green, a history professor at the Community College of Southern Nevada, puts it this way, "They became embroiled in this terrible fight where neither man [Maxson nor Tarkanian] controlled his logic or emotion. In a sense, they destroyed each other. The fight also divided the town."

Only one year later, Dennis Finfrock also resigned, unable to tolerate the friction any longer.

The UNLV Athletics Department began a long decline, though the arena and stadium continued to hold their own. In the vacuum after Finfrock left, Maxson promoted me to Director of Thomas and Mack Center and Sam Boyd Stadium. That was the good news. The bad news was I now reported to an athletic director—in his first job as AD.

for signature Las Vegas events.

The obvious choice for the job of replacing me was Libonati. He had a big job ahead of him. By 2001, Thomas and Mack was feeling the pressure from Grand Garden, Mandalay Bay Events Center, and The Joint at

... Money For Nothing

In the next eight years, the basketball program stumbled and the football team never rose above mediocrity. UNLV's football team went 19-57 and basketball 116-89. Attendance and revenue plummeted. The AD, who now dictated how arena and stadium revenues were dispersed, began raiding capital accounts. From 1992 to 1997, the arena and stadium doled out more than $10 million to subsidize an Athletic Department in freefall. (This pattern continues today, 20 years later.)

I had zero say in how our profits were spent, but it was my responsibility to make an impossible situation work.

Fortunately, we kept growing revenues, predominantly through concerts at Sam Boyd Stadium.

The pass-through to Athletics deferred critical maintenance and by the turn of the century, the arena and stadium were falling apart. I turned to Acting President Kenny Guinn (later governor of Nevada) with a plea to stop the bleeding. He complied and changed our reporting to the vice president of finance who could intervene. After Guinn left the interim position at UNLV, he helped make a case to the state legislature for $40 million of funding to modernize both venues.

Thomas and Mack Center upgraded all mechanical and plumbing systems and added a new scoreboard, an acoustic blanket on the ceiling, a widened concourse, and new restrooms and concessions. Sam Boyd Stadium was greatly upgraded, with a new concourse, all new restrooms, 16 VIP suites, 500 club seats, a state-of-the-art press box, a new grass field, an LED scoreboard, and double the food and beverage concessions.

the Hard Rock. The Palms was opening and was sure to have a theater, and the Orleans had announced a new 7,500-seat arena. A big chunk of the arena and stadium concerts were being picked off by Grand Garden and other venues sprouting up. Daren had been an underdog before, but this challenge would require some real out-of-the-box thinking—which was what Libonati spent most of his time doing anyway. It was time to make a radical move.

"I called Mike See at Tickets.com, TMC's vendor, and said, 'I need a list of the six best ticket software companies.' See wanted to know, 'Why are you asking me this?' I said, 'Because one day I'm going to hire you away and we're going to do our own ticketing.'"

By doing the ticketing in-house, Libonati believed the building could set its own ticket fees, better market concerts, and generate substantially more revenue. He proposed going head to head with Ticketmaster.

On hearing Libonati's plan, Tickets.com tripled its venue-rebate offer, guaranteeing Thomas and Mack Center and Sam Boyd Stadium $750,000 to keep their business. Libonati was only reassured by the "generosity."

Next, at a venue-industry conference, Libonati stopped by a software presentation by Paciolan, an Irvine, California-based, ticket company and proposed a partnership. Paciolan agreed to bankroll all the startup equipment. The venues would pay a minimal guarantee to Paciolan, plus a rebate of 50 cents per ticket. The upside would be big for both.

But Libonati still needed $300,000 seed capital, which he sweet-talked out of Carol Harter, the president of UNLV, promising the venture would pay it back in three months.

And so, UNLVTickets was born.

Libonati describes its impact. "It allowed us to become a marketing machine for every event. We had TV commercials running every night that we pre-bought annually. We went from a $250,000-a-year profit with Tickets.com in 2001 to $1 million, then $1.5 million, then $2 million, $3 million ..."

Not only did it generate sizable revenue from its own events, but UNLVTickets started servicing events at other Las Vegas hotel-casino venues, such as local companies Boyd Gaming and Station Casinos.

He used the additional revenue from ticketing to compete head on with the newer arenas, making Thomas and Mack Center, the oldest of all Las Vegas venues, a very healthy operation.

Had Libonati patented his idea, he'd undoubtedly be in a different tax bracket. But he wasn't greedy. He shared the concept with AEG, which ended up creating AXS tickets. He showed it to Spectacor, which invested $20 million and built its own system for its 300 venues. He showed it to IBM, which also invested $20 million. In short order, Ticketmaster bought out Paciolan and a lot of people got rich. But not Libonati.

"I did it because I knew all I had to do was turn the turnstiles. If I turned the turnstiles, my food and beverage made 10 bucks a head, my ticketing 6 to 8 bucks a head. Multiply times 18,000 people for a sold-out concert. I could lose on the show, but I knew I was going to win in the end. Those turnstiles were my slot machine."

In 2010, for the second time, Libonati moved on, but UNLVTickets still nets $2 million annually for UNLV and Athletics.

Scalpers, Bots, and Service Charges—The Nasty Side of Live Music

Michael Rapino, CEO of Live Nation, which owns and operates Ticketmaster, talks about the challenge of distributing and selling tickets today. "There are only twenty thousand seats at Madison Square Garden and four million people want those tickets. And then, they go on the Internet and see eight pages of scalpers and get confused. [They think] Ticketmaster must have given [the brokers] the tickets. Fans must direct their anger somewhere. And that's been the massive inefficiency in the business."

"There is no other industry in the world where the [product] is worth more the second it's sold." In 1998, Tom Ross, one of the founders of the music department of the L.A.-based talent agency CAA and a booking and artist manager, described the business in his keynote speech at the Pollstar Conference, an annual gathering of the live-music industry. "The business has created a national scalp. And when the national scalpers and brokers can come and move 2,000 tickets to every event in every city, let's put it on the table [share with the act and promoter]."

Why don't artists simply sell their tickets for what they're ultimately worth on the resale market?

"It's because the artists, who are some of the greatest brand managers in history, are very obsessed," says Michael Rapino. "Bruce Springsteen wants to be able to say to his fans, 'Of course, I charge an affordable ticket.' Artists like Bruce Springsteen are brilliant with their brands. They want to find that fine line, which for Bruce is between $95 and $125. But that leaves $400 to $500 that Springsteen isn't getting directly. We're not getting it either. Eight million dollars sitting on the sidelines. The reason I can't buy that Bruce Springsteen ticket is I'm literally fighting computers from Asia and Eastern Europe trying for it, because it's worth four times more the second it's sold."

"StubHub is like Napster—a business built on other people's investment," says Live Nation COO Joe Berchtold, likening the $8 billion secondary ticket market to the live-events version of piracy. "The people behind the content [should] own the right to control how to price it."

The business that was once known as scalping has become so sophisticated that for on-sale dates, brokers use "bots," Internet software that automates simple repetitive tasks, such as purchasing tickets, at a much higher frequency than the tickets could be sold to individual consumers.

The undisputed king of bots was Ken Lowson. Lowson and his team used bots, and 30 computers, to buy up millions of tickets and generate $25 million in profit. "Lowson studied the ticketing websites compulsively, installed super-high-speed Internet lines to improve latency, used computer systems from all over the world to boost propagation, and had programmers write scripts that automated orders, quickly filled in CAPTCHA fields, and bought up hundreds of the best tickets in seconds," says Dave Brooks with *Billboard*.

Lowson makes a point about scalpers. "If the ticketing companies don't sell the good tickets to the scalpers, there's no one to push the fans back and up in the venues. I'm talking about the upper-level seats that are generally priced higher than they should be. Who's gonna buy a shitty seat that can't make money? Not a broker. It's gonna be a fan."

Lowson was busted by the feds on a flimsy charge, pled out to one count of conspiracy, and now runs a new company, TixFix, which, while still fan-based, also purports to work with artists and entertainment providers.

It's no wonder fan ire is often directed at Ticketmaster. Ticketmaster serves more than 12,000 venues worldwide and it's owned by Live Nation; in 2016, 73 million fans attended a Live Nation event. Concert fans resent service charges that are 15%-25% of the cost of the ticket. They're frustrated with a lack of access to tickets and the subsequent cost from secondary ticket sites like StubHub.

The fact of the matter is, primary ticketing can address this huge dissatisfaction; there are solutions.

For one, do away with the service charge. Tie the buyer to the ticket, exactly as airlines do when they sell a ticket that's absolutely not transferrable. Put every seat on a manifest. Then distribute the true value of what venues and promoters provide in the deal (contract) and inside the price of the ticket.

Secondly, if artists want to take care of their fans, do what Garth Brooks does. Price it fairly and put as many shows on sale until the demand is filled.

Lastly, do away with pre-sales. What makes someone with a VISA or American Express more valuable than a regular fan?

Peace and Police

In 1979, 11 fans died during a stampede at Cincinnati's Riverfront Coliseum at a Who concert. In the aftermath, venues around the country banned general-admission shows and started to take crowd management seriously.

From the late 1930s through the mid-'60s, the only organized event-services business was known as Frain Services, a union ushering company. Their buttoned-down blue-and-gold uniforms were synonymous with ushering all over the country. However, in the mid-'60s, rock 'n' roll crowds required a different approach. Little old ladies or older men weren't a deterrent to rabble rousers. "Peer-security" companies quickly developed.

Cory Meredith, CEO of Staff Pro, remembers concerts in the '60s. "Police and fans clashed a lot, mostly over drugs. To make sure the police weren't around, promoters hired football players or bouncer types to handle protecting the stage and managing the crowd on the floor. In those days, peer security was more like bouncing."

Damon Zumwalt was a good football player and wrestler in San Diego in the late '60s. A DJ at a local dance was having trouble with kids who arrived drunk and belligerent. The DJ and Zumwalt went to the same high school in San Diego. The DJ asked Zumwalt, "What can I do to stop these fights?"

Zumwalt recruited a shot putter who looked like Rosie Grier and weighed about 290, a couple of Samoans who were 300-350 pounds, and a wrestler he found on the beach. "Their size was a deterrent, but my focus was more on their popularity," said Zumwalt.

Soon, more promoters were impressed with his crowd-management acumen.

"I didn't intend to start a crowd-management company," recalls Zumwalt, "but everybody started calling after I helped Concert Associates with summer shows like Marvin Gaye, the Fifth Dimension, the Animals, and Country Joe and the Fish. The guys I recruited were champions from different sports, physically impressive and leaders in their communities. They were also in the same age group as the patrons attending the rock shows. Thus, we coined the phrase 'peer-group security.'"

In 1967, he created a company called Peace Power. His guards wore jackets with a peace sign on the back. "The idea was for the kids to act with love and peace. The reality was, some of them wanted to crash doors. And if they got in front of the stage, they'd run over you. That wasn't peace." Three years later, he changed the name to Contemporary Service Associates.

Today, Contemporary Service Corporation is the world leader in crowd management and event security with 100,000 employees providing services at 150 stadiums and arenas, 110 universities and colleges, 45 convention centers, and some of the world's most prestigious special events, including collegiate bowl games, NCAA Final Four tournaments, U.S. Open tennis, 30 Super Bowls, and 10 Olympic games. CSC operates more than 50 branch locations throughout the United States and Canada.

In the mid-'80s, insurance costs were increasing and venue managers were looking for a better way to make certain that fans were treated well. The International Association of Auditorium Managers (now International Association of Venue Managers) began to refine crowd manage-

The phenomenal Claw that traveled around the world to stage U2's 360 Degree tour included a stop at Sam Boyd Stadium in 2009—attended by former president Bill Clinton.

The original Aladdin Theater for the Performing Arts, which opened in 1976.

Gary Naseef, Las Vegas' pioneer rock promoter, booked hundreds of shows at the Aladdin Theater in the late '70s and early '80s.

National tours relied on three Las Vegas indoor venues in the '70s: the Aladdin Theater, the Sahara Space Center, and the Las Vegas Convention Center.

(top) Loggins and Messina at the Sahara in 1974
(center) Sly & the Family Stone at the Sahara in 1974
(bottom) Fleetwood Mac at the Aladdin in 1977

GANA PRODUCTIONS
presents
Vega70

JANIS JOPLIN
B.B. KING
Country Joe & The Fish
The Youngbloods
Illinois Speed Press

TICKETS:
ALL WALLICHS MUSIC CITY STORES • LAS VEGAS, ALL USUAL PLACES.

ALL TICKETS/$7.50
CASHMAN FIELD/LAS VEGAS • JULY 16 1970/GANA PRODUCTIONS, 1021 EAST BRACKEN, LAS VEGAS, NEVADA.

Cashman Field was scheduled to host Janis Joplin and B.B. King outdoors in 1970, but the concert was canceled by the city fathers.

Thomas and Mack Center became the dominant tour stop in the '80s, and continued its run into the '90s.

The author (left) and his boss, Dennis Finfrock, opened "TMC" in 1983 and ran it as a profit center for UNLV.

Thomas and Mack Center under construction.

Yes,
TMC, 1984

Genesis,
TMC, 1984

Waylon and Willie celebrating
Willie's 50th Birthday, 1984

Van Halen, TMC, 1984

AC/DC,
TMC, 1986

Guns N' Roses,
TMC, 1992

Bon Jovi,
TMC, 1987

Following Page: Garth Brooks strung together a series of 13 sellouts in Las Vegas (seven at TMC and six at T-Mobile) and later had a long run at Wynn Las Vegas.

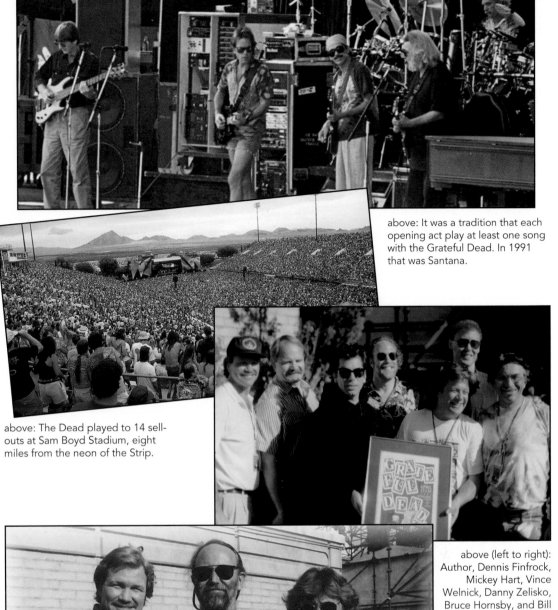

above: It was a tradition that each opening act play at least one song with the Grateful Dead. In 1991 that was Santana.

above: The Dead played to 14 sell-outs at Sam Boyd Stadium, eight miles from the neon of the Strip.

above (left to right): Author, Dennis Finfrock, Mickey Hart, Vince Welnick, Danny Zelisko, Bruce Hornsby, and Bill Graham at the Dead's—and Vegas'—first stadium concert, 1991.

(left to right): Author, Grateful Dead road manager Bob Barsotti, and promoter Danny Zelisko at the Dead's third concert (1993) at Sam Boyd Stadium.

The biggest stars in music came to town in the '90s through the turn of the century.

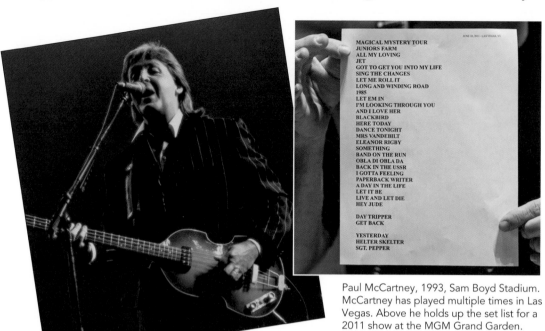

MAGICAL MYSTERY TOUR
JUNIORS FARM
ALL MY LOVING
JET
GOT TO GET YOU INTO MY LIFE
SING THE CHANGES
LET ME ROLL IT
LONG AND WINDING ROAD
1985
LET EM IN
I'M LOOKING THROUGH YOU
AND I LOVE HER
BLACKBIRD
HERE TODAY
DANCE TONIGHT
MRS VANDEBILT
ELEANOR RIGBY
SOMETHING
BAND ON THE RUN
OBLA DI OBLA DA
BACK IN THE USSR
I GOTTA FEELING
PAPERBACK WRITER
A DAY IN THE LIFE
LET IT BE
LIVE AND LET DIE
HEY JUDE

DAY TRIPPER
GET BACK

YESTERDAY
HELTER SKELTER
SGT. PEPPER

Paul McCartney, 1993, Sam Boyd Stadium.
McCartney has played multiple times in Las
Vegas. Above he holds up the set list for a
2011 show at the MGM Grand Garden.

Sting (opening for the Dead), Sam
Boyd Stadium, 1993

David Bowie, TMC, 1995

Spice Girls, TMC, 1998

Pearl Jam, TMC, 1998

Tina Turner, TMC, 1999

Eric Clapton, 2001, first performance for Clapton in Vegas and last event for author at the Thomas and Mack Center.

Phish, TMC, 2003

In Las Vegas' next live-music incarnation the arenas got smaller, bringing fans closer to the action in venues like The Joint at the Hard Rock and Pearl at the Palms.

below: Van Morrison at The Joint

left: (left to right) Billy Conn, Jackson Browne, and Danny Zelisko, Backstage at Pearl

below: Kings of Leon at The Joint

bottom: Kanye West at The Joint

House of Blues, with its distinct U-shaped balcony that sits right on top of the stage, giving fans a tight and intimate view.

Brooklyn Bowl—a bowling alley, restaurant, lounge, and the busiest concert hall in Vegas.

The Joint at Hard Rock was Vegas' first small theater dedicated to live music; it's now in its second incarnation at twice the size of the original.

Las Vegas has no peer in the number and quality of A-list residencies.

top: Celine Dion created the blueprint and set the standard for several ensuing residencies in the Colosseum at Caesars Palace

far left: Kenny Chesney has frequented The Joint since 2009

Rod Stewart (above) and Jennifer Lopez (left) also played extended residencies in the Colosseum and the Axis Theater at Planet Hollywood, respectively.

Life Is Beautiful (above and below), which takes place in September in downtown Las Vegas, is funded by Tony Hseih, of Zappo's fame (and fortune). Stevie Wonder opened the 2015 festival.

above: The main stage, Kinetic Field, at Electric Daisy Carnival, the huge annual festival at Las Vegas Motor Speedway, eight miles north of the city.

right: Legendary DJ Producer Armin Van Buren (left) and EDC founder Pasquale Rotella

below: Incredible nightly fireworks display at EDC

above: MGM built Las Vegas Village on a 15-acre parking lot across from the Luxor for the Route 91 Harvest (country music) Festival.

below: Metallica headlines Rock in Rio Vegas (2015); the first—and maybe the last—time the huge international music festival played the U.S.

Just a couple dads, talking about their kids: At Rock in Rio in Lisbon, the author and Bruce Springsteen were staying at the same hotel. Pat introduced himself, said he produced Springsteen's show at Thomas and Mack, and didn't get much reaction. Then he said he also produced the World Cup Jumping and Dressage Finals, and the star lit up. His daughter Jessica is a champion show-jumping rider who's represented the U.S. in international competition. After chatting for 10 minutes, Pat politely asked for a photo.

ment and facilities adopted a best-practices guide. Recruiting became a priority. It was no longer appropriate to hire "warm bodies," put T-shirts on them, and expect them to manage a drunk or drugged fan or an unruly crowd. Today, crowd-management companies screen extensively, test for drugs, and require eight hours of instruction before an employee puts on a uniform shirt. Full-time employees receive intensive security and customer-service training.

In his book *Moments of Truth*, Jan Carlson, CEO of SAS Airlines from 1981 to 1994, professes that the numerous interactions customers have with front-line employees, "50 million moments of truth," ultimately determine whether a company succeeds or fails.

It's more difficult to ensure customers' expectations are met at a live event than with almost any other experience, because their expectations are broadly based on their experiences with all the things for which they pay. From filling a car with gasoline to flying around the world, from grabbing lunch at McDonald's to dining out at Masa, from buying CDs to TVs, these are all consistent experiences. Perhaps they're not all great experiences, but they all have a consistent opportunity to get it right.

At live-music events, artists are in a different city every night, at a different venue with its own culture. The fans, meanwhile, might never have bought a ticket online or seen a show at a theater or stadium. Even if they've been to the venue, traffic patterns, parking, and current information are often new and inconsistent. Then, finding seats, getting drinks, buying T-shirts, these all happen before the show starts. Today, a venue's plan needs to be committed to ensuring it delivers on as many "moments of truth" as possible.

Bill Overly uses the moments-of-truth as a mantra for his crowd-management company, We Serve. Overly graduated from UNLV in 1980 and worked 28 years for the state of Nevada conducting workmen's-comp investigations and doing regulatory work. On the side, he was employed by FINCO, managing crowds for events at Caesars Palace. He formed We Serve in 1988, providing a critical service at a time when Las Vegas was about to explode with live music. Today, his company is ubiquitous at live-music events in Las Vegas.

"At every event, we're managing thousands of moments of truth," he says. "Part of the experience is visual. When I pull into the parking lot, I get a first impression and that's visual. I might not speak to that parking attendant, but I'm going to form an opinion based on how he looks. And with the advent of phones and videos, I can share that opinion. As I get closer to the performer, I should find that the staff is more inclined toward security than friendliness. The employee needs be more cognizant of who I am, what my intentions are, and why I am where I am."

Rick Nogues grew up in Tampa, Florida, and went to college at Central Florida, where he played baseball. "One night in the Sun Dome, I was showering after practice when the locker-room door flew open and a security manager yelled, 'Does anybody want to work security?' It was a Metallica concert. I needed the cash and it sounded like fun, so he threw a T-shirt to me. I got two minutes of training on how to be a security guard and out I went into the crowd."

He worked at the Sun Dome for several years, eventually becoming chief of security at a 2,000-seat theater. He was involved with the Super Bowl in Tampa and for MLB in Europe, Asia, and Australia. In 1996, with 12 years of event experience under his belt, he moved to Las Vegas. "I'd always dreamed of getting into special events with the police," he says. "I slowly worked my way through the department. In 2005, Metro offered me a position to oversee special events."

What sets Nogues apart from most cops is his philosophy on dealing with people. Under his leadership, police are more than a last resort. "All the pieces of an event need to fit together. It comes down to customer service. If you look, you can see when something isn't going right for a fan. They spend a lot of money on a show. It's important to them. I can help people enjoy the moment. I've only been in one or two fights in 20 years. I don't want things to escalate. I want to solve problems."

For events, Nogues has 2,500 cops, paid time and a half, to choose from. Under Nogues' leadership, the Clark County Metropolitan Police Department has developed a rapport with Las Vegas audiences that means fewer problems for both fans and police. "You need a team that understands the plan and believes in the goal of everybody's safety and enjoyment. Everyone is empowered to implement the plan," he says.

Two major Las Vegas events demonstrate the importance of police temperament and planning: New Year's Eve on the Strip and Electric Daisy Carnival.

Fifteen years ago, it was a risk being on the Strip on New Year's Eve. It was a massive drunk-and-disorderly crowd. Today, even though the crowds are larger, year-round planning and coordination and service-oriented police tactics are the recipe for managing 300,000 revelers at a three-mile-long party. Metro closes the Strip for New Year's Eve and creates a three-mile mall by placing bike racks as barricades. Inside them, police are no more than 50 feet from any problem. Outside the barricades, people can freely move up and down the Strip.

Electric Daisy Carnival is similar. In addition to a year's worth of detailed planning for EDC, it comes down to an approach and attitude. "Our goal, from uniforms up to the commander, is to have a good time. Say hello, take pictures, walk around, help people who need help. We're not there to stand back in a corner by the grandstand with crossed arms. We're there to be a part of the event. A lot of pictures have wound up on social media of our guys, smiling, taking pictures with and for fans, and being a part of the experience."

To ensure everyone is on the same page, each major event has a series of "Table Top Exercises," both before and after the shows, with as many as 50 people, including Metro and Highway Patrol, promoter, fire and rescue, venue, hotels, government, crowd-management company, even cab companies. Some of the exercises are extreme, playing out crisis scenarios. One of those exercises might be an evacuation due to high winds. In 2013, that exercise paid dividends.

High winds that year became increasingly dangerous. Yet, there was no panic. There was a plan. Nogues recalls that night. "I told my men, 'We just talked about this two weeks ago. Let's go to work.' We got everyone away from the stages and put them in the infield and grandstands. One of the DJs played music, so people could still dance and work off their buzz. It just kind of handled itself." To say that was a modest account is an understatement.

Production—"See Me, Feel Me"

Sitting stage right, 12 rows up in MGM Grand Garden, my regular concert companion (my daughter Nicole) and I anxiously awaited one of the most anticipated concerts of 2012.

Pink Floyd was one of the best-selling rock bands in history. Its breakout album, *Dark Side of the Moon* (1973), remained on the charts for an unprecedented 741 weeks until 1988, and sold 45 million albums, among the top three of all time. They followed up with *Wish You Were Here* (1975), *Animals* (1977), *The Wall* (1979), and *The Final Cut* (1983). Their last years together were contentious, resulting in the departure of singer, songwriter, and bassist Roger Waters.

Their most critically acclaimed album was *The Wall*; it was also a commercial smash, selling 30 million. The album is based on a story with the central figure of Pink—a gestalt character inspired by Waters' childhood experiences, the most notable of which was the death of his father in World War II. This first metaphorical brick led to more problems; Pink became drug-addled and depressed by the music industry, eventually transforming into a megalomaniac, a development inspired partly by the mental and physical decline of original Floyd lead guitarist Syd Barrett (and perhaps Brian Jones of The Rolling Stones). At the end of the album, the increasingly fascist audience watches as Pink tears down the wall, once again becoming a regular and caring person.

The Wall—Live in Berlin was a concert performance by Roger Waters and numerous guest artists held in Berlin on July 20, 1990, to commemorate the fall of the Berlin Wall eight months earlier. The massive production was staged on vacant land between Potsdamer Platz and the Brandenburg Gate, a location that was part of the former no-man's land of the Berlin Wall. The show had a sell-out crowd of nearly a half-million people.

Pink Floyd's style combined philosophical lyrics, sonic experimentation, and extended songs, all performed at elaborate live shows.

We weren't going to see Pink Floyd, but Roger Waters and an arena version of the same production. *The Wall* had it all. Iconic songs, superior sound, and an extravagantly themed production.

But was this show better than previous productions?

In the late '60s and '70s, promoters made it up as they went. For each tour, they rented the stage, provided sound and lighting, and hired stagehands. The bands traveled in cars, vans, and maybe trucks; Jimi Hendrix, it's rumored, toured the country in a station wagon. Acts arrived and plugged into what a promoter had rented and set up. Few ceilings could rig any equipment, so trusses were built to hang lights and the sound sat on the stage. For outdoor shows, the production was bigger, but there was no roof to protect the acts from the elements. As production evolved, rigging roofs were manufactured and traveled with bands.

Then a new business began to refine touring production.

Companies in the U.S. and Europe assembled production crews that traveled by truck with rented sound and lights. "They put an ad in the newspaper for technicians, paying $25 a day, three square meals, and a hotel room, even on your day off, all charged back to the band," recalls iconic production manager Steve Lemon. "These companies didn't pay a thing out of their own pocket."

While the efficiency of touring improved, the sound was still erratic and inconsistent. Lemon describes the problem. "You have your sound system on stage and sound for the front of house. The front of house is always fighting the volume level on the stage. The guitar player wants to hear himself, the lead singer needs to hear himself, yet nobody on stage can hear. If you're the artist, you can't hear what the crowd is hearing, because a massive PA is hanging above you about eight feet in front of stage. If you're too loud on stage, if you're burning 110 DB or something stupid and dangerous, it has to be adjusted by the sound console."

In the late '80s, sound quality made huge strides with the advent of inner-ear monitors. Inner-ear monitors eliminate feedback, reduce pushing your voice, have optimal volume quality, and optimize audience mix. Lemon says, "We've taken a lot of the stage noise out of the equation. The sound you hear in the front of house is much better, because the engineer doesn't have to push to make the main sound heard."

In 1977, Steve Lemon's career, singing and dancing in light opera and musicals, ended with a broken leg playing softball in a physical-education class. In order to receive credit for a class, he transferred to shop, where he was asked to show up for a job that weekend, foot boot and all. For three days, he made $300. At that pay scale, he was up for more.

The job, at the San Diego Sports Arena to unload trucks for the Icecapades, changed his life. "I was sitting in the back of the truck and I started asking questions. 'What does this guy do? What does that guy do? Holy shit. What's that guy doing way up there?' His friend says, 'He's rigging. Nobody wants to do that.' At that point in time, if you wanted to be a rigger, all you had to do was show up. I said, 'I want to learn this rigging thing.' He said: 'Report down there tomorrow, 9 a.m.'"

Lemon reported at nine sharp.

"I was talking to the riggers. 'My gosh, you get to go on the road as a rigger?' I kept angling, trying to position myself to get a job on the road."

As luck would have it, on the day before a crew was heading out, one of the riggers developed kidney stones and was in the hospital.

"I go over to the hospital. 'Dude, how are you? What's going on?' He's in real pain and he says, 'I need you to leave right away.' 'Okay, sorry. I didn't mean to—' 'No, no, no. Not that kind of leave.' He reaches into his pants and hands me an airline ticket. In those days, all you needed was the paper ticket. It didn't matter whose name was on it. You could be almost anybody and get on an airplane."

Steve Lemon never looked back. Forty-five hundred shows later, he marvels about how the business evolved.

Lemon learned a lot in the air. "You have a bird-eye's view of everything. By watching the pieces of the puzzle below, I learned how a show came together."

His next move came in 1985, when he was tabbed to be production manager for the Tears for Fears tour (an English duo with the hit "Everybody Wants To Rule the World," touring with Hall & Oates). "I was already advancing a lot of shows, so I was ready."

The production manager has the biggest budget and the most responsibility on the tour. As Lemon aptly puts it, "The production manager has the biggest target on his shirt."

He says that the key to a production manager's success is "a strong assistant who sees most of the action."

Then there are the floor stage manager who's in charge of the lights, sound, and video, and the stage manager who handles the performance of the band.

Since 1985 when Lemon was put in charge, technology across the board has evolved dramatically, particularly, of course, computers. "At the time, the computer was more a toy than a communication tool. Today, the production manager receives 200 to 300 emails a day. And each one requires two to three minutes between reading and responding."

Loading a show in and out has also improved dramatically. "In the '80s, two loading docks to get two trucks side by side was rare. A big arena like Thomas and Mack Center, for example, had one. We learned to drive our trucks right into the building, as many as four at a time. Back then, six trucks was a huge show. Today, 26 trucks is average."

One invention came from iconic production manager Jake Berry. Equipment used to be loaded off trucks with a forklift. Today, all carts are on rollers; crews roll them off and roll them back on. The current massive productions wouldn't be possible without this bit of ingenuity. In fact, the new Barclays Center in Brooklyn has a turntable. The truck drives onto the turntable, which revolves the truck 180 degrees. The truck backs a bit into a dock. When it's off-loaded, it pulls right out.

Working conditions for traveling crews have also drastically improved. Band crews used to fly from show to show. They finished a load-out at 2:30 a.m., caught three hours of sleep in a hotel, then made a 6 a.m. flight to start the next load-in at 8 a.m. Enter the crew tour bus. At first it was an RV. Today, it's a decked-out bus that sleeps 12. After the load-out, they hop in the bus, hit the sack, and wake up at the next venue, ready to go.

On a typical concert day, load-in is done in waves. The riggers are first, setting points. With the second wave come the lights, sound, and video. The third wave is carpentry. Then the sound is checked.

On tours where the production is huge with a lot of dancing or an artist has lost or is losing his or her voice, the Black Box is often used. The Black Box allows the singer to rest from time to time. The musicians and/or an off-stage singer play the voice. Neil Young used to print on his ticket, "Every note of tonight's show is performed absolutely live." He wanted fans to know that he didn't use the Black Box.

Another critical piece that must keep improving is the people. "There's no formal training to do what we do, but we're working on it," says Lemon.

In 2009, after more than 30 years traveling for concert production, Steve Lemon finally got off the road. "A lot of people in this business get addicted to the road. They love doing it for the good of the music and the experience of the fan. We all love to stand in the middle of a concert crowd and experience the singing or chanting, which gives you goose bumps. But it's a hard life. It's the old story of the guy sweeping up behind the elephant in the circus. People ask him, 'Why don't you quit and take a less, you know, messy job?' And he responds, 'What—and get out of show business?'"

Rock Connects the World

I have few pictures of the concerts or festivals I went to growing up, and certainly no video. Today's fans store and share every event they attend, creating an instant digital album of memories. Smartphones have become the window to the world, the lens through which we view and share life experiences.

Technology has made the concert experience both more social and seamless. Mobile devices with high-speed connectivity have greatly improved ticket purchasing. Almost every artist has a website and e-newsletters notify you when they're touring and when tickets go on sale. Signing up for a newsletter can get you early-buying privileges.

Social media has created fan power and in doing so has dramatically changed the live-music experience. Seventy percent of Millennials feel that social media improves live music. The majority share music moments from live events on social networks; 47% of fans text during shows. Per a 2014 Ticketmaster survey, YouTube is the number-one social platform at 86%, followed by Facebook at 84%; fully 91% of fans share their concert photos and video via Facebook.

Fans aren't only grabbing pics and vids, but texting, tweeting, snapchatting, gramming, and vining. Today the audience is controlling the experience, instead of letting the experience limit them. Having a small recorded segment, despite distorted quality and muffled sound, is a cherished "I was there." Everything you need to know about a show before, during, and after is in that three-by-five electronic device in your hand, including set lists (setlist.com), background (Wikipedia), lyrics (Google Lyrics), and song titles (Shazam.com).

Fans become the stars of their own production, snapping selfies and pictures from the time they leave home. At festivals, they can monitor the Doppler of an approaching downpour or track a sporting event on Slingbox.

Social media is amped up at festivals where Twitter is the main reliable source of information, keeping followers apprized about line-ups, tickets, and logistics, along with getting questions answered and offering support. Facebook focuses on sharing lineup updates and promoting festival-related activities; it's the medium of choice for sharing experiences. Music festivals have a high number of followers on Instagram and Snapchat is closing in. Organizers use creative photos and videos to support festies' own posts. Some festivals also have professional videos (music performances and after movies), allowing fans to create custom-digital memorabilia shared on YouTube and Vine.

Custom apps for festivals provide fans access to all relevant information and include some features like digital postcards, location services, notifications, and contests. Festival organizers have integrated RFID technology into entry wristbands that allow festies to charge all services to one source and producers to track that data.

Not everyone is enamored of all this connectivity.

"People live through their cellphones now," said Kevin Preast, senior vice president of event management at Tampa's Amalie Arena. "You see people watching the entire show through the lens of their phones. They seem more focused on sharing the experience with other people than they do enjoying the experience on their own."

In addition, artists and fans alike often get tired of bright mobile devices being shoved in their faces at live events. The overuse of cellphones has for years aggravated artists like Jack White, Alicia Keys, and Mumford and Sons.

Others are more accepting. "You can spend all your time complaining about it and trying to get people to meet you on your level, but really, there's an audience there," says singer-songwriter Josh Ritter. "It's not my job to mediate their experience. It's just my job to play as well as I can."

As mobile-device use evolves, so will a more balanced protocol.

"Etiquette and social norms around something radically new like a smartphone—of course they're going to take some time to develop," insists Yondr founder and CEO Graham Dugoni; Yondr helps create phone-free spaces at venues and events. "The implications, socially and psychologically, are becoming apparent."

As venues add wifi and install DAS (Digital Antennae Systems), mobile devices will become even more ubiquitous and not only to the live-music experience. Just as important is the quality of experiences at all special events.

The Vegas Live-Music Experience

Since the late '80s, the city and all hotel properties have made the experience of all 44 million annual Las Vegas visitors the highest priority. The hotel-casinos have few peers around the world in creating and delivering unique experiences. If there are 50 million "moments of truth" at SAS Airlines, there are a billion in Las Vegas.

What motivates people to visit Las Vegas? What makes Vegas special? Why do people travel long distances to see live music in Sin City?

A laundry list of reasons has always included the weather, convenient direct flights and the proximity of the airport to the hotels, a diverse room product, endless gambling opportunities, nearby attractions, and true affordability. However, since the Mirage opened in 1989, the hotel-casinos have shifted, to a certain extent, from a value-driven to an experience-driven strategy.

It started with shopping and the success of the Forum Shops at Caesars, which opened in 1992. The new strategy immediately encompassed dining, when celebrity chef Wolfgang Puck's Spago opened with the Forum Shops. At that time, some of the hotels still had the old-fashioned "gourmet rooms," along with Italian and Chinese, but the main attractions were bargain breakfasts, cheap steak dinners, and loss-leader buffets. Spago led a wave of culinary expansion that, in 25 years, has transformed Las Vegas into one of the top cities for fine dining on the planet, home to the finest collection of world-renowned chefs and restaurants.

The growth of fine dining has been a principal piece of the evolution of the Vegas experience where today, 70% of visitor spending is outside the casino; 25 years ago, it was the exact opposite. Since 1995, food revenues alone have grown to nearly 20% of total resort revenue.

What's more, in the past 25 years or so, spending on gambling has steadily declined, from more than 70% to less than 30% of a visitor's budget. Casino revenue is more profitable than entertainment-venue revenue, as the overhead is dramatically less. But the public has spoken and their preference is to spend discretionary income on *experiences*, and taste continuously evolves. What set Las Vegas apart from every other destination in the world was how it adjusted to this paradigm shift.

"You've got a different audience every day," says Bill Hornbuckle, the president of MGM Resorts. "Visitors are skewing younger, and with more cash to spend. The average age of a Vegas visitor has been falling—even as America gets older—hitting 47.7 years old last year, from 50 in 2009."

The proliferation of major malls and shopping districts helped make the daytime experience as important as the nighttime in Las Vegas. All the luxury brands are well-represented in millions of square feet of mall space on the Strip: the Forum Shops at Caesars, Crystals at Aria, the Grand Canal Shoppes at the Venetian, Miracle Mile Shops at Planet Hollywood, and at 1.9 million square feet by itself, the Fashion Show Mall, largest in Nevada. Two huge outlet malls also anchor both sides of the Strip.

The new themed hotels all opened with theaters dedicated to extravaganzas like Cirque du Soleil or superstar headliners like Siegfried and Roy and David Copperfield. Today, residencies include Céline Dion, Elton John, Britney Spears, Santana, Jennifer Lopez, and perennial favorites Donny and Marie Osmond. A hundred more shows encompass tributes, impersonations, illusions, comedy, hypnosis, off-Broadway, and of course adult.

And in the past 15 years, three more visitor motivators have developed: conventions, nightclubs, and special events.

With more than 10.5 million square feet of convention and meeting space (most in the U.S.), Las Vegas hosts nearly 60 of the 200 largest conventions (most in the U.S.) and 20,000 meetings annually (most in the U.S.). As such, Las Vegas has reigned as the U.S.'s top trade-show destination every year since 1995.

In 2002, the Vegas nightclub scene kicked into high gear when Paul Oakenfold first played the Rain nightclub at the Palms. It was the first celebrity-DJ residency. Soon, Rain was hosting anywhere between 2,000 and 5,000 people a night. Rain spawned some of the world's hottest nightclubs—Hakkasan, XS, Drai's, Tao, Light, Marquee. It's hard to find a hotel now that doesn't have 200-400 party-goers in a line to get into one of dozens of Vegas clubs.

As for special events, visitors can see The Rolling Stones in any major city. Every city has a convention center. Two dozen cities host rodeos and bull riding, monster trucks, NASCAR, and professional sporting events.

Only Las Vegas, however, has them all, in the world's most diverse venues—most of them a short cab ride from one another.

CHAPTER ELEVEN

THE LIVE-MUSIC BUSINESS' CIRCUITOUS ROUTE TO LAS VEGAS

Live music can be traced back to the caveman.

Until credible forms of transportation developed, however, touring was an arduous ordeal undertaken by very few entertainers. For example, in the gold rush days, before transcontinental railroads connected the west and eventually the east, performers from the East Coast had to travel by ship around Cape Horn, at the southern edge of South America, to play in distant California. With the advent of the railroad, Buffalo Bill Cody crisscrossed the land with his Wild West Show, living in his own personal train car.

As transportation infrastructure improved, the traveling-entertainment business developed further. The railroads offered discounts for entire railcars to the traveling troupes. By 1905, the year Las Vegas was founded as a whistle and watering stop on the Salt Lake to Los Angeles railroad (one of the last major routes in the intercontinental network), troupes and circuses had train travel down to a science, performing in theaters, fairgrounds, bars, ballrooms, and clubs in every part of the country.

Acts like Guy Lombardo, Benny Goodman, Les Braun, and Louis Armstrong were full-time fixtures on trains and, when roads came into play, buses. Royalties from record sales barely dented the cost of the large bands, which could number as many as 12 members. They had to travel constantly, usually playing in ballrooms, to make ends meet. Most cities had a ballroom that featured a bar and wooden dance floor. People gathered to watch, listen to, and dance to acts they'd heard on records and the radio.

By the '40s and '50s as the war ended and people started to spend more time staring at television screens, the big-band era faded and it was awhile before major concerts took its place. Elvis was the first "rock star," taking the live-music business by storm in the mid-'50s. However, even with cars, buses, trucks, and airplanes for touring, the experience of pioneer rockers on the road was sketchy at best and scary at worst. They had to work with unscrupulous promoters, who often provided little or no production and stiffed the acts after their shows.

In the '60s, concert touring improved with the advent of two types of promoters: local/regional and national. Across the country, the local or regional promoters used small venues to present the first version of concert-dances. One of those was Pat O'Day.

Pioneering Promoters

From a very young age, Pat O'Day dreamed of a career in radio. He got his start as a DJ in 1956 on a 250-watt radio station in Astoria, Oregon, doing the morning news and afternoon program. The station allowed him the freedom to choose his own music. He chose an "emerging style," rock 'n' roll.

He took his show into school gyms, where student contingents voted the songs "up or down." His radio show provided a perfect vehicle to start promoting dances. Dances were the first organized concerts.

Moving across the Columbia River to the more populated Kelso-Longview area in Washington state and KLOG radio, he turned a sports format into rock 'n' roll and combined it with his fledgling dance business. The $100 a week he net from dances doubled his salary as a DJ. O'Day's knack for *self*-promotion made him a natural *concert* promoter. In late 1956, he made the move to Yakima, Washington, and KUTI where he was DJ and program director.

His radio show was tops in the region. Unfortunately, KUTI was sold to an industrialist from Chicago who, like a lot of others at the time, didn't "get" rock 'n' roll. In his zeal to defend the format, even with a one-year-old son and another on the way, O'Day found himself out of a job. He took a job at the cross-town rival. KLOQ gave him complete autonomy on the records he spun. It wasn't long before they claimed KUTI's rock 'n' roll audience.

O'Day's dance business was put on hold as Pat Mason, a promoter from Oregon, had established dances at the Yakima National Guard Armory. Rather than fight it, he joined, recording Mason's commercials and acting as emcee for his "sock hops" (no shoes on the gym floor).

"I went out of the box and developed a beefed-up system," recalled O'Day in his book, *It Was Just Rock and Roll*, "with two turntables, stacks of 45s and 33-1/3s, heavy-duty cabinets capable of handling cranked-up volume and enhanced bass, and a bag full of gimmicks to get the kids on the dance floor."

While working for Mason, O'Day met many of the rockers of the time—Bill Haley, Jerry Lee Lewis, Fats Domino, and Don and Phil Everly. Their stories of experiences on the road were frightening: no sound systems set up, poorly promoted shows with no tickets sold, and getting stiffed when tickets were sold.

O'Day cites a conversation he had with Fats Domino. "Fats, if a promoter came to you and said, 'Here's my checkbook. Here are my finances. Can I handle all your shows, everywhere, every night? And I promise I will make everything perfect for you. What would you say?' Fats rolled his eyes, looked at me, and said, 'Yes sir!' That's what I'd say. But there ain't no such promoter.'"

As luck would have it, the program director for KAYO in Seattle heard O'Day's show and offered him a job sight unseen. His $650 monthly salary barely sustained the four mouths he now had to feed and Seattle didn't have a dance scene.

"I had this vision that wouldn't stop running across my mental screen in an infinite loop: dances, lots of dances, dances across the state, dances with local rock bands then beginning to proliferate, dances with stars, dances with Pat O'Day at the mike. Dances, dances, and more dances."

The venue that kicked off a 22-year run of shows was the Spanish Castle, a former roadhouse from the 1920s and '30s. The deal was O'Day paid 25% of ticket sales to rent the 2,000-capacity venue. Even after the rest of the expenses, he was left with a fat profit and he knew he was onto something.

Capitalizing on his growing relationships with the acts, he expanded and started promoting in Bremerton at Recreation Hall. He was now promoting two concerts a week, one at each venue. O'Day's strategy was simple: Develop a chain of venues that deliver a safe, quality, and consistent experience for the young audiences and the performers.

Starting in 1960, rock 'n' roll from the East Coast made its way west. Groups like the Wailers, the Blue Caps, and Johnny Burnett headlined the dances. By the mid-'60s, O'Day was doing close to 20 events a week, with acts like Jerry Lee Lewis, Roy Orbison, Bobby Vee and Jan and Dean, Leslie Gore and Mel Carter.

O'Day recalls an infamous oversold Jerry Lee Lewis show he promoted at Recreation Hall in Bremerton. "Just as the opening act concluded, the fire marshal came up to me in a rage. 'Pat, you know 1,000 is the limit and you sold your 1,000[th] ticket an hour ago. Why are you still selling tickets?' I told him, 'I personally closed the box office myself! I have the tickets in my briefcase!' I began looking for the leak. As I stepped into the hallway, I was nearly knocked over by a swarm of young people racing toward the auditorium floor."

O'Day quickly got to the bottom of it. "Noticing the large number of people being turned away, Jerry Lee sent his assistant looking for a step-ladder, which they lowered from his dressing room. The assistant then slipped out front to let the disappointed crowd know of another way in. As the fans clambered up and through the window, Jerry Lee greeted them with an outstretched hand waiting to be paid. He was running his own private scalping business, collecting double what he did at the box office."

O'Day expanded into eastern Washington, but was challenged by lo-cal promoter Terry Bassett. Rather than compete, they joined forces. Then Tom Hulett, a great sales guy who played semi-pro football for the Seattle Ramblers of the Pacific Coast Football League, signed on.

Right at that time, Elvis blew up. John Meglen, now co-president and CEO of Concerts West AEG Live, recalls, "The story I heard was that they pitched Colonel Parker, Elvis' manager, about throwing all the money into the pot, and they'd promote Elvis everywhere. The Colonel said, 'Okay, give me a million dollars upfront.' They borrowed the million from Les Smith and entertainer Danny Kaye at Kaye/Smith Enterprises in Seattle, who owned 10 radio stations and were among the four original owners of the Seattle Mariners."

Eventually, O'Day, Basset, and Hulett partnered with Jerry Wein-traub, a film producer and talent agent (who was married for 50 years to singer Jane Morgan). The joint venture grew to become one of the biggest national touring companies, Concerts West Live.

Concerts West Goes It Alone

In the '70s, the music industry was scattered across the country in different universities. Meglen remembers some of them. "Rob Light, current head of music at Creative Artists talent and sports agency, was at Syracuse University and Clint Mitchell, current partner at William Morris, was at the University of Montana. I knew the northwest guys. Dan Bean was at the University of Washington; and Gary Bongiovanni, Gary Smith, Pollstar and Jeff Apregan were at Fresno State. Many of them came out of these college concert programs.

The touring business is based on "stables" of artists. A stable is a group of artists who fall under the rubric of some type of handler—a band manager, business manager, agent, attorney. John Meglen describes how "stables of talent" were used to develop tours. "Concerts West worked with managers to book their stables of talent. For instance, Jerry Weintraub managed John Denver, Neil Diamond, Sinatra, Bob Dylan, the Pointer Sisters, and the Carpenters. Terry Basset's best friend was Irving Azoff, so we got all his acts: Boz Scaggs, the Eagles, Jimmy Buffett, Chicago, and Dan Fogelberg. Peter Grant managed Led Zeppelin, Bad Company, and Dave Edmunds. Ninety-five percent of our business came from these three stables."

Concerts West didn't stick to one region like other concert promoters. It did shows nationally and paid local promoters a $2,500 flat fee. In the '70s, Concerts West was promoting more than 700 events a year, working with Elvis Presley, Eric Clapton, and The Rolling Stones, among others. This was a real touring company.

However, local promoters were infuriated when Concerts West poached their territory and threw them a couple grand as a bone. Thus, in the '70s, as touring continued to develop, the Concerts Wests national tour model gave way to upwards of 30 regional promoters: Bill Graham (San Francisco and Northwest), Feyline (Denver-Las Vegas-Southwest), Jam Productions (Chicago, Midwest, Vegas), Evening Star (Phoenix, Southwest), Cellar Door (Atlanta and the South), and Electric Factory (Philadelphia and the East).

In Las Vegas, the onerous Rock Concert Ordinance and scarcity of quality venues left Sin City to promoters like Feyline, Beaver, GANA, and

Michael Schivo Presents. Schivo, who held a Rock Concert License, partnered with many different regional promoters.

In those days, promoters worked a system that included talent agencies (CAA, William Morris, Premier, Monterrey), venues, and managers representing acts. A manager cut deals with record labels, developed strategies to break the artist, and chose an agency to route tours. He had (and has) the final say on all tours. The agencies' value was their ability to efficiently route a tour and maximize the net profit for the artist.

As bigger and better venues became available to promoters, more offers were made for the auditoriums and coliseums. Generally, agents and managers were loyal to promoters who took chances booking acts when they were breaking in clubs and small theaters. A promoter could count on the loyalty of acts as they graduated to bigger venues. Regional territories were carved out for promoters, which were respected by agencies and other promoters.

This system continued into the '80s. However, agents, under pressure from managers to deliver a bigger net profit for the artist, started to whittle away at promoter profits. Here's how it worked. A promoter

---

A Lot of Firsts ...

Frank Barsalona booked the first American concert tours of the Beatles and The Rolling Stones, then created a concert circuit that served as a farm system for a generation of rockers. The company he founded in 1964, Premier Talent, was the first established exclusively for rock acts; previously, they'd been represented by established agencies catering to nightclub singers and comedians. As the rock business grew and routing was still uncharted territory, Barsalona drew the map.

Barsalona established an independent concert system uncoupled from the record companies by creating a network of young, rock-savvy, concert promoters around the country—Bill Graham in San Francisco, Ron Delsener in New York, and Don Law in Boston were part of his crew. The tours he routed with that network

---

made an offer that included a guarantee for the act. The promoter recommended ticket prices, expenses for the show, and a promotion plan. In exchange, an agreed-on promoter profit was calculated as a percentage of the net profit; in the '70s, it was 35% of the net.

Booking agent Tom Ross described the business in his 1998 keynote address at the Pollstar Conference. "The acts just wanted to go out and play music. And the landlords, the people who owned these rooms, made a lot of money. We didn't know how much money until we started making this a business. Then we tried to go back and give control to the acts. We went to 50% of the gross, 60% of the gross, then 70% of the gross. Then 80-20 of net, 85-15 of net, 90-10. We've driven our business so hard that we've had to go to the ancillary businesses to make our profits. This is the only business where if, as a promoter, you went to a bank and said, 'Here it is, this is the business,' the guy would look at you like you're from outer space."

The business Ross was describing was the beginning of promoter consolidation.

Barry Fey put it this way, "When I started in the late '60s, I'd give the

... for Rock

provided his clients with freelance income (10% of which he took as his commission), gave artists in need of seasoning minor-league performance venues, and established the basic landscape of the rock-concert circuit in the U.S., which hasn't eroded at all.

"You cannot exaggerate the role Frank played in creating the infrastructure of the rock 'n' roll world as we know it today," Steven Van Zandt, the longtime guitarist with Bruce Springsteen's E Street Band, said in an interview in the *New York Times*. "It was his unique vision that rock 'n' roll was here to stay, and that it wasn't just going to be about records, but about how good a band plays live."

If Bill Graham is the godfather of promoters, Frank Barsalona is the Christopher Columbus of live-music touring.

bands $5,000, $10,000, whatever it was and that was that. I'd keep everything over that, if there was anything. Then the bands got wise and it became, say, $10,000 guaranteed, plus 50% of the gross over $50,000. They wanted a piece of the back end. Then it went up to 60% and 70%. Eventually, it got to where the big bands were fine without a guarantee, but they wanted 80% of the net after expenses. So, if you grossed $300,000 and expenses were $100,000, there was $200,000 left, they got $160,000 and I got $40,000. But then, they decided they *wanted* a guarantee against 80%, which quickly became 85%. And then, the dreaded 90-10." He continues, "That's when the band and managers became abusive and wouldn't let us earn a living. They became unconscionable. They turned us into thieves."

What he means by that is as the acts squeezed more and more from promoters by demanding and getting higher guarantees, promoters started to steal—scalping tickets, creating back-door incentive deals with ticketing companies and venues, falsifying settlement sheets, and all in plain view of everyone in the industry.

It was hardly an ideal model for acts to maximize touring profits. In fact, few acts profited from touring. "Touring in those days never covered the bills," said Geddy Lee with Rush. "You toured to get your name out there. To hopefully move you into the next stage of things."

By the late '80s, the live-tour deal had to change. In 1989, Arthur Fogel, a Canadian music promoter, figured out how.

And Now for Something Completely Different

Fogel's days as a drummer were numbered; he didn't see the future. So he took a job managing the Edge, a nightclub in Toronto. Though the place seated only 200, on most nights when popular acts were playing, there were more like double that number of people.

"The days at the Edge were a bit of the wild west," recalls Fogel in the documentary, *Who the F**K is Arthur Fogel*. "I learned how to fight figuratively and literally. I learned how to identify theft. I learned that there are some real sick people out there in the world."

That gig earned him a spot on the Martha and Muffins tour, then with Concert Promotions International (CPI). As a promoter, he did everything, including booking, settling shows, promotion, and coordinating production with the acts. He loved the action on the road, moving from town to town and the continuous tension of challenges on the rock 'n' roll highway.

CPI was a concert promotion company formed in 1973 by Billy Ballard, Michael Cohl, and David Wolinsky; Ballard was the son of Harold Ballard, owner of Toronto Maple Leafs. Arthur Fogel joined in 1981. In 1986, he was appointed president of the Concert Division.

CPI became known for well-organized successful shows, while providing good value for the act. As important, Fogel was honing his skills and developing a vision for a different touring world.

CPI's expertise and culture mandated an expansion beyond Canadian borders. To Fogel's way of thinking, touring was fragmented; in effect, it left too much on the table. He wondered, could you build a business model where one promoter can take an act around the world? No less an act than The Rolling Stones gave Fogel his answer and in so doing, rewrote touring history.

In 1989, The Rolling Stones were thought to be on a creative downslide. Even so, their value as a touring act was unquestionable. CPI, using the credibility it had established in the business, made a pitch: They offered an unprecedented guarantee of *$65 million* to promote a tour of up to 60 dates in the U.S. and Canada and more worldwide, as well as to handle merchandising, a sponsorship deal, and a pay-per-view TV special.

Fogel recalls, "Everyone thought we were nuts. 'The Rolling Stones are over; they're finished.' Well, we were either going to blow up the company and blow our brains out or it was going to be the best move we could ever make."

How could they afford a $65 million guarantee? And how could they pull off a national tour in the U.S., much less Europe and the rest of the world? And how would the 32 members of the National Concert Promoters Association, represented by impresarios like Bill Graham, respond?

Donald K. Donald, part owner in CPI says, "Bill Graham didn't have quite the same kind of understanding of the potential and vision for the numbers and the money. CPI was able to present a business plan to The Rolling Stones far greater than Bill Graham even believed was possible."

CPI won the tour bid.

"I have to be honest with you," says Fogel. "I didn't give a shit that it was outside the system. I loved that. If you're confident of a strategy and a plan, you must put your blinders on and your defenses up against all those who want you to fail. Failure was not an option."

CPI was now committed to doing something neither they nor anyone had ever imagined, let alone undertaken. "I don't think we ever understood how big and complex this would be," says Fogel in retrospect. "The thing of the moment was to shoot first and ask questions later, and then we'll figure out how to put it altogether."

The Symphony for the Devil Tour went off without a hitch. The Rolling Stones played to more than 3 million fans in 20 different countries, grossing $170 million, the largest concert gross up until that time. What's more, CPI had entered into a true partnership with the artist, which ran opposite of the way the business was run and in doing so, they eliminated the middleman. With a huge win under their belt, CPI continued to develop international tours, virtually unchallenged. CPI's only competition was with itself.

While CPI took a chunk of business from them, local promoters still thrived—until an even bigger paradigm shift in live music occurred. In the early '90s, a mesmeric mogul, Robert Sillerman, changed the concert business from a network of individuals into a single empire—SFX Entertainment.

A Paradigm Earthquake

In 1989, radio and TV station owner Robert Sillerman started his rollup of music, forming Capstar Communications.

Seven years later, he applied for and received permission to operate more than one class of radio station in the same market. The Telecommunications Act of 1996, allowing for ownership of multiple stations in single markets, fueled a binge by Capstar, which bought up so many stations that it became the nation's seventh largest radio chain. The name was changed to SFX Broadcasting.

In 1996, SFX made its first concert-promoter acquisition, Delsener/Slater, one of the top concert promoters in the Northeast. The $20 million deal gave SFX a company that staged concerts at several venues and operated an 11,000-seat amphitheater on Long Island, New York. Within a few months, SFX also acquired Indianapolis-based Sunshine Promotions for $55 million. A new division, SFX Concerts, was formed to operate the two companies. SFX's plan was for its chain of radio stations to advertise the events promoted by this division.

SFX continued the expansion of its concert division when four more promoters were acquired, including Bill Graham Presents, Contemporary Group, and Concert/Southern Promotions, for a combined cost of more than $230 million. Only two weeks later, a $155 million deal to buy PACE Entertainment Corp. was announced. PACE was the largest producer of touring theatrical productions outside New York City; it also promoted concerts and motorsport events and owned 11 amphitheaters around the country.

Shortly thereafter, SFX spent another $227 million to purchase concert promoters Avalon Attractions, Don Law's Blackstone Entertainment, souvenir company Event Merchandising, Inc., the Oakdale Theater, and Falk Associates Management Enterprises (FAME), an agency that represented basketball stars such as Michael Jordan and Patrick Ewing. After these acquisitions, SFX asserted it had gained control of more than 40% of the concert market.

SFX's national buying rampage was the talk of the traditionally fragmented and regionally based concert-touring business. Some questioned the premium prices being paid for concert promoters, whose profit on a concert was usually as thin as 3%-4% of the gross. Others wondered about Sillerman's agenda, insisting he was merely repeating his radio game plan of consolidating a fragmented industry, so he could drive up prices and sell out when the market peaked.

Live-music insiders predicted a negative impact on developing acts that wouldn't have a club system to break into a market. Talent agents feared their acts would book tours directly with SFX, eliminating the need for their services in dealing with multiple promoters across the country.

Tom Ross, head of CAA's music division, railed against SFX and Sillerman. In an interview for the book *Power House—The Untold Story of Hollywood's Creative Artists Agency,* Ross said, "I felt Bob Sillerman was an enemy of the agency system and they were going to bypass the agents.

They were going to go direct to the acts, make their deals, and leave us in the cold. I was very outspoken about not letting him control us. I believed it was going to shrink the playlist of radio, shrink the opportunity for our artists to grow, and result in the same acts on the same stations in every city across the nation." The CAA hierarchy didn't react kindly. On November 8, 1998, CAA announced Ross would be leaving CAA after 15 years.

Most observers predicted that SFX would ultimately have to raise ticket prices to turn a profit, possibly causing a backlash among audiences in the process. SFX's position was that the best seats would likely become more expensive, but the non-premium seats could be reduced in price and the overall balance would remain the same.

SFX continued its spree when it made a deal to buy Cellar Door Companies for $105 million. Cellar Door was one of the last holdouts against the SFX onslaught. Jack Boyle, Cellar Door's head, was placed in charge of SFX's music division. The company also formed a new unit, SFX Live, to market entertainment events on a national basis. *The New York Times* portrayed the move as "the biggest transformation in the history of the concert business."

In the face of SFX's increasingly firm grip on the market, 11 of its competitors formed the Independent Promoters Organization (IPO) to collectively bid for the major acts. Members of IPO included number-two U.S. concert promoter Universal Concerts, Metropolitan Entertainment, Belkin Productions, and others. Some performers, including Eric Clapton, Céline Dion, and Shania Twain, avoided SFX venues at their agents' insistence.

Major arenas around the country had the same issue. Because SFX controlled most outdoor amphitheaters, the company was now leveraging acts to tour in the summer and fill their dates in its own outdoor venues.

Consolidation not only ushered in an unprecedented era of ticket-price increases, but the touring season was weighted to the summer where SFX's bulk purchases were targeted for their amphitheaters.

During SFX's sweep, in Las Vegas, Thomas and Mack Center tour stops dwindled from a peak of 24 in 1985 to 12 in 1996. However, Vegas wasn't hurt by consolidation. The start of Sillerman's mega-consolidation of the live-music industry coincided with the opening of MGM Grand Garden Arena. But MGM didn't need a network. It had established itself as a top-10 tour stop, landing almost every major tour.

In fact, SFX woke up the arenas. In the early '90s, a group of five major arenas met regularly to share best practices, TMC among them. SFX's influence on the touring calendar created an urgency among all arenas to act. The group of five became 20, then 30, and now stands at 40. As a result, Concerts West's two principals, John Meglen and Paul Gongaware, proposed an alliance that created the ArenaNetwork.

As predicted, in 2000, Sillerman sold SFX to the giant radio broadcasting company Clear Channel for $3.3 billion in stock and the assumption of $1.1 billion of debt. In 2005, Live Nation was spun off from Clear Channel. In 2009, Live Nation merged with Ticketmaster to form Live Nation Entertainment.

Buying SFX allowed Clear Channel to use its radio assets to promote upcoming concerts and secure better concert tours with the promise that

Vegas Roll Call

MGM's live-music track record meant that whether your name was AEG, Live Nation, Clear Channel, SFX, CPI, or Danny Zelisko, it was the Grand Garden where your act was playing. Now that arena is T-Mobile, also owned by MGM.

The smaller theaters aligned themselves with an assortment of promoters, depending on the venue. The Joint (Hard Rock) started with Andrew Hewitt and Bill Silva, before AEG Live took over. The Pearl (Palms) opened with Hewitt-Silva and then Danny Zelisko, whose company was briefly owned by Live Nation. (Station Casinos now owns the Palms and books with Live Nation.) AEG Live established the Colosseum with Céline, Elton John, and Rod Stewart and continues to promote at the Caesars' venue. Axis (Planet Hollywood) is booked by Live Nation, Brooklyn Bowl (The LINQ) by AEG Live, and Chelsea (Cosmopolitan) by C3.

the acts get more radio play. Clear Channel expected that expanding its footprint in live entertainment would allow it to leverage its scale to negotiate better contracts.

A 2005 *Wall Street Journal* report had this to say, "But Live Nation's value has also fallen by as much as 81% in the five years since Clear Channel acquired its corporate predecessor, SFX Entertainment Inc., for $3 billion. The media giant, based in San Antonio, wasn't able to execute its vision of creating a pop-culture juggernaut by using its thousands of billboards and radio stations to cross-promote concerts. And the concert business in recent years has been staggered by over-aggressive pricing and sky-high fees paid to artists.

"The result is that Clear Channel Entertainment has been one of the least-profitable components of the $9.4 billion parent company, generating just $16 million net income in 2004 on $2.8 billion revenue. Live entertainment 'is a much lower-margin business than the outdoor [advertising] and radio businesses,' says a company spokesman."

WSJ went on to say: "So the business can do poorly even when it seems to be doing well. The concert business set revenue records in 2004, thanks to high-profile tours by Prince, Metallica, Madonna, and others, as well as pricey tickets. But in terms of profit, it was an especially bad year, because attendance couldn't keep pace with rising prices and fees paid to performers."

Clear Channel took a $2.4 billion loss spinning off Live Nation.

Live Nation Entertainment has grown into the world's largest music-promotion company, Live Nation, and the world's largest ticketing company, Ticketmaster, which it acquired in 2010. It now includes live-music events, venue operations, ticketing services, sponsorship and advertising sales, and artist management and services.

In a podcast with Recode Media, Live Nation CEO Michael Rapino discussed the concert business at length. "Ten years ago, we did a few thousand shows. Now we're doing 30,000. But we've always had a very simplistic strategy on content called 'the concert.' That was, one, to go global. And we want to be in a multi-channel business. So we do 8,000 club shows, we have a huge country and live-touring division, an Insomniac division [electronic dance music], a festival division in Europe, and a jazz division."

No Economics like Veganomics

Las Vegas' number of diverse venues allows a variety of acts to have a shot at the huge market, from casino lounges to Sam Boyd Stadium, from the 1,000-seat Club at the Cannery to the Rock in Rio festival. That market is now 44 million visitors and two million locals, many looking for a "Vegas music experience." Those locals have the highest discretionary income in the country. Kerry Bubolz is president of Las Vegas' first major-league sports franchise, the NHL's Golden Knights. One of the first things he learned about his new city is that Las Vegans have extra money. Concerning the discretionary income for the 22 U.S. NHL teams and their local markets, Las Vegas ranked 8 or 9, Bubolz discovered. "When adjusted based on cost of living and no state income tax, Vegas was number one."

Why have Las Vegas hotels made such a big investment in theaters, arenas, and festival sites and why should live music be important to you, even if you don't like music?

Economics, when applied properly, can be a great way to get around our biases when it comes to making prudent and sensible decisions on the allocation of resources. Veganomics is a good way to describe an economy highly dependent on tourism. The local brand of economics supports the private and public investments made to drive visitors, which in turn strengthen the job market, increase the tax base, support services such as education, health, and roads, and stimulate even more growth.

Jeremy Aguero graduated from UNLV in 1996 with a degree in Hotel Administration. He's a fourth-generation Las Vegan. In his first job at Coopers & Lybrand (now Price Waterhouse Coopers), he embraced the unpopular data-intensive projects no one else wanted. From there, he started the company he owns today, Applied Analysis, which specializes in fiscal and policy consulting. Today, Jeremy is the most recognized economist in Las Vegas with a distinguished group of clients, including the Las Vegas Convention and Visitors Authority, Nevada State Bank, Southwest Gas, the Las Vegas Water District, Clark County, City of Las Vegas, City of Henderson, and the Governor's Office.

Las Vegas has a unique economy that's highly dependent on exports

The New ...

The growth of fine dining has been central to the ongoing evolution of Las Vegas. As legalized gambling has expanded across the United States, Las Vegas has responded by expanding its amenities beyond gaming to maintain its position as a top tourist destination.

Two decades ago, gaming revenue made up more than half of all revenue for resort hotels along the Las Vegas Strip. Today, the casino accounts for just a third of revenue, with high-end shopping centers, world-class venues that draw the biggest names in entertainment, and restaurants headed by the top chefs in the culinary world bringing in more than 50%. Since 1995, food revenues alone have grown from 11% to nearly 20% of total resort revenue.

While the growing selection of fine-dining destinations has been a boon for Las Vegas tourism, the benefits don't end there. Local residents now have access to the world's best cuisine via a short car ride. Two decades ago, that would have required a trip to Los Angeles or New York.

(tourism). Tourism has been a big part of Aguero's work in Las Vegas. "Traditional economic theories do not always work here. We're unique," he says. "Other cities export cars, food, money, fuel. We attract visitors. Not only is tourism critical to the direct impact of generating revenue and profits for the hotel-casinos, the indirect and induced impacts and the taxes paid by visitors fund a big portion of the economy." Aguero explains the differences, putting them into live-music terms.

"'Direct' impact is the money visitors spend on a hotel room, food, entertainment, etc. while they're here. 'Indirect' refers to everything spent to produce a concert—promoter, venue services, advertising, and the like. 'Induced' means everything someone who works at the concert, full- or part-time, spends throughout the community, at a grocery store, movie

... Las Vegas

Additionally, restaurants and bars have provided economic opportunities and jobs for southern Nevadans as they proliferated before the Great Recession and, following a brief decline after the downturn, became a $10 billion industry in southern Nevada.

Full-service restaurants, which include everything from the celebrity-chef establishments on the Strip to neighborhood diners, make up about a third of the sector. Since 2002, the number of full-service restaurants in southern Nevada has nearly doubled from 760 to 1,410, which isn't all that surprising when you consider that Americans are spending more on dining out than ever before. Employment growth at those restaurants has followed a similar trend, expanding from 25,440 jobs in 2002 to 47,870 jobs that paid $1.2 billion in wages last year.

Whether it's a high-end restaurant run by a Food Network star or a modest family-owned restaurant around the corner, the bottom line of southern Nevada's growing restaurant industry is that we have many more choices for eating out today than just a decade ago. That's great news for our economy and our appetites.

theater, or doctor's office. That spending wouldn't happen if he or she didn't have a job at the concert."

Detroit measures output from cars made and sold. Las Vegas' productivity is measured by the expenditures of its visitors. The Convention and Visitors Authority conducts extensive research to understand the spending of people who visit Las Vegas. The LVCVA determined that the average visitor in 2015 spent $857. However, a visitor for a special event spends substantially more (direct impact). According to the LVCVA, a National Finals Rodeo fan spends $2,320, college basketball tournaments $1,460, R&R Marathon $1,420, NASCAR $1,390, Electric Daisy Carnival festival $1,390, and Life is Beautiful festival $1,194. Granted, visitors who travel to Las Vegas for one concert probably don't spend as much as someone who attends the NFR or Electric Daisy Carnival. Still, they spend more, sometimes much more (for example, for a Stones concert where two high-end tickets cost $1,400) than the average visitor. And according to *Pollstar* magazine, in 2016 more than three million concert tickets were sold to all live music events in Las Vegas.

How does that impact differ from a concert elsewhere? When fans go to live music events in Chicago, Dallas, L.A., or Seattle, they might be traveling, but from much closer to the venue. Most don't stay in a hotel, gamble, or shop. They go directly to the show. They might have dinner beforehand and go to a bar afterwards, but that doesn't have anywhere near the direct economic impact that a visitor who travels to Las Vegas by plane to see a show or attend a festival does.

In the end, though it took a long and winding road to finally arrive in Las Vegas, the live-music experience is here to pay.

CHAPTER TWELVE

MUSIC TO THE MASSES

The problem with amplitude-modulation (AM) radio was static. Lightning and electrical products regularly interfered with station signals, causing a disjointed mess of spine-tingling noise. In 1933, Edward Armstrong of Columbia University found a solution: FM. Frequency modulation boosted the bandwidth of the signal to eliminate interference from other energy waves.

Several issues with Armstrong's idea immediately arose: No one owned a radio that could receive its signal, stereo reproduction of sound had little demand, and the radio industry, fearing FM might overtake AM technology, fought Armstrong tooth and nail till the bitter end.

After spending 30 years of his life trying to bring FM to the market and distraught over his failure, Armstrong jumped out of a window of his 13th-story New York apartment. Ironically, his legacy as an anti-corporate anti-mass-medium renegade is exactly what FM was born to be.

RCA, which stands for Radio Corporation of America, was the first major player in the radio industry. RCA also invented the record player and the 10-inch 78-RPM record. It made 78 revolutions per minute around the turntable, played for three minutes, and was made of wax, plastic, and silicone. The record was played on a gramophone, which had a mushroom-shaped speaker attached to a turntable with a two-inch pin (needle).

In the '40s, Columbia Records came up with a quieter record that played for 25 minutes per side. Not to be outdone, RCA produced a seven-inch 45 RPM that played three to six minutes per side. By the '50s, music was distributed primarily through these "single" records. Kids congregated around a small record player listening to hits they were hearing on Top 40 radio. "What amazed me was the sheer technical ferocity of the stuff," said George Martin, Beatles record producer. "I could actually see the loudness of the record."

Top 40 AM radio stations played hit records and, thanks to its broadcast range, the reach was enormous. WLS in Chicago could be heard by 20 million people. The single record and AM radio combined to sell an astounding 10 million 45s of Elvis' 1956 hit "You Ain't Nothing but a Hound Dog." Rock 'n' roll was off and running.

One problem for artists who wanted to get on the radio was that their songs could be no more than two minutes and thirty seconds.

The stereo 33-1/3 LP (long-playing) "album," which produced less noise and had finer reproduction quality, debuted in 1954. It started the demand for high-fidelity sound and the 25 minutes per side allowed artists to produce concept albums. In 1955, Frank Sinatra released what's considered the first concept album, *In the Wee Small Hours*, which tells the story of what it's like to lose your love. That love was Ava Gardner. The cover art also reflected the concept, with a sad Sinatra smoking a cigarette on a deserted city street at night.

In 1961, the FCC approved stereo broadcast for FM. In 1964, the FCC required owners of AM-FM stations to have at least a half-day of FM programming. Between 1960 and 1965, the number of FM radio sets grew from six million to 30 million, then to 93 million in 1970.

AM also ignored the politics of the time, mainly the war in Vietnam and racial tensions, while experimental FM stations tackled it head-on. At midnight on WBAI in New York, for example, Bob Fass was growing a counterculture audience with improvisation programming that bounced between dead silence and rock to forums for whoever walked into the station. Dylan, Arlo Guthrie, and Judy Collins made the show regularly. During the '60s, the station hosted innumerable anti-establishment guests, including anti-war activists, feminists, and comedians, and broadcast complete albums late at night. In San Francisco, Tom Donahue's show on KMPX was similar: "free-form" FM radio that was almost entirely DJ-centric.

Tom Ross, former CAA agent, elaborates. "That's what alternative radio was. That's when a DJ would say, 'Here's a cut I heard last night and I want to play it for you.' DJs took chances. They weren't driven by profits and advertisers. They were driven by the love of musicians, of the art."

FM radio was critical to the growth of touring music, which provided high-fidelity sound over broadcast radio, broke new music, and promoted concerts; almost exclusively, promoters advertised on FM radio stations. The quality and format, along with the departure from traditional top 40 hits, ushered in an unprecedented era of discovery and creativity. Album sales outpaced the 45 and eventually eliminated them. The entire work of an artist was now marketable.

Tapes, CDs, MP3

In the '70s, the album was king, but it had drawbacks. It easily scratched, it wasn't portable, and in today's lingo, it was "read only"; you couldn't do anything but play it.

"The cassette tape was a good example of technology that didn't even pretend to be an advance in terms of sound quality," says music writer Greg Milner. It was, however, portable and recordable.

"We made cassettes and shared them with friends," says Dave Grohl of the Foo Fighters. "We passed them around, then went see those bands when they came into town. We felt like that music was ours. A blank cassette cost a dollar. You could record your own playlists using any theme you chose."

The portability of the cassette tape and tape recorder drove sales of the pre-recorded cassette past the album, assisted by the convenience of the car cassette player and the Sony Walkman. Listening to records in your car was real progress, though those of us who lived through that era could have done without the frustration of the tape-eating players.

Cassettes also ushered in the recording of concerts. Each Grateful Dead show was highly improvisational, with no two shows the same. Fans recorded the shows and gave them away through the Grateful Dead's free-tape exchange. The band didn't want to be cops, so they organized an area behind the mixer for legal recording. Recordings from the band's 50 years of performances are easily available online.

In my own case, I managed to avoid paying for albums in college, as my playlist vehicle was an Akai reel-to-reel tape recorder my bother brought home from Vietnam. My roommate bought every record and let me record them. Both sides of the tape gave me three hours of mixed music. Before the CD, I recorded more than 180 hours of cuts from different records.

The record industry was opposed to the compact disc when it arrived in 1982. Its durability, mobility, and sound quality weren't enough to offset the potential for piracy. However, bands like Dire Straits embraced the new technology as a breakthrough for audio reproduction. By the end of the '80s, music lovers were rebuying their record collections on CDs. Album sales began to decline.

The CD revolutionized the music industry by introducing a quality recording platform that required little maintenance and played in machines at home, in the car, and on the beach. The CD dominated record sales for more than two decades—when sales of digital tracks finally surpassed those of analog discs.

Twenty years later, consumers decided, once again, that they preferred convenience to quality. Around the turn of the 21st century, the MP3 file emerged as the format of choice and the iPod the distribution piece that revolutionized the way we listen to music. Apple sold 275 million iPods the first nine years they were on the market.

Vegas Rock Radio

Tony Bonicci grew up in Livonia, Michigan, a half-hour from Ann Arbor. He married his high-school sweetheart Linda and in 1978, not yet 20, they moved to Las Vegas. Their first house was a travel trailer in a park behind the Hacienda Hotel. The plan was to learn a trade in the construction industry. Bonicci recalls, "We came out and I didn't get a job immediately in the trades, which was challenging, so I created a bunch of little businesses until I got a construction job."

Linda went to work selling ads for KFM 102.

"I remember playing softball for their softball team and this yellow 450 SL pulls up. I ask Linda, 'What does that guy do for a living?' She says, 'He's the sales manager for KLUC.' I wanted in."

Linda didn't relish the idea of competing against her husband, which limited his choices. He tried two radio groups and was turned down by both, but Morgan Skinner at KORK at least called him to tell him why. "He said he didn't have a budget, and I don't know where this came from, but I just said, 'Perfect.' And he said, 'Why is that?' I said, 'Because I work for free.' 'What do you mean you work for free?' I said, 'If I sell something, you can pay me.' He said, 'When can you drop by?'"

Bonicci worked at KORK AM-FM for a year before joining KENO-KOMP. The station had a top-40 format and both AM and FM, whereas his wife was kicking ass at the all-FM rock station across town at KFM.

Bonicci recalls Vegas when he joined KOMP. "There wasn't much of a music scene in town. It was a big boxing scene. Vegas got some shows at the Convention Center and Aladdin, but nothing on the Strip at all. There was one rock, one top 40, and one country station—not a lot of radio competition."

While top-40 stations had a standard format, an album-oriented rock (AOR) station like KOMP played a mix of the best new and old rock. Though there were no big venues to host the major touring acts, the smaller clubs advertised on KOMP to promote events like battles of the bands, where just about anything went. The KOMP audience was always looking for a place to party.

In 1983, the 18,500-seat Thomas and Mack Center opened and with it a new era of live music and more business for a rock station. "Thomas and Mack concerts became a huge revenue source for radio. They proved how starved audiences were for rock music and that they'd come back repeatedly and spend money," remembers Bonicci.

The sophisticated promoters TMC attracted allowed the DJs on stage to make announcements before the shows and let the station hang KOMP banners. They did contests. If you wore a KOMP T-shirt or designed the coolest banner welcoming the band, you were upgraded to the front row. They sponsored "official post-concert parties" at clubs. "It was a partnership," says Bonicci. "We played their record more, because fans wanted to hear it. We had the acts or promoters on the air regularly. We flew listeners to other concerts on the tour. In turn, the promoter gave us a welcome, which means we were the exclusive station. We were highly motivated to sell out TMC."

In 1988 at age 30, Bonicci became general manager of KOMP, just as he caught wind of a new AOR station in town, KKLZ. "Our staff pretty much ignored it—until the rating book came out and they crushed us. They had the first rock morning show with two DJs. These guys were doing bits, parodies mixed with songs. My guy, Big Marty, was doing his thing, but he was by himself."

The war was on.

At concerts, KKLZ staff tore down KOMP banners. On its AM station, called the Crusher, they ran a spot saying, "KOMP is dead." They sent KOMP programmers dead roses.

"They told their audience to come to our promotions and cause trouble," Bonicci says. "They called Big Marty Fat Marty and Mike Cullotta Piña Colada. I'd like to say they were the only bad guys, but I can't say our guys didn't do the same thing. It wasn't friendly competition at all. It was ugly."

The consolidation of the concert-promotion business by SFX changed the radio scene enormously. Corporate promotion didn't have the personal touch. "We were no longer offered exclusives," says Bonicci. "Everything had to be shared with other stations. The meet and greets weren't as good. The bands became more detached from their audience. They no longer come in and do on-air interviews. They're now unapproachable rock stars."

By contrast, Bonicci continues, "Country stars are always appreciative. At the Academy Country Music awards, the artists thank the radio stations for their success. For the rock bands, it's all about them. We used to love bands. Today, rock listeners like the songs more than the bands."

In the early days of FM, a low-key half-stoned-sounding DJ picked what he liked to play. In the late '70s and early '80s, program directors laid out playlists for DJs. Around that time, KOMP turned to a consultant to create tight playlists of hits people wanted to hear. That created commercial rock. Bonicci says, "When you're doing free-form, you only reach a niche audience. Our goal was to play the songs everyone wanted to hear. Rock music was better off."

Not everyone agreed. Lost was the opportunity to hear new music from established bands and from bands trying to break into the business.

In addition, like the oil, airline, telecommunications, and concert-promotion industries, the radio business underwent extreme consolidation over the past 20 years. After media ownership was deregulated in 1996, Clear Channel went on a buying spree, purchasing more than 70 media companies, plus hundreds of individual stations. After 20 years of mergers, acquisitions, and bankruptcies, we now have iHeart radio.

With 850 stations, iHeartMedia is the largest radio-station group in the United States. The 850 stations reach more than 110 million listeners every week and 245 million every month. Its closest competitor, CBS Radio, owns 117 radio stations in 26 markets.

A testament to iHeart radio's dominance is its annual festival in Las Vegas. Nearly 10,000 fans journey to Las Vegas compliments of the radio network. The iHeart Festival uses a rotating stage as a mechanism that keeps the show on a schedule that's all about instant gratification with a general focus on radio hits.

Amazingly, some stations in Las Vegas escaped the radio gold rush. Tony Bonicci's KOMP, in fact, remains independent.

"I Want My MTV"

On August 1, 1981, MTV went on the air. MTV founder Bob Pittman remembers the first hour as an "unmitigated disaster. The VJ's announced, 'That was Styx,' right after we played REO Speedwagon. They said, 'This is The Who' and a 38 Special video would begin."

Worse, the quality of the videos was bad.

Kevin Cronin of REO sets the scene. "The first time we made a video in 1978, they set up a couple of cameras at sound check and we ran through a song. That was a music video. For *High Infidelity*, we made four videos in one day. They were horrible."

Music videos were either live with the band lip syncing or funny, crass, undignified, or borderline unsuitable. Duran Duran was the first of many Brits to introduce sex. Per the authors of *I Want My MTV*, Rob Tannenbaum and Craig Marks, Duran Duran's "Girls on Film" is the most influential music video ever made, setting up three decades of rock-video titillation.

"It had glamour, it had polish, it had sex, it had good-looking boys, it had girls sliding on poles. It was dirty. In hindsight, it had ingredients that were MTV-able. I'm sorry. I can only apologize," admits the director Kevin Godley.

Music videos weren't an original idea. The Beatles made several music videos—"We Can Work It Out," "Paperback Writer," "Rain," "Revolution," and "Hey Jude" (with a cast of dozens) among them—in part to placate a world of rabid fans when they stopped touring. In the later years of "The Adventures of Ozzie and Harriet," at the end of the show, their son Ricky Nelson usually performed one of his hits. The Monkees television series was more style than substance. Devo's "Whip It" cost $16,000 to produce and was both hideous and funny, but the visual image launched their career.

It's hard to gauge the impact of MTV on live music. Before MTV, you had to shell out $15-$40 to see Rod Stewart perform. Now he was in your living room 20 times a day.

Developing the MTV brand required a lot of luck; it was a hard sell to advertisers and cable operators. Advertising executive George Lois said, "Hard to believe, but after its first year of operation, MTV was an abject failure." It was projected to lose $10 million, but the number in red was closer to $50 million. No one knew what MTV was.

Good slogans capture the essence of a brand in a very few words. But the phrase must be compelling. The phrase chosen for MTV was a third generation of a Maypo Cereal ad: "I want my Maypo." But its impact would be no greater than the person delivering it. And no one person would have a greater impact than Mick Jagger.

Les Garland, executive vice president of MTV programming from 1982 to 1987, was dispatched to get Jagger on board.

"I get my meeting with Mick. 'Okay, Garland, tell me what you want.' I go, 'I'd like you to go on camera and help us with our new TV ad campaign, and all I need you to do is say, 'I want my MTV.' And he goes, 'You mean, you want me to do a commercial?' I go, 'It's more of an endorsement, for a new phenomenon called music videos.' He says, 'Yeah, that's a commercial. The Rolling Stones don't do commercials.'

"I go, 'Well, that's not true. I was at Atlantic when Jovan perfume sponsored your tour.' 'Well, we got paid for that.' 'So what you're saying is, you do commercials for money?' And that got a little laugh. I said, 'Mick, we don't have any money. But if this is about money, I'll give you a dollar.' And I threw a dollar on the table. He looked up and said, 'I like you, Garland. I'll do it.' We shot it the next day. And it blew everybody's mind. From there we called Pat Benatar. 'Mick Jagger's in.' David Bowie. 'Mick Jagger's in.' We used Mick to get the cooperation of everyone else."

As cable television grew, the demand for music videos waned, but new formats for the delivery of music and videos were about to become mammoth tools for discovering bands and artists and promoting live music.

Platforms Keep Progressing

In the early part of this millennium, a new format, subscription-based satellite radio, was born. On February 19, 2007, the two competing services merged, becoming Sirius XM. Today Sirius XM Radio provides 69 streams, or channels, of music and 65 streams of sports, news, and entertainment. Music streams on Sirius come in a variety of genres, all commercial-free and uncensored. When Sirius XM merged in 2007, they had 14 million subscribers. Today, subscriptions are over 30 million.

YouTube was founded by Chad Hurley, Steve Chen, and Jawed Karin in 2005. It began as an angel-funded enterprise from a makeshift office in a garage. The concept was to create a site where people could download and view any and all video content. In September 2005, YouTube reached its millionth hit. On October 9, 2006, Google purchased YouTube for $1.65 billion. Fans began discovering, watching, and listening to music on YouTube, creating another platform for promoting music. In April 2009, Usher introduced the world to Justin Bieber via a video on YouTube Now. Justin Bieber's "Baby" has had more than 820 million views. Also in 2009, YouTube and Vivendi teamed up to launch a new music-video service, Vevo.

Thirty percent of videos account for 99% of YouTube views and 60 hours of new videos are uploaded to the site every minute. It's the third most visited website on the Internet after Google and Facebook. In March 2013, the number of unique users visiting YouTube every month reached a cool billion.

MP3 is a coding format for digital audio that uses a form of lousy data compression. The idea was to compress a file in a way that keeps as much of the data needed to reproduce a quality music recording as possible. After decades of work on the challenge, MP3 files were created in the early 1990s and are now the dominant format for downloading both legal and illegal music files, as well as streaming.

In the mid-1990s, slow dial-up access, with bad browsers and web pages taking seconds to load, made anything on the Internet, much less music downloads, unimaginable. Napster, founded in 1999 by Shawn Fanning and Sean Parker, was launched as a pioneering peer-to-peer (P2P) file-sharing site that emphasized sharing digital audio encoded in the MP3 format. The file-sharing service that allowed users to download MP3s in seconds peaked at 60 million users.

Napster caught the record industry napping, as it were, as they clung to huge profits the traditional CD was reaping. The audience got to the technology before the industry. "The music industry was fairly constrained for 75-100 years in terms of how music was found, sourced, developed, created, distributed, marketed, promoted," said Brandon Barber, director of product management for Napster. "It was a locked paradigm. Napster created an avenue for consumers to get out of that, which was superior in almost every way."

Napster created a social network of music enthusiasts who could download most any song, as well as otherwise difficult-to-obtain older songs, unreleased songs, and concert bootleg recordings. Users justified downloading digital copies of recordings, because they had already purchased them in other formats, such as LP and cassettes, before the compact disc emerged as the dominant format.

CDs cost $16. Napster was free. And so began the music-format revolution. Napster only wanted to be a digital musical-distribution service, but never got there. Its primary service was shut down by court order in 2001, but the Napster brand survived, as did new file-sharing sites such as Gnutella, Freenet, Kazaa, and Bearshare.

For their part, the record companies never recovered from the paradigm shift in how music was acquired. They spent the next 10 years tripping over themselves looking for a way to break into commercial downloading. They couldn't rescue themselves. Apple's Steve Jobs had to.

The record industry blamed illegal downloading for the fall in sales, but Jobs saw Napster, MP3, and the Internet differently. He believed fans would download and pay for songs they liked if the experience was easy, affordable, and consistent, as opposed to traveling to a record store and paying $16. The magic of the MP3 was that the file shrunk so dramatically, you could store 5,000 songs on your three-by-four iPod. He talked the record labels into a distribution model with a 99-cent song. Free music downloading might be piracy, but the record industry recognized it wasn't going away. Apple had already launched the iTunes Music Store and synced it with the iPod.

The iTunes Music Store opened on April 28, 2003, and instantly transformed music distribution. In its first week, iTunes sold one million songs. This became the norm for purchasing music until again, music became (almost) free.

iTunes hastened a revolution that record executives feared—it shifted the business from expensive high-revenue CDs to cheap low-revenue singles. However, consumers now had a legal way to download songs. This was how fans would buy music in the future, whether the record industry liked it or not. In the more than 10 years since iTunes made its debut, the global record industry has shrunk drastically, from $38 billion in revenues to $16.5 billion in 2015.

Although iTunes disrupted free-for-all piracy, music was still pirated, though at a slower rate. However, with the rise of technology companies across different industries, music startups emerged that wanted to further improve the music listening experience for consumers.

In January 1993, Internet Underground Music Archive launched the first free MP3 downloadable songs. It was developed for unsigned artists to share music and reach an audience without a record label. In 2002, Last.fm launched a platform that built a profile of each user's taste and recommended similar artists.

Then came streaming. Streaming is delivering content, usually audio and video, to computers and mobile devices over the Internet. When streaming, you're listening to songs in "real time" instead of downloading and storing the file to your computer to listen later.

In September 2005, Pandora Radio introduced a streaming service using algorithms to create personalized "radio stations." Subscribers either accept viewing ads or pay a $10 monthly fee. Today, Pandora has 4 million subscribers.

In October 2008, Spotify launched a streaming service, offering a seemingly infinite catalog of music and now, with 39 million paid subscribers, is dominating the streaming space. Artists are paid per play.

Like Pandora, Spotify is free with ads or $10 per month. Spotify's competitive advantage was getting the record labels on board early. Recently, it has taken curating music to another level with two new weekly playlist features. Using algorithms based on your listening habits, Discover Weekly recommends music customized to your taste and Radar Release recommends new releases. Discover Weekly hit 5 billion listens just 10 months after launching.

In the '60s, you could buy a small round yellow-plastic disc that fit in the middle of your 45 single, so you could stack as many as a dozen on the tonearm. After each play, the record player released the next on top. Today, streaming allows you to put 5,000 records on your record player. From them, pick your hits and create your own playlists from hundreds of million of songs. Or take Spotify's advice via Radar Release or Discover Weekly playlists. Or listen to a full record. Or … the options are endless.

I can't think of a more significant technological breakthrough in bringing music to the masses. Five years ago, I was buying albums and CDs. Even with a 300-CD changer, the experience was one-dimensional. I just listened to the CD or the same playlists from my recordings on iTunes. Streaming has increased the amount of new music I listen to and helped me discover nearly 50 new (to me) artists.

It's clear plenty of other music lovers feel the same way. Streaming services are on the rise, with participation growing from 56% of the Internet population in 2012 to 69% in 2014. Streaming services have become a major source of music discovery. When asked how they found new artists and bands in the past year, 42% of survey respondents cited audio or video streaming services like Pandora, Spotify, and YouTube.

In 2015, Jay Z launched Tidal as a high-fidelity option, with most of the company owned by artists. It doesn't have a free option; rather, two tiers are defined by audio quality: $10 a month for a compressed (standard) format and $20 for CD-quality streams.

The last (for now) to the party is Apple, which launched a streaming service in March 2015 with 40 million songs and already has 17 million subscribers. The service allows any music you've got—whether previously purchased via the iTunes Store, ripped from a physical CD, or uploaded to iTunes Match—to appear in your Apple Music library.

The Future's in Streaming—and the Next Big Thing

This modernization of music distribution has generated a wave of music innovation we haven't seen since the '70s. Not only is there unlimited access to music, but the continued development of algorithms means discovering music is more convenient and effective than ever. I might have discovered six bands or artists over the past 10 years listening to commercial or satellite radio. Using Spotify's Weekly Discovery and Radar Weekly, I've become a fan of more than 50 acts in six months. The Information Age has given way to the Recommendation Age and curation will only get better.

Terrestrial radio will continue to prosper. People want to hear that song. They want to listen to personalities covering issues that matter to them, often with comedy relief. News, traffic, weather, and sports are all programming that streaming can't deliver, especially over the car radio.

Radio still reigns when it comes to listening to music in America, but it continues to feel the squeeze from Spotify, Apple, and YouTube. In Nielsen's annual "Music 360" survey of more than 3,500 consumers, the polling company found that 27% of respondents preferred radio, 20% digital, and 10% physical collections. But the survey also found that streaming in all its various formats surpasses radio if you combine them: Listeners fixed on-demand services (Spotify, Apple Music, etc.) at 12%, programmed audio (Pandora) at 11%, streaming video (YouTube) at 10%, and streaming live radio (iHeartRadio, TuneIn) at 4%. Respondents said they were using streaming media to listen to music 37% of the time versus 27% for traditional radio and a combined 30% for their own music collections.

Today, 46% of people buy their music from iTunes and from other online sites. More convenience and choice are growing CD and album sales on Amazon. I still prefer the experience of a record store. In Las Vegas, Zia Records may not have the selection of Amazon, but I love the personalized service, the prices, and the sensual experience of shopping for music.

According to Nielsen's media report, just three albums sold more than a million in 2016, the lowest since 1991. However, revenue from streaming has increased dramatically—so much so that Sony is making

$25 million per week just from streaming. Record labels have become data companies, looking at streaming platforms to find new hot artists to sign, monitoring listens, ads, and skips across platforms.

My first record was "I Want to Hold Your Hand." It was a 45. But I didn't get to see the Beatles. Few did. Over the past 50 years, more than a half-dozen recording formats introduced me to the music that became a part of 800 live music events I've seen or been involved with.

New technology is already connecting the dots. Ticketfly announced a partnership with Pandora that sends notifications on concerts or festivals nearby to fans listening to music on Pandora. Dave Brooks of Amplify Media wrote that Ticketfly's mission has been "to challenge the titans and counter Ticketmaster by putting new powerful tools and data in the hands of customers. Few other executives [Andrew Dreskin, Ticketfly CEO] in live entertainment have the *cojones* to challenge TM and its parent company, Live Nation."

Most of Ticketfly's accounts are clubs or festivals without contracts with Ticketmaster. Still, the company has racked up some impressive numbers: Last year, five-year-old San Francisco-based Ticketfly sold 11.2 million tickets, valued at $250 million, for 80,000-plus events in North America.

The results of the Ticketfly-Pandora affiliation have been staggering. The automated integration program has served up 190 million impressions to 66 million unique listeners (free of charge). Six percent of those who receive a push notification buy tickets in the moment, 32% buy within the next 30 days. More than 70% of those receiving the notification say they didn't know the event was happening and 85% of those who bought tickets hadn't been to the venue before.

How long will it take Ticketmaster to form a partnership with Spotify or Apple? What are the implications of algorithms homing in on most likely purchasers and why couldn't the offer include a flight to Las Vegas, a room, and dinner reservations?

The continued development of music distribution will be a springboard to more artists being discovered and touring, and fans purchasing a package while they're listening online. Imagine the impact on Las Vegas, as new generations of music fans flock to experience the best live music on the planet.

CHAPTER THIRTEEN

UP CLOSE AND PERSONAL

I arrived a bit early to Brit Floyd, a Pink Floyd tribute show, at The Joint. While listening to the melodic and psychedelic pre-show, I reflected on all the concerts I'd seen in Las Vegas. During the 18 years I worked at Thomas and Mack Center and Sam Boyd Stadium, I played a part in more than 500 of them. But my job wasn't to enjoy them. Rather, it was to make sure they were enjoyable—for the fans and bands. Only occasionally did I actually attend a show at one of the hotels or out of town.

In 2001, I left the 150 nights per year away from home for Las Vegas Events, where my job is to secure events, not manage them. Las Vegas Events, a private non-profit organization, was created in 1983 to aggressively compete to bring events to Las Vegas. Annually, we produce the Wrangler National Finals Rodeo and have secured and support another 40 events, including four conference basketball tournaments, NASCAR, the Rock and Roll Marathon, Electric Daisy Carnival, Life is Beautiful, USA Sevens Rugby, NBA Summer League, and World Cup Jumping and Dressage, to name a few. After making the transition from working nights to days, that left most of my nights free to enjoy all the music the Entertainment Capital of the World now offers. I have lots of choices, but my favorite venue is the theater.

There are more than 500 operating theaters around the country, some built in the 19th century.

In 1870, the Arch Street Opera House in Philadelphia opened, eventually changing its name to the Trocadero Theatre or "the Troc." Originally used for burlesque and vaudeville performances, the theater thrived as an art-house cinema through the '70s before making the transition to a dance club during the sweat-soaked mid-'80s. It was a short-lived phase, as it quickly became a popular destination in Philly for live music.

The Showbox in Seattle was established in 1939, lasting through some of music's most polarizing periods. In its 78 years of existence, it has featured everyone from Duke Ellington to the Ramones and Kanye West. It played a crucial role in the grunge era, helping to propel acts like Pearl Jam and Nirvana.

Inhabiting the 12-acre stretch of history that is Rockefeller Center, Radio City Music Hall opened two days after Christmas in 1932. The 6,000-seat venue has seen more than 300 million people pass through its doors for theater, films, and concerts. The Great Stage is 60 feet tall and 100 feet wide, covered by the gorgeous gold curtain, undoubtedly one of the world's most visually impressive indoor concert halls.

The Greek Theatre in L.A. was built by Samuel Tilden Norton in 1929 in the image of a Hellenic theater. The award-winning 6,000-seat venue is hidden inside the picturesque Griffith Park, the second-largest city park in California.

A second L.A. venue, the 2,220-seat Wiltern Theater located on the western edge of the city, opened in 1931. It was originally built with the intention of hosting vaudeville productions, but has become arguably L.A.'s best live venue—and has been for at least 30 years.

A sacred place indeed, the Tabernacle opened over a century ago as the Broughton Tabernacle. The church remained popular in the Atlanta area until after the 1996 Olympics, when it was remodeled into a House of Blues. The original pipe organ can be seen behind the stage

The intimate 400-seat Troubadour has been home to the debut performances of an endless list of legends. Since its 1957 opening, the West Hollywood nightclub has created a storied history that includes the debut performances of Buffalo Springfield, Joni Mitchell, James Taylor, Metallica, and Pearl Jam.

Many concert posters plaster the walls of the 1,150-seat Fillmore in San Francisco. Dating back to the '60s, the Fillmore was instrumental in launching careers, including legends like Carlos Santana, the Grateful Dead, Otis Redding, Jimi Hendrix, and Cream.

Thomas G. Ryman built the 2,362-seat Ryman Auditorium in Nashville for $100,000 in 1892. At first, it was for earmarked dignitaries—the Metropolitan Opera, John Philip Sousa, Charlie Chaplin, and Harry Houdini. In 1943, the Grand Ole Opry radio station moved to the Ryman. Since then, it's gone on to welcome just about every country star, from

Hank Williams and Johnny Cash to Taylor Swift. Chicago promoter Andy Cirzan calls it "the legendary mother church."

For all those years, while cities across the country were redeveloping or building theaters, the Las Vegas "theater" was a casino showroom. In this copycat town, they were all essentially the same: three or four tiers, with banquet tables on the floor and perhaps the first tier, booths for two or four people on the next tier or two, and regular theater seating against the back wall or in the balcony. The largest showrooms could accommodate 1,000 guests (Caesars' Circus Maximus sat 1,100) for dinner shows. Locals and visitors could dress up to see revues like *Minsky's Burlesque, Folies Bergere*, and *Jubilee!* or take in headliners large and small, from Frank Sinatra to Jayne Mansfield (performing, so to speak, with her husband Mickey Haggarty, a former Mr. Universe). For live music, it was the intimate lounges—up to three acts a night going into the wee hours, at least one of them a residency, such as the Mary Kaye Trio, the Treniers, or the iconic Louis Prima and Keely Smith (with Sam Butera on the sax).

What Vegas lacked for decades was live touring music—other than rare one-offs in the Convention Center Rotunda, at least until the advent of the bona fide theater at the Aladdin.

Aladdin Theater for the Performing Arts

The Aladdin Theater for the Performing Arts was attached to a hotel that couldn't quite find its way. Consequently, the theater didn't live up to the hype of its opening.

From its inception in 1962 when the inventor of the game Yahtzee, Edwin Lowe, opened the $12 million 450-room Tally-Ho Motel without a casino to when it was transformed into Planet Hollywood in 2007, the Aladdin Hotel-Casino had one of the most checkered histories of all the properties on the Strip. It weathered a revolving door of owners, several bankruptcies, mob infiltration and skimming, several expansions and remodels, an implosion, and a new megaresort and mall built from scratch, until finally the Aladdin was bought for pennies on the dollar by Planet Hollywood, which subsequently sold out to Caesars Entertainment.

Through most it, from 1969 to the present, the 7,000-seat Theater for the Performing Arts Center, now known as Axis, has remained Las Vegas' original theater and concert venue.

Gary Naseef promoted more than 100 shows there in the late 1970s, from Alice Cooper and Leo Sayer to Emmylou Harris and Joan Baez, from Donovan and Supertramp to Parliament Funkadelic. Post-Naseef, between 1980 and 1983, the theater, almost by default, continued to book major concerts. The Convention Center was rarely available and the Sahara was out of the concert business. Frank Zappa, Van Halen, Grateful Dead, Elton John, Journey, ELO, Tom Petty, and Rush were among the 15 concerts the venue hosted per year with promoters like Decaeser-Engler, Beaver Productions, and Feyline.

When Thomas and Mack Center opened in 1983, concerts mostly migrated over, but some events, too small or inappropriate for a cavernous 18,500-seat arena, continued to be held at the theater.

And even in 1986, when the hotel-casino was shut down for more than a year after evidence surfaced of hidden mob ownership, the theater kept on trucking, putting on a dozen concerts—Uriah Heep, Journey, J. Geils, and of course the Dead.

HC Rowe grew up in Clearwater, Florida, where he earned a business degree. He started a small construction company specializing in renovations and ran that until the soaring interest rates of the early 1980s forced him to adjust his life ambitions.

He moved to Las Vegas and one of the first people he met was Steve Wynn. Rowe recalls the meeting. "The first job I took was as a lifeguard at the Golden Nugget. When I met Steve Wynn, he was telling me about his grand plans for building a theater and to sign Sinatra. I said, 'That's great! I've got a construction background.' When he started building, he needed a stage manager and asked me if I wanted the job. Of course I said yes and I stayed with him for 10 years."

At the same time, Rowe kept busy working production for the newly opened Thomas and Mack Center installing spotlights. Rowe remembers the pre-opening days at Thomas and Mack Center. "There was a lot of energy and excitement there, but also a lot of inexperience, including my own. I was extremely excited about being involved in live entertainment. We built the platforms, installed the spotlights, hung trusses for rigging and cabling, and did a little bit of wiring. I got called a lot."

Rowe was involved in the arena's grand-opening show, "Christmas with Class," which included Frank Sinatra, Dean Martin, and Diana Ross. "All the riders [all the things a band needs written into the contract] came in for lighting," recalls Rowe, "but the equipment we needed wasn't available in Las Vegas. Someone got hold of Steve Wynn, who got hold of Kenny Rogers. He was out on tour, so they slotted their production trucks to come to Thomas and Mack and drop off lights and sound. That kind of stuff doesn't happen today."

In 1993 at the four-year-old Mirage, Steve Wynn erected a temporary tent for the first of nearly a dozen Cirque productions that would appear on the Strip. He'd also sold the Golden Nugget, leaving Rowe looking for the next big thing. Rowe was hired on at the Aladdin.

"I was responsible for getting the theater up and running after a bankruptcy. I started meeting with Bill Silva, Barry Fey, and Danny Zelisko. It was very difficult to get people to play there. Vegas was looked on as a place where your career was on the backslide. We started off pretty slow, but once we got a handful of shows, we started getting some traction."

This was new territory for Rowe, but he learned quickly and, with multiple promoters, booked a lot of classic-rock shows. The stage was only 32 inches off the floor. To this day, if you sit in one of the 110 seats in the "golden circle," it's like watching a show in someone's living room.

"What a great hall. You really forget you're in a casino when you're inside," says Danny Zelisko, who promoted his share of concerts there.

But the theater had only 7,000 seats versus 18,500 at the Thomas and Mack Center and 15,000 at the newly opened MGM Grand Garden.

In 1998, the Aladdin was sold to a new owner, who imploded everything but the theater—symbolic of how it was defined more by the diverse concerts in demand at the time than any integrated plan with the hotel and casino.

The Aladdin reopened in 2000, which included a multi-million-dollar renovation of the theater. The first celebrity to appear at the new Aladdin's Performing Arts Center was Enrique Iglesias. But the general contractor for the renovation sued the Aladdin for defaulting on a $7.5 million payment. Even then, the theater continued a long tradition of seeming to be oblivious to what was happening around it. It started right back in booking an array of concerts, including Prince, Whitney Houston with Bobby Brown, Sting, Lionel Richie, Tom Petty, Stevie Nicks, and Alicia Keys. In 2005, Vegoose did four "After Dark" shows there, including the Meters, Dave Mathews with Tim Reynolds, and Trey Anastasio. Each year, however, the theater was doing fewer shows.

Axis Goes Pop

Jason Gastwirth is not your typical Las Vegas hotel executive. He grew up on Long Island, played piano and flute, graduated from Harvard, then earned an MBA from Stanford. Before landing in Vegas, he amassed experience in strategically aligning businesses. Looking to stay close to home while his wife pursued a cardiology fellowship in Scottsdale, he was offered and accepted a position as head of entertainment and casino marketing at the Venetian, which was looking for a high-level strategic thinker.

In 2009, Gastwirth joined George Maloof at the Palms as Chief Marketing Officer before he was offered another opportunity as Chief of Staff for Gary Loveman, CEO of Caesars Entertainment. He held that job for six months; then he was approached from within to manage Caesars' entertainment division.

Gastwirth jumped in, centralizing the company's 40 venues, before turning his attention to the theater at Planet Hollywood. He promoted a few shows—Journey, Linkin Park, Peter Gabriel, Nicki Minaj—before having an epiphany.

"I always felt that Britney Spears would be a great residency. We started down the road with Britney, in parallel with discussions with Base Entertainment [which had the contract to produce events in theater]. We secured capital to upgrade the theater and forged a partnership with Live Nation to be our co-promoter."

The original theater had an intimate feel, but to create a "Britney feel," the stage was extended, reducing the venue capacity to 4,600, then the floor in front of the stage was dug out to create a 600-capacity general-admission experience. Today, *Britney: A Piece of Me* is the permanent show at the renamed Axis at Planet Hollywood. Spears performs 50 shows per year.

"It became a property that has attracted younger people, which, for our portfolio, was very important," says Gastwirth. "We've seen a significant upside from what we're doing in the theater. We have record income from entertainment. We're a commercial promoter, not just a casino entertainment promoter. Caesars Entertainment, based on gross ticket revenue, is now the third largest live-entertainment promoter in the world."

After 50 years, the theater that has been home to more than 500 concerts, yet constantly burdened with a hotel that could not quite find its way, may have discovered its niche.

The Joint—Love All, Serve All

The average fan attends 2.5 concerts a year. It's a big occasion and expensive. Ask concert fans about their favorite type of venue and they'll almost always tell you that smaller is better. Their second choice is festivals where they get better value through seeing more bands and having a social experience. Their least preferable are arenas and stadiums.

Ironically, arenas and stadiums are where artists earn up to 70% of their income. In 1994, Vegas didn't have niche venues like the Pantages in L.A., the Fox Theater in Atlanta, the Beacon in New York, or Ryman Auditorium in Nashville. Understanding what Vegas lacked and not wanting to compete with stadium concerts and MGM Grand Garden, Peter Morton didn't want to just build a new music venue, but to brand a hotel around it.

The idea for the first Hard Rock Café was hatched in London in 1971, where Peter Morton was unable to find a good hamburger. He and fellow American Isaac Tigrett envisioned an American-themed diner with a rock-'n'-roll brand. In 1979, after Eric Clapton gifted the restaurant a guitar, the café began covering its walls with rock memorabilia. Since then, Hard Rock has amassed one of the largest collections of rock memorabilia in the world. Currently, 191 Hard Rock properties in 59 countries include 157 cafés, 22 hotels, and 11 casinos whose genuine rock memorabilia became an essential part of the décor and allure.

Morton and Tigrett's virtuosity wasn't in the Hard Rock's food, but its marketing, which began with T-shirts with a circular logo including Hard

Rock Café and the city where it was bought. Today, merchandise sales exceed food and beverage profits.

In 1990, Morton opened a Hard Rock Café on the corner of Paradise and Harmon in Las Vegas. It quickly became a popular spot for locals and visitors as its location, on the way in and out of the airport, kept the lines for merchandise and food out the door.

In the early '90s, the design of Las Vegas hotel-casinos was still aimed at the 50-plus customer. Morton envisioned attracting a much younger crowd that had passed on Las Vegas in the past. *Jubilee!* and Engelbert Humperdinck were out and Radiohead and Dylan were in.

Like Steve Wynn's creation the Mirage and Sheldon Adelson's convention-targeted Venetian, the Hard Rock Hotel became the template for more to come, including the Palms, Cosmopolitan, and SLS.

Vegas historian and culture critic David Schwartz puts this into perspective. "The hotel he opened in 1995 became a cultural icon and an indispensable link in the evolution of Las Vegas. Morton connected the city with a new generation, emphasized amenities and a branded lifestyle, and was the first to marry an international brand with a Las Vegas resort, something that other brands have found isn't so easy. It's clear that an adult vision of uninhibited fun was the path Las Vegas chose. Most of what's happened on the Strip since the end of the 1990s resonates with Morton's break-the-mold concept: a resort that catered to a younger and more affluent visitor, one who—and here's the revolutionary change—wasn't necessarily a gambler."

Everything in the original Hard Rock Hotel was like walking around the inside of a drum. The Center Bar was so crowded, you'd have thought they were selling $1 drinks. Restaurants, rock displays, slots, tables, everything surrounded the iconic bar. Loud rock music was ubiquitous and every square inch of the walls was decorated with "the world's greatest" collection of rock memorabilia.

It goes without saying that a Hard Rock Hotel in Las Vegas wouldn't be complete without a live-music joint. In fact, that was a good name for Las Vegas' first rustic 2,000-seat theater.

On March 10, 1995, the hotel opened with The Joint hosting an all-star evening: Guns N' Roses bassist Duff McKagan backing up Sheryl Crow, Duran Duran, Al Green, and Melissa Etheridge. The Eagles were next. A year earlier, they played Sam Boyd Stadium on their Hell Freezes Over tour. There was so much emotion in their stadium performances, because it was the first time they'd been together in 14 years. Watching them a year later in the ambience of this new intimate 2,000-seat bar reminded me of everything I love about this city.

In the first incarnation of The Joint, the entry was on the exterior of the circular casino. From the entry, you could see the whole intimate venue, including the stage, bar, and three levels of seats. The variations of seating, from general admission to reserved, created a tight custom feel to each concert. The sound and acoustics were everything you'd expect from a shrine built to rock 'n' roll. And of course, the memorabilia! I was always proud to see the poster displayed from the original 1991 Grateful Dead-Santana shows at Sam Boyd Stadium.

In all, The Joint hosted more than 600 diverse concerts in the original venue—James Brown, Johnny Cash. Alicia Keys, Radiohead, Billy Joel, Guns N' Roses, Coldplay, Metallica, and of course The Rolling Stones, who played the original venue three times.

In 2006, Morton sold the Vegas Hard Rock to Morgan's Hotel Group, which invested $750 million in 875 new rooms in two towers, expanded the meeting and casino space, and replaced the original Joint with a venue with double the capacity. The bigger hotel-casino footprint eliminated the intimate cylindrical layout and eventually the Center Bar.

John Meglen of Concerts West AEG Live recalls, "When we first got involved with Hard Rock, they were building a 2,500-seater. We basically stopped them and said, 'Not only is that a bad move, but if that's what you're doing, we're not interested.' We talked them into a 4,000-seater.

"When you're averaging $150 a ticket, playing at a 4,000-seater, you gross $600,000," says Meglen. "Compare that to a $75 average ticket and 8,000 seats," again referring to the fact that Las Vegas venues can command a higher-priced ticket. "It gives you the same gross. Remember how we used to say, 'In Las Vegas, a $100 bill looks like a $10 bill anywhere else?'"

The man most familiar with the new Joint, Bobby Reynolds, was born and raised in southern Westchester, 20 miles north of Manhattan. He didn't know there was a business behind live music until he started his career. Studio 54 opened in New York in 1977 as a haven for celebrities and excess. In 1993, it was completely different, a 400-seat club called the Ritz and it was 17-year-old Reynold's first job. He did everything—security, runner, production assistant, whatever it was, it was his job. Guns N' Roses, Brett Newby, Blues Traveler, and a new band, Dave Mathews, all played the Ritz while Reynolds was cutting his teeth.

Reynolds moved to Vermont and enrolled in a military academy, Norwich College. His job options were washing dishes or Student Affairs. In Student Affairs, he promoted his first show: He convinced the military to book its first event, a movie. Within three months, he had an office and a phone and convinced the conservative campus to promote comedy, then bands. Reynolds had found his calling, which didn't require a college degree.

His first internship was at QBQ Talent Agency, where "internship" meant a cheap entry-level do-everything-for-nothing job. "I was earning $200 a month and the Metro North Train fare was $176 a month. I was the happiest slave that's ever lived."

While at QBQ, Reynolds got to know Jim Maloney, who was leaving to go work at House of Blues (HOB). In those days, House of Blues venues were in Boston, Chicago, New Orleans, and L.A. In 1997, Reynolds moved from New York to Myrtle Beach, South Carolina, for his first fully paid job as an assistant on the HOB opening team, where he moved up the gopher ladder for a couple of years, until Kevin Morrow, a good friend and vice president of entertainment for HOB, offered him a life-changing job. Within a few days, Reynolds had packed everything he had into two boxes and was on a one-way flight to Los Angeles. He was still an assistant, but headed to the second biggest live-music market in the country.

Reynolds recalls one of his first nights on the job. "A band called Quest was booked three nights. I was shadowing Kevin, who had a VIP table on the balcony rail where he hosted agents, managers, and celebrities. At Kevin's table were other agents, Chris Rock, and Shaquille O'Neal. I was, like, this is unbelievable. I'm a New Yorker. Quest is playing three nights sold out and I'm standing by my boss like the Secret Service." Reynolds started to book local bands four nights a month.

In 2001, Reynolds left HOB in L.A. for HOB Orlando where he became a junior talent buyer. In 2005, he got an offer from AEG to move to Chicago, where he booked and promoted shows all over the Midwest.

In 2007, AEG got the contract for buying talent for the Hard Rock's new 4,000-seat The Joint. When Reynolds heard that his name was being tossed around, he reacted like any man who'd been on the 15-year promoter-development plan: "Oh, man. I want to kill this!" He explains, "The Joint was our competitor. When I was working for House of Blues, I got to know The Joint very very well. I knew the Hard Rock very very well. I was a customer and I'm still a customer. And to book that room was, like, you got to be kidding me. This is amazing. Amazing! I started booking it."

Soon, opportunity knocked again when John Meglen asked how Reynolds would feel about moving to Vegas. Reynolds recalls, "It probably took me, I don't know, five seconds to say, 'Hell yeah!'"

That year, 2007, wasn't the best time to be in the entertainment business. It wasn't the best time to be in any business. While Las Vegas was about to suffer in a big way from the recession, Reynolds and The Joint managed to hold their own. The results set the foundation for Reynolds' formula for success. "It's simple. Show up every day and really give a shit. We went to all the shows. We met with the radio stations, the papers, the writers and tastemakers, long before blogging was as prolific as it was. I was at all our shows. To this day, I still am. I can speak intelligently about a lot of events, because I *go* to them. If I'm not producing the show, I go first and foremost as a fan. But I always go with an eye on what I'd do differently, what I'd do better. Oh, that's a good idea that I'm going to steal. I'm going to try to integrate that idea into some things that we do.

"You'll never convince me that doesn't make a difference. We won a lot of our fights with a much duller sword than our competitors."

Reynolds has arrived. For AEG, he books The Joint, Brooklyn Bowl, T-Mobile Arena, Mandalay Bay Events Center, and MGM Grand Garden. In all, he books upwards of 150 shows a year and is now, finally, well-compensated.

"In this business, you make nothing until you make something," says Reynolds. "Some of my best friends are big agents in L.A. We used to mess around together when I was driving my Saturn and they were driving their Toyota Corollas in '99. We were making $24,000 a year, living in Los Angeles, out 8 nights a week, checking out bands, checking out venues, checking out shows, and having a blast. And these guys were making zero and they sign a band and, instead of making zero, they make two bucks and that blows up and now they're doing really well."

Unlike an arena show, AEG Live doesn't pay an artist a guarantee for a single show. For example, an artist like Elton John, in the 4,000-seat setup, won't make as much as he would playing for one night in an 18,000-seat arena. But how many times can you play that arena in a year? Once? Twice? Add your production and travel expenses. The 4,000-seat Vegas option is: Do 50 shows and get paid $400,000 a night. And you can still do the arena appearance or two.

Chas Smith, Hard Rock vice president of operations, believes the partnership is strong. "Bobby knows what we need to drive the property. We talk like we're married sometimes, yelling at each other or like, 'Dude, thanks so much for the great show!' Bobby's smart. He knows the demos that work. Like booking Metallica or a Def Leppard residency, that's right in our wheelhouse."

Personally, Chas Smith prefers a harder rock in his concert cocktail. But like most production managers, it's the satisfaction of a great show, not his own fan experience, that motivates him. Since March 2000, he has worked his way from stagehand to operations director. "The original Joint was tight and intimate," he says. "We once did a private party for billionaire David Bonderman on his 60th birthday for 500 and tightened the room up further. Mellencamp opened for The Rolling Stones."

What sets The Joint apart from every other theater in Vegas and the country is the lore. From the time you enter the Hard Rock, you're immersed in rock 'n' roll history. And the collection grows with every performance. "We're doing a Neal Schon case for Journey. We're taking Steven Smith's drum kit and putting it in a separate display," says Smith. Jerry Garcia's ponytail is at the front door.

The new Joint retains the intimacy, charm, and authentic rock experience of the original, but its 4,000-capacity means bigger and more acts. There are three levels, all with great sound, a tiered floor (more than twice the size of the former) to ensure everyone standing can see the show, three massive bars, seven high-end suites, and a great load-in for the band and crew. The stage is enormous and anchored on each side by two huge video screens, giving the major acts AEG books plenty of space for arena-size productions. For more intimate shows, there's an intelligent curtaining system, which takes it from 4,000 capacity down to 3,000.

On February 7, 2009, the first incarnation of The Joint closed with Mötley Crüe. The new Joint opened April 17, 2009, with a concert by Avenged Sevenfold, followed by Kenny Chesney, The Killers, Paul McCartney, and Bon Jovi. In the seven years to follow, AEG booked as many acts (600) as they did in the first 14, primarily due to the addition of a steady stream of residencies, like Keith Urban, Mötley Crüe, Guns N' Roses, Def Leppard, Prince, Kiss, Rascal Flatts, and Journey.

House of Blues—Unity in Diversity

Standing on the stairway that leads to the floor, I stopped and listened to the fans who'd purchased about 200 four-seat tables. They and the 500 or so on the floor seemed to be at a "happy hour" in which Joe Walsh was going to eventually perform. The conversation was as loud as the show. And therein lies the difference between HOB and Pearl, the Park, or the Colosseum.

With the success of The Joint, live music was paying attention to what was happening in Las Vegas. The second nationally branded music venue to open in Las Vegas did it in a new hotel-casino, Mandalay Bay.

To mark the opening of the House of Blues, Dan Aykroyd, Jim Belushi, and John Goodman—and 300 friends—made a grand entrance astride their Harleys. Roger Smith with *Rolling Stone* was there to catch the action: "All that horsepower couldn't upstage the event's real spectacle: Bob Dylan and Bono doing an encore of 'Knockin' on Heaven's Door.' As Dylan's band began, the U2 singer walked on, grabbed a six-string, and freestyled a bit: 'Here we are in the House of Blues/Black tie and cowboy shoes/Not much to win, but a whole lot to lose/Feel like I'm knockin' on heaven's door." It was a roof-raising finish to a 75-minute set that began just after midnight and included "Gotta Serve Somebody," the new "Million Miles," and the Grateful Dead's "Friend of the Devil." Grand opening, indeed.

While live music is just a piece of Mandalay Bay's brand, the HOB is an anchor that still rocks today.

The House of Blues grew out of founder Isaac Tigrett's (co-founder of the Hard Rock Café) affection for the distinct American art form known as the blues. One of Tigrett's goals was to introduce the world to the music of the rural South, including the blues, rhythm and blues, gospel, jazz, and roots-based rock. The first House of Blues opened on November 26, 1992, in Cambridge, Massachusetts. The original partners were Dan Akyroyd, Aerosmith, Paul Schaffer, River Phoenix, and James Belushi. When Mandalay Bay opened, its centerpiece for live music was the sixth rendition of HOB.

What sets House of Blues apart from other Las Vegas theaters is its programming and restaurant. In addition to producing 100 concerts annually, it's booked solid with unique events like its Sunday Gospel Brunch, Nothing but the Blues, and Midday Studio Sessions. Gospel Brunch is so popular, there are two performances a day. The shows feature local talent performing both traditional and contemporary Gospel songs to an all-you-can-eat buffet with Southern specialties like the signature chicken and waffles. And if you're in the mood, you just might end up on stage waving a napkin and dancing off some of that cuisine.

A funky folk-art atmosphere in the restaurant features slow-smoked St. Louis ribs and shrimp with crispy-fried grit cakes.

The sightlines in the theater are unique, thanks to the small floor, while the U-shaped balcony sits right on top of the stage, giving fans a tight and intimate view. Markings with historical significance (of the HOB culture) cover every inch of the venue. HOB is dedicated to educating and celebrating the history of Southern culture and African-American artistic contributions to music and art. The "crazy-quilt" stage curtains pay respect to enslaved Africans who used the underground railroad as a passage to freedom; it was constructed in an abstract arrangement and took 1,000 hours to complete. Under every stage in the House of Blues is a metal box filled with Delta Mississippi mud. This box is welded to the structure on the stage to ensure that all artists have the roots and the spirit of the South planted beneath their feet.

Juke joints are a major inspiration for the House of Blues' look and feel. Many Southern juke joints are full of hand-painted signs and décor; in HOB Las Vegas, a highly eclectic collection of art, posters, furniture, wall murals, and other sorts of decoration are displayed from the entry to the top of the stage with the slogan, "Unity in Diversity."

The Music Room (main hall) provides fans the unique experience of viewing acts they might have seen as arena and stadium headliners. Upwards of 1,500 diverse acts have played the hall, including Eminem, James Brown, Guns N' Roses, Britney Spears, Limp Bizkit, and Kid Rock. After a two-year residency at the 4,000-seat Joint, Santana settled into one at HOB.

On July 5, 2006, Live Nation acquired House of Blues. As a division of Live Nation, the company operates the 11 clubs throughout America.

The Pearl

After a strong 10-year run with his first hotel-casino, the Fiesta in North Las Vegas, New Mexico-bred George Maloof envisioned a spot on the Strip. Instead, he opted for 25 acres a mile east, across from the Gold Coast and kitty-corner to the Rio. After all, Peter Morton had started something at the Hard Rock a mile east of the Strip. A mile west of the Strip, Maloof would take it to what Malcolm Gladwell, in his book of the same name, calls a "tipping point."

Gladwell describes a key component to the tipping point: "The success of any kind of social epidemic is heavily dependent on the involvement of people with a particular and rare set of social gifts."

George Maloof was raised in Albuquerque with three brothers, Joe, Gavin, and Phil, and a sister, Adrienne. He listened to some country, but mostly rock. The first album he bought was *Led Zeppelin IV*. He went to lots of concerts promoted by Bill Graham, Evening Star, and Feyline.

His father owned a Coors beer distribution that covered all of New Mexico. Maloof started work as a 10-year-old in the beer warehouse, eventually delivering beer as he matured. He grew to love the action and excitement he felt on the family trips to Vegas. In 1977, he went to UNLV and majored in hotel management. As soon as he graduated, he began working on his dream of owning a hotel, buying 25 acres in North Las Vegas and going after financing. Raising the capital took longer than expected, so he opened a casino in Central City, Colorado that provided a huge learning curve for entering the competitive Las Vegas market.

On December 14, 1994, the Fiesta opened and just as quickly, Maloof realized it was too small. In 1996, he added a buffet and 700 slot machines. In 1997, he doubled the size of the casino. In 1999, he pulled out all the stops, spending $26 million for a food court with six restaurants and "the world's largest" tequila bar at Garduño's Margarita Factory. He opened Roxy's Pipe Organ Pizzeria, which featured a huge 70-year-old pipe organ that was once part of the Roxy Theater in New York. Maloof remembers the organ. "My uncle collects pipe organs. He bought the original organ from the Roxy Theater in New York. We opened a big concert hall and played the organ every night while people ate all the pizza they could."

In 1996, he was already dreaming of his next property. In 2000, a conversation with Stations about a joint venture in Green Valley turned into an offer to buy the Fiesta. That purchase gave Maloof the funding he needed to open the hotel he'd been envisioning, the Palms.

Maloof spent six months writing a marketing plan. His first thought was to do another Fiesta, but being close to the Strip, he landed on a hybrid. Rather than an architectural theme, the new property would fill a specific niche: nightclubs and entertainment to draw visitors from the Strip, but good-value gambling and dining to attract locals during the day.

In 2000, Las Vegas' hotels took a defensive posture when dealing with the press. The Palms changed that. Norm Clarke, a noted Las Vegas gossip columnist, arrived in 1999 and spent a year trying to get people to talk to him. Maloof embraced Clarke. "Nobody would talk to the guy. I helped him. He helped me. We kind of scratched each other's back."

Macy Gray opened the Palms on November 15, 2001.

Maloof reveals his marketing strategy. "I planned to focus on celebrities. We wanted to find a TV show that would promote the property." Then MTV came along with "Real World," the first reality-TV show in which eight twenty-somethings live together in a new city, in front of cameras 24 hours a day. An early season, 2002, was filmed from a Sky Suite atop the Palms hotel tower, which had a $10,000 room rate per night. It was like a half-hour commercial 20 times a week. The casino was also shown in Britney Spears' music video for her hit song "Everytime" and in Eminem's music video "We Made You"; the Palms' Fantasy Tower was the setting for the shooting of Katy Perry's music video "Waking up in Vegas."

It's hard to believe, but in 2001, Las Vegas had no real nightlife as we know it today—until Rain at the Palms. Not one hotel on the Strip had a nightclub. Paul Oakenfold did the first Las Vegas DJ residency at Rain. But the club wasn't limited to DJ's. Pink, Kiss, No Doubt, and even hip-hop artist Snoop Dog played there. Today, DJ-driven nightclubs and day clubs account for a huge portion of non-gaming revenues. Las Vegas now consistently dominates the top-10 highest-grossing nightclubs in the world.

The Palms was an immediate hit with television, celebrities, visitors, and locals, which created a pleasant problem: demand. Demand for more rooms, more restaurants, more shows. "We were doing shows in Rain and getting so busy as a nightclub that it wasn't mixing right. That's when the idea for a theater developed. But the vision wasn't to build just any theater. Let's build a 'pearl.' Let's make it the nicest live venue in the world," says Maloof proudly. "We didn't model it after another theater. We wanted every seat to be perfect, with a good mix of VIP seats. No obstructions. Nothing that would affect the experience of the guest. We wanted a flat floor so you could sit or stand. And we wanted exceptional sound."

The three-level Pearl's capacity ranges from 1,100 to 2,500; no seat is farther than 120 feet from the stage. The lighting, video, sound system, and acoustics rival that of larger venues. There are 18 private and semi-private suites that offer exclusive bars, lounges, and restrooms.

The theater is also hard-wired to the Studio, a state-of-the-art recording facility that enables the artists who perform at The Pearl to easily create albums live from Las Vegas. Céline Dion, the Killers, Britney Spears, Maroon 5, KISS, Pink, Panic at the Disco, and 100 other acts have recorded in the studio.

In 2005, the new $600 million Fantasy Tower opened with a number of one-of-a-kind suites. My favorite (it's not exactly in my budget; I was there for a reception) is the two-story 10,000-square-foot suite that encompasses the only basketball court in a hotel; it's fully loaded with a locker room, scoreboard, and multi-screen entertainment system. On the 48th floor of the Fantasy Tower was the nightclub, Moon, with an outdoor view of the Strip.

The Pearl's grand opening, on November 15, 2005, was a celebrity-studded affair with Gwen Stefani, Avril Lavigne, Morissey, Goo Goo Dolls, and the Deftones. In the first year, The Pearl did 70-plus concerts, including Evanescence, KISS, Tool, Foo Fighters, Fergie, Alicia Keys, and Smashing Pumpkins. The theater stayed hot the next three years, averaging 70 diverse shows a year, like Def Leppard, Steely Dan, STP, Backstreet Boys, Lady Gaga, One Republic, and Usher.

Maloof scored a major coup when Pearl hosted the 2007 MTV Video Music Awards. MTV's two-hour show featured 25 acts, including Britney Spears, Justin Timberlake, Kanye West, Kid Rock, and Hillary Duff. The September production enhanced the already-hot Palms brand, which now included a steady stream of celebrities and concerts, the "Real World" episodes, and a plethora of NBA players, thanks to the family's ownership of the Sacramento Kings.

Like many other Las Vegas companies, Maloof and the Palms rode the economic bubble, building a third tower with 600 units marketed primarily as second-residence condominiums. Palms Place opened in May 2008 with typical Maloof pomp and circumstance. But the party was bittersweet. The U.S. housing crash, which started a tsunami of economic catastrophes across the country, had already taken its toll on Las Vegas. It got worse before it got better and it got as bad as it gets in Las Vegas.

The heavy debt load was too much for Maloof. A 2011 restructuring gave private-equity firms TPG Capital and Leonard Green and Partner each a 49% share, leaving the Maloofs with 2% ownership. Like many hotels that survived the meltdown, entertainment in The Pearl was scaled back.

Billy Conn joined Pearl in 2011. Conn grew up on the south side of Chicago in a family that was always jazzed up. The records of Dizzy Gillespie, Maynard Ferguson, Buddy Rich, and many others filled the house with music. But like most kids of the time, Led Zeppelin, Aerosmith, and Hendrix were on Billy's own phonograph.

At 15, he started waiting in line at Chicago Stadium to buy tickets for concerts that he upsold for as much as double. In addition to the profit, he found himself in the front 15 rows for Led Zeppelin, Styx, and Rush. A chance meeting with Chicago photographer Dean Simmon piqued his interest in concert photography. Conn honed his photography craft in

Chicago venues like the Aragon and Beginnings before hitting the road to do tour photography.

In 1993, he moved to Las Vegas to work special events at Caesars—Wrestlemania, the Davis Cup, outdoor NHL games, and the infamous November Bowe vs. Holyfield fight where a parachutist crashed the party. Conn recalls that debacle. "You see this guy buzzing in with his shirt off. The parachute gets caught in the ring. He stops the seventh round and lands, from the back, on Rock Newman, Riddick Bowe's manager. Newman's wife is six months pregnant and sitting next to Louis Farrakhan. They think it's an assassination attempt. They bring out the brick phones. They beat that guy to a pulp."

Conn had a part in opening New York-New York in 1997 and the reopening of the Aladdin in 1999. Later, Conn coordinated corporate shows for Paris, then moved over to M Resort, and wound up at the Hard Rock where he worked with Neil Moffat to bring dance music to The Joint, before migrating over to the Palms.

In 2011, George Maloof was gone from the Palms and Conn was challenged with programming The Pearl. At the time, his only competition was with his former venue, The Joint, but The Pearl's ambience and liberal position on the length of the show made it artist friendly.

Conn turned to Danny Zelisko. In 2011 and 2012, Conn and Zelisko averaged 50 shows a year, with a focus on classic rock: Steely Dan, Deep Purple, Steve Winwood, Eddie Vedder, Procol Harum, Alice Cooper, Joe Bonnamossa, Bonnie Raitt, Jackson Browne, John Prine, ZZ Top, Chicago, and John Fogerty. In 2013, they did 70 shows. Conn also did shows with Live Nation and AEG.

In May 2016, local Las Vegas giant Station Casinos announced it was purchasing the Palms for $316 million. Station has booked every range of live music at its 11 hotels. The Pearl will continue to be a jewel.

Brooklyn Bowl

Peter Shapiro is a rare, thriving, independent promoter in an industry ruled by behemoths like Live Nation and AEG. An upper-middle-class New York City kid, his career began to take shape after attending a Grateful Dead concert in 1993. It motivated him to follow the Dead and make the documentary, *And Miles to Go Before I Sleep—On Tour with the Grateful Dead*, a movie about the Deadheads.

In 1996, Shapiro bought his first club, Wetlands Preserve, in the Tribeca neighborhood in lower Manhattan, which featured jam bands, hip-hop artists, and community activists. The club barely broke even, but the exercise forged new relationships. A former ironworks foundry in Williamsburg, Brooklyn, was the site for the original Brooklyn Bowl. It took two years to construct before it opened on July 7, 2009. Shapiro recalls, "It was a huge barn, no electricity, barely any plumbing. We just said, 'This is it.' You don't often find barns like that, even in the outer boroughs."

The 600-capacity venue quickly drew rave reviews for its great food, run by the popular city-wide chain Blue Ribbon. The bars served only draft beers brewed in Brooklyn. In 2010, it was reported the establishment was the biggest seller of Brooklyn-based beer.

Many major acts, including Guns N' Roses, Elvis Costello, the Roots, and RJD2 have performed there. It's the busiest concert venue in the city and sells tickets mainly to locals. In its short history, Brooklyn Bowl has averaged 100 shows a year, including John Legend, Jane's Addiction, Robert Plant, the Avett Brothers, My Morning Jacket, Kanye West, Beck, and Spoon.

On March 8, 2014, Shapiro opened his second Brooklyn Bowl in the new LINQ Promenade on the Las Vegas Strip, an open-air retail, dining, and entertainment district located between the Quad and Flamingo hotels. The 80,000-square-foot venue has two stories, a capacity of 2,000, 32 bowling lanes, and six bars. The 40-by-26 stage is huge for the size of venue and the Bowl has great sound, lights, sightlines, and crowd flow and friendly employees. It's the busiest concert venue in the city and, even though it's on the Strip, it sells tickets mainly to locals. From hip-hop to metal, jam bands to classic rock, Brooklyn Bowl is super-eclectic. In its short history, the venue is averaging 100 shows a year.

A large part of Brooklyn Bowl's charm is that it's not in a casino. Not having to walk past smokers at row after row of slot machines to get to a concert venue is a nice change. And while it's a show room first, you might stumble onto a cool funk band from New Orleans while you're bowling with your friends, drinking some ice-cold beer, and polishing off an order of legendary Blue Ribbon fried chicken, featured on the Food Network and in every entertainment and culinary magazine in Vegas.

Entering Brooklyn Bowl, you ascend a staircase where you're treated to a visual backdrop that has a carny/rocker hangout feel with distressed wood, industrial metals, and vintage finishes. There are several outdoor patios, lounges, dining rooms, and VIP spaces. A creepy collection of antique knock-down punks from an old carnival keeps watch as diners chow down on fried pickles and slurp ales.

The bowling lanes are spread out over two floors, each with a great view of the stage, and table service is more like a nightclub than a bowling alley. "Bowling doesn't distract from the show, because the pins are essentially silent," says Tony Lizzio, the Bowl's sound and video director.

Peter Shapiro also created the four-day Lockn' Music Festival in Virginia, opened a third Brooklyn Bowl in London next to O2 Arena, reopened the Capitol Theater in Port Chester, NY, and enticed the Grateful Dead back after a 20-year hiatus with three sold-out stadium shows.

Says the Dead's Phil Lesh, who played the Lockn' Festival, "Pete thinks like a musician. He understands the spirit of the music."

"Pete is the reincarnation of the '60s and '70s entrepreneurs. He's as close as we have to Bill Graham," says Steven Van Zandt of Springsteen's E Street Band.

Chelsea

Rehan Choudhry is first-generation American. In 1970, as soon as his parents got their medical degrees, they moved to the United States from their one-bedroom 400-square-foot apartment in Pakistan—which they shared with six other people. They did their residencies in Chicago and Houston and lived in Sioux City, Iowa, before moving to Washington, D.C.

Choudhry's father adopted American music, attending concerts for all the top bands—Pink Floyd, Led Zeppelin, Hendrix, The Rolling Stones, Dylan. "Every night when I woke up crying as a baby, my dad came in, turned on Pink Floyd, and carried me around until I fell asleep," Choudhry explains how he got into music. "When I started playing my first guitar, a red Fender Stratocaster, at 12, I was learning Hendrix and Zeppelin songs, not New Kids on the Block."

At 14, he went to his first music festival. The HFS-tival was held every summer from 1990 through 2006 in D.C.'s RFK Stadium. Rehan experienced the festival in 1994 and 1995 where he saw 25 bands for $25. "We camped out in front of Tower Records each year for 24 hours. The show was general admission, so the all-night was the only way to get in before it sold out."

Choudhry continues, "I remember the feeling of being around that many people with that much energy and that much love for music. I had no idea there were this many people that dressed, looked, acted, and liked music the way I did. Going to a concert is like seeing a movie. You go into the theater, you sit down, it performs, it ends, you leave. The festival environment was different. This was being part of a subculture that nobody knew existed until they got there. This was a defining moment in my life. I just wouldn't realize it for several years."

After earning an MBA at Vanderbilt, Choudhry received an offer from Caesars Entertainment in Atlantic City to run marketing and business development.

His first event was the 2009 Food Network, Atlantic City Food and

A Gambling City in Decline

Rehan Choudhry explains his view of the fall of Atlantic City. "Instead of doubling down on diversifying the experience of the Boardwalk, hotels milked existing customers and stopped reinvesting in their properties. Some of the casinos had the same carpet for 30 years. Why reinvest in these properties when you're raking in $30 million a year in taxable revenue? They were crushing it. There's absolutely no reason to reinvest unless it becomes a competitive environment. They didn't believe it was going to become a competitive environment—that surrounding states like Pennsylvania, Delaware, and New York would approve casino gambling. The year I got there, it declined 8%. The year I left, it declined 22%."

Wine Festival, a four-day affair with six chefs, 115 vendors, and a tasting village. He went on to produce a tennis exhibition with Venus Williams, Andy Roddick, and Pete Sampras, a figure skating event with Nancy Kerrigan and every major figure skater, a fashion show with Hugo Boss, and the first gay and lesbian festival in A.C. "The idea was to make Atlantic City known as a lifestyle destination," he says.

In his three years in Atlantic City, he learned a lot. But the city was in decline.

In 2010, Choudhry's "lifestyle-events" strategy caught the attention of John Unwin, CEO of the soon-to-open Cosmopolitan in Las Vegas. Unwin offered him the entertainment-director position. A month later, he was in Las Vegas.

"I'd never run entertainment before. I'd never booked a concert before," recalls Choudhry. "Worse, when I got out there, they had no entertainment strategy. They had no sense of what entertainment was going to look like."

They did know, however, what it *wasn't* going to look like—live music.

Choudhry wasn't swayed. His plan was 98% music.

Choudhry's perspective on the market was that residencies were dated. There's only one Céline. The market can't bear another theatrical show of any scale. But no one was promoting frequency music, different low-cost acts booked every week. His idea was that Cosmopolitan would be an incubator for the next-generation Célines. The three "incubator" venues had 100-250 capacities and were right on the casino floor. Book & Stage, Chandelier, and Bond Bar booked bands that cost anywhere from $1,000 to $2,500 a night, two shows a night for four nights.

Choudhry also proposed two big concert venues: the Boulevard Pool for 4,000 people, which overlooked the Strip, and the Chelsea, which was just a ballroom at the time.

The budget for the grand-opening concert was $30 million; the owners, Deutsche Bank, wanted to make a splash. With a $30 million budget, it was more like a tsunami! Jay Z and Coldplay co-headlined the (drained and covered) Boulevard Pool and the Chelsea Ballroom. Beyoncé was a surprise special guest. Kanye was a surprise special guest. John Mayer showed up and played two songs with Jay-Z. The dinner before the show featured Florence Welch from Florence and Machine and Ben Folds Five.

The budget also included Brandon Flowers, the Black Keys, the Strokes, and Mumford and Sons. Those who were there experienced one of the greatest Las Vegas shows ever.

While the opening was off the charts, many elements of the venues made producing concerts difficult. Choudhry redesigned the venues.

The Chelsea on the third floor of the West Tower now has a comfortable capacity of about 3,200, where he booked acts such as Bruno Mars and Childish Gambino. From the general-admission floor to the opera boxes, the entire space is cozy but vertical, ensuring that there isn't a bad seat in the house. It also has an air of urban sophistication; it may be a concert venue, but you want to hang out there as well. It's been described as "a working theater dropped into the middle of a glass factory."

International design firm AvroKO utilized a monochromatic color palate, playing with both industrial and wood textures throughout the lobby and VIP areas. Lengths of rope travel across ceilings and walls, as they did in old-school theaters when backdrops and scenery were moved by pulleys. Now, of course, they're more decorative than functional in the Chelsea, but in true New York-theater style, a grand metal-worked staircase leads from the lobby up to the VIP section. And in true Cosmopolitan form, a stunning chandelier catches your eye as you ascend the stairs.

The first year, the Book & Stage hosted Foster the People, Ellie Goulding, Young the Giant, J. Roddy Walston, Black Rebel Motorcycle Club, and KT Tunstall. Those acts today make $150,000 to $350,000 a night.

The bars in the lobby and VIP section aren't simply watering holes to quickly grab a drink and get back to the show. Seating areas with ultra-cool furniture encourage guests to take a break from the action and socialize in a setting that feels like a real living-room space. Masculine leather chairs, chaise lounges, and little but distinct touches such as mannequin heads donning vintage headpieces, or a row of vintage wooden theater seats, create an atmosphere of conviviality and comfort.

Choudhry proudly reflects on the music influence at Cosmopolitan. "It wasn't supposed to be about music, but we became known globally for music. It completely changed how people booked venues and their ability to see the value in smaller bands. It had no competition. I could book anyone, because nobody was competing for the offers. I put the offer in for the Strokes, for the Black Keys, for Adele, and nobody competed with us. We had the easiest job in the world, because we were booking band after band. Everybody wanted to play at the Cosmo. It took another year and a half for everybody to catch up."

Foundry

In July 2016, I had an opportunity to see Ted Nugent for the first time. Better yet, it was at one of Las Vegas' newer clubs, the Foundry at SLS.

The 1,600-room SLS was a $415 million renovation of the old Sahara, which opened in 1952. The Sahara had struggled for years until Sam Nazarian purchased it in 2010 and reopened it with a design in stark contrast to the 58-year-old hotel-casino.

The uniqueness of the Foundry is its shape, which places the 2,000 people closer to the front of the stage than any other theater in Vegas. The custom built 25- by 65-foot stage has top-shelf sound and lighting, five LED video screens, three full bars, and VIP table service.

Nugent mixed his conservative view of America with his superlative guitar, playing old blues tunes from Chuck Berry, as wells as his own hits, "Cat Scratch Fever," "Great White Buffalo," and my favorite, "Stranglehold." From the first riff, he had the predominantly local capacity crowd on their feet and held them until the last two songs in his encore.

The Foundry's niche consists of diverse shows like Lil Wayne, Cult, Kansas, and AWOL Nation, with tickets priced a little less than The Pearl, Chelsea, and House of Blues.

Kurt Meilen of Live Nation told the *Las Vegas Sun*, "Entertainment in other cities serves a wider range of tastes across a greater number of formats, but here in Las Vegas, the broader population of tourists is looking for immediate name recognition." It remains to be seen if the Foundry bears that out or if it'll diversify the calendar and maximize its appeal to music fans living in and coming to Las Vegas.

Smith Center

For 20 years, building a state-of-the-art public performing-arts center had been a dream for many Vegas movers and shakers until Don Snyder made it his mission. Snyder has been a philanthropic jewel to Las Vegas, coordinating the funding and opening of the Fremont Street Experience, UNLV fundraising for a new academic building and School of Medicine, and the Smith Center. Plans were initially conceived in 1994, but a $150 million donation from the Donald W. Reynolds Foundation in 2005 kickstarted a private-public partnership for the center. A car rental tax funded $105 million of the bonds. The remaining funding for the $470 million project was raised privately.

The Smith Center's design team visited venues across North America and Europe to finalize design and operation. They modeled the center after multiple historic venues, including Palais Garnier in Paris, the Musikverein in Vienna, and La Scala in Milan.

On March 10, 2012, the Smith Center for the Performing Arts finally opened in downtown Las Vegas' 61-acre Symphony Park. The neo-art-deco design was chosen to echo the design elements of Hoover Dam. The center features a 17-story carillon tower containing 47 bells and sits on five acres. It consists of three theaters in two buildings. The 2,050-seat Reynolds Hall features stunning balconies, a dramatic stage, and a full orchestra pit. Cabaret Jazz is a unique venue with a beautiful view overlooking Symphony Park, but the notable treatment of the floor sets it apart. Most venues on the Strip have carpeted aisles. The Smith Center has a reflective surface to create a more live room. The 200-capacity Troesh Studio Theater has large and beautiful windows and a floating dance floor.

In 2016, the Smith Center joined the Colosseum and Axis in Pollstar's top-50 grossing theaters in the world, hosting acts like Ringo Starr, John Fogerty, and Jennifer Hudson, who hadn't played in Las Vegas.

The Smith Center hosts international music and dance companies and is the home of the Las Vegas Philharmonic and Nevada Ballet Theatre. The performances primarily attract locals.

The Park Theater—Size Matters

Since 1993, MGM Resorts has steadily increased its investment in live music. In addition to MGM Grand Garden, Mandalay Bay Events Center, and House of Blues, it opened the state-of-the-art 19,000-seat

T-Mobile Arena and the 5,200-seat Park Theater. Between Grand Garden Arena and T-Mobile, MGM sold more than a half-million concert tickets in 2016.

A new theater wasn't even on the drawing board until they considered a renovation of Mandalay Bay Events Center, which was going to cost $100 million. In the end, it was more economical to build a new theater.

The Park opened with a sold-out Stevie Nicks and the Pretenders concert. Chrissie Hynde sported an Elvis T-shirt and replaced Tom Petty in Nicks' "Stop Dragging my Heart Around" duet. The theater complements the urban neighborhood feel of the Park, the nicely landscaped area that includes T-Mobile Arena and a dozen shops and restaurants. The Theater is inside the Monte Carlo, which will also undergo a $450 million renovation. It is kitty corner from T-Mobile Arena, across the plaza from New York-New York and surrounded by parking garages with 12,000 spaces.

The Theater wasn't just built for live music. "Our convention group was telling us we were losing business," says Mark Prows. "We really needed a 4,000-seat venue. What drove the 5,000-seat decision was making sure we could compete with the Colosseum. It needed to be a little bit bigger."

Floor-orchestra, low-orchestra, and high-orchestra seating can all be retracted for general-admission shows. The worst seat in the balcony is no more than 145 feet from stage. The concourse has seven bars and bottle service in the VIP seats. The stage is 40 feet deep by 140 feet wide, 20 feet wider than the Colosseum, and is draped by an 80-by-40-foot LED video system, which is customizable into any configuration.

The theater's 5,200-seats equip MGM to compete for single concerts and residencies. Already booked for residencies are Bruno Mars, Ricky Martin, and Cher and single-night appearances of Chicago with the Doobie Brothers and Boston. Prows expects another five in 2017.

More Coming ...

There will be at least two more venues when the Raiders' stadium gets built and if Madison Square Garden delivers on its announcement to build a 17,000-seat music-exclusive arena.

The proposed arena is a collaboration among Las Vegas Sands Corporation and the Madison Square Garden Company with Azoff MSG Entertainment, Live Nation Entertainment, and Oak View Group that will build a first-of-its-kind large-scale venue. The new Madison Square Garden will offer "bunker suites" that have exclusive entrances, premium seating, private restrooms, and access to menus prepared by top chefs and sommeliers. The group isn't contracting with performers just yet, but the long-term relationships all involved parties have had with groups and individuals bode well for attracting top names. "We would look at Las Vegas as a unique opportunity to create those kinds of long-term and long-standing residencies," says David "Doc" O'Connor, president and CEO of the Madison Square Garden Company.

The planned site is perfectly situated, with thousands of hotel rooms at the Venetian-Palazzo and nearby Wynn, TI, and Mirage. The Sands Expo & Convention Center will be physically connected to the venue via its upstairs lobby and a bridge across Koval Lane.

In the past two decades, Las Vegas has hosted every major concert tour. However, the real work horses have been the theaters. With the humble beginnings of the 1,800-capacity Joint to the just-opened 5,200-seat Park Theater, Las Vegas has added close to 40,000 seats in capacities ranging from 1,800 to 7,000 seats. In just 2016, those theaters have sold 1.3-plus million tickets.

Fans want an intimate, unique, and pleasant concert experience. Las Vegas adds a sprinkle of great food, nightclubs, shopping, weather, and special events and wraps it all up with the most diverse offering of rooms in the world. A 20-year foundation has been laid with the best promoters, venue managers, and hotels ready to do battle for the top live music acts in the world.

No other urban area on Earth can lay claim to the title Rock City.

CHAPTER FOURTEEN

THE RETURN OF THE RESIDENCY

Las Vegas' early live music had a good mix of what today is called "residencies." But that tradition went into hibernation and didn't emerge again for more than 20 years. As usual, it was Caesars Palace that maintained the tradition, then mothballed it, then revived it.

John Meglen is the vice president for the music division of monster promotions company AEG Presents. His first memories of Vegas revolve around promoting the Beach Boys in the early '80s to 1,000 fans in Caesars' Circus Maximus showroom. "Most popular bands sidestepped Vegas in the '70s. It was branded an 'entertainment graveyard' where you went when you were old and a has-been," he says.

Meglen's journey to become the top promoter of live music in Las Vegas took a circuitous route. He grew up as an army brat in the middle of two sets of sisters. His dad was a West Point colonel and his mom a dancer from New York City. In the early '70s, he played guitar, influenced by Buffalo Springfield, Crosby, Stills, Nash & Young, and other folk-rock bands. He started his career at Spokane High School while serving on the dance committee where he bought his first act, Tower of Power. The concert netted the committee $1,500.

He enrolled at Washington State with plans to be a veterinarian. But he derived his real education from his side job with the Campus Activities Committee of the Associated Students.

Meglen says, "I was interested in creating an open mic. I became familiar with open mic at Spokane University where every Friday night, the students gave musicians an opportunity to perform in front of a live audience. I took my guitar and played a couple of songs a night." He approached the music department, which sent him over to the faculty adviser for the Associated Students, who gave his idea the green light.

Meglen started the Coffee House Committee. "There was a room in the basement of the Student Union they called Butch's Den. The room held maybe 75 people. I booked three bands. The opener got ten dollars, the second act twenty-five, and the headliner thirty-five. That migrated into mini-concerts."

While Meglen cut his teeth there, he fondly remembers the things he liked best. "You don't learn the business first. You learn the fun parts first: picking up the band at the airport, making posters out of bed sheets and hanging them from the overpasses on campus, and getting excited about how to make the environment great, how to get everybody excited about it."

It didn't hurt that he was paid regardless of how the shows did. But WSU got its share too. When Meglen joined the Associated Students, they had a budget of $250,000. When he left, they were generating a $250,000 profit. The Activities Committee had some leverage; promoters had to go through them to do concerts on campus. Meglen began to build his music-industry Rolodex.

He joined the National Campus Activities Association (another NCAA), where he became the block-booking coordinator for the Northwest region. The live-music who's who were also building Rolodexes on campuses across the country. Rob Light, current president of CAA Music division, was at Syracuse. Bobby Brooks, CAA agent (now deceased), was at St. Johns. Clint Mitchell, current partner at William Morris, was at University of Montana. John Bongiovani and John Smith who created and operate *Pollstar*, a live-music publication, were at Fresno State. At one of the NCAA conferences, Meglen met Tom Hulett of Concerts West, who gave him his first job. Or did he?

He quit school, packed up all his stuff, and moved to Seattle. With four guys in a two-bedroom apartment, his space was on the living-room couch. "Every day I drove down to the Concerts West offices in Bellevue, Washington, and just sat there. It became obvious after a while that I hadn't actually been offered a job, but I just kept showing up. For six weeks, I walked around the office asking for things to do. I just started doing things for people.

"After two months, I went to the CFO, Bill McCeggle, and asked, 'Is there any way I can get paid?'" Meglen started at $200 a week as a promoter production rep and immediately started touring.

In 1978, buildings were "four-walled." The promoter rented the building, but few services were included. Promoter reps managed the ticket office and outlets, which meant ordering hard tickets (tickets printed, counted, and distributed by hand). They hired crowd management and police, rented staging, sound, and lights, loaded the show in and out, then cleaned up afterwards. Meglen's first tours were Alice Cooper and Jimmy Buffet. His first full tour as production manager was 1979 with Bad Company.

In 1977, Meglen went to work for CPI, which had started its own national touring division, regularly booking tours with four major acts: The Rolling Stones, Pink Floyd, David Bowie, and Paul Simon. Those tours came from the same management companies: Joe Razkopf and Bill Zisko.

The Live-Music Glass Ceiling

Linda Crane grew up in New Jersey in an Irish Catholic family. As a kid her taste progressed from the Partridge Family, Bobby Sherman, and the Carpenters to edgier groups like Meatloaf, Queen, and eventually Springsteen.

"I used to tell my grandmother, I'm going to marry a celebrity. I'm going to Hollywood and I'm going to be in entertainment," she says. She had a Katy Perry look and sang in a band in high school, but it was the degree in theater that got her a first job at the Garden State Arts Center, a 10,000-seat amphitheater in Holmdel, New Jersey, 10 miles from where Springsteen and Bon Jovi lived.

In 1984, at 21, she began working her way up the venue ladder, starting as part-time assistant stage manager. She managed musicians and the union payroll, fulfilled band riders for catering, and did the laundry for acts like Rod Stewart, Jimmy Buffett, and Don Henley. She was promoted to a full-time position and for the next 10 years, she learned the live-music business.

In 1993, she jumped at a chance to work for the Nederlander organization, which promoted shows at the Arts Center. She managed backstage production, the booking calendar, and concert settlements.

An opportunity with Caesars World came along and with it a move to Los Angeles and a position as assistant vice president of Caesars World Entertainment. Her first challenge with Caesars was the glass ceiling.

"That's the part they never tell you or maybe we're being naive. I had a hard time being accepted in the role," she says. "I was a woman in a man's world. They just didn't take me seriously."

In those days, Caesars' Circus Maximus was hosting residencies for Cher, Freddie Prinz, David Copperfield, and Diana Ross. But one of Crane's first bookings was on a tip from the casino.

René Angélil was a Canadian high roller at Caesars Palace; he was also a musical producer, singer, and the manager and husband of a developing French-Canadian singer. Crane recalls, "The casino was telling us that they had this customer who managed an act that was starting to break. They wanted us to go check her out. We were very particular about who we'd play at Caesars. They had to command a certain ticket price. We bent the rules, but not a lot." The young girl was just getting started and barely spoke English, but she passed the audition.

Ten years later, Céline Dion would open a new 4,000-seat venue at Caesars for the residency to end all residencies.

It's ironic that Linda Crane and John Meglen worked together in the early '90s at the Garden State. Ironic because Crane would break Céline at Caesars and Meglen would put together the deal to make her the biggest box-office attraction in Las Vegas history.

Vegas' Own Pop Diva

Céline Dion was born on March 30, 1968, in Charlemagne, Quebec, Canada. The youngest of 14 children, she grew up in a close-knit musical family. Her parents formed a singing group and toured Canada while Céline was still an infant.

At 12, Dion recorded a demo tape of a song she had written with her mother. They sent the tape to manager and producer, René Angélil. After hearing the tape and seeing Dion perform for him in person, Angélil signed her.

Dion recorded her first English-language album, *Unison*, in 1990; it sold a million copies. Her real breakthrough came in 1992, when she recorded the theme to *Beauty and the Beast*, a duet with Peabo Bryson. It was featured on her second English album, *Céline Dion*, which sold 12 million copies internationally.

In 1993, Dion capitalized on her newfound fame, releasing the top-selling *The Colour of My Love*. In 1994, Dion happily merged her personal and professional life when she married Angélil, 26 years her senior. Angélil and his second wife had divorced in the 1980s and around this time, he and Dion began a romantic relationship. Engaged in 1991, the couple tied the knot at Montreal's Notre Dame Basilica in an elaborate ceremony that was celebrated throughout Canada.

Dion's international stardom was solidified by her performance of "The Power of the Dream" at the 1996 Olympic Games. That same year, her album *Falling into You*, including the number-one hit "Because You Loved Me," won Grammy Awards for album of the year and best pop album. In 1997, her hit streak peaked with the release of the blockbuster film *Titanic*, for which Dion sang the theme song, "My Heart Will Go On." By the time the film had raked in a record number of Oscars, Dion's ballad had become ubiquitous on radio stations around the world.

Included on both the *Titanic* soundtrack album and Dion's own *Let's Talk About Love* (1997), "My Heart Will Go On" sold a combined 50 million records worldwide.

In the first months of 2000, Dion announced she was taking time off from her career to focus on her family. During that break she and Angélil went to see *O*, the second of six shows Cirque du Soleil would produce in Las Vegas. Céline was so moved and impressed by *O* that she insisted on going backstage afterwards to meet the performers. At dinner, she turned to Angélil and said, "When I come back, I would love to do a show like that."

"Wait a minute," he said. "Why don't we create a show that stays in Las Vegas and let people come here?"

Each Cirque du Soleil production is a synthesis of circus styles from around the world, with its own central theme and storyline. Shows employ continuous live music, with performers rather than stagehands changing the props. Cirque shows are also unique for their custom-designed theaters. Until Cirque, no Strip property was investing in custom theaters for themed production shows. But with Cirque's success, all the major casinos, plus Cirque itself, were looking for that "next big thing."

A few weeks later after Cirque director Franco Dragone heard about her experience at *O* and the meeting she had with the cast, he sent her a letter. "Thank you for coming to my show and if you ever come out of retirement, I would love to work with you."

Angélil wasted little time, approaching Arthur Goldberg, president and CEO of Park Place Entertainment (now Caesars Entertainment). They shared an enthusiasm for creating something for Céline and decided to do it on their own—build a venue and produce a show in-house.

Goldberg's successor, Tom Gallagher, also shared Goldberg's vision for a Céline residency, but wanted to limit the role to building a venue, with an outside promoter producing the show.

AEG learned that Céline Dion was looking for a backer for an unusual project in Las Vegas, where she'd perform at a new theater for five years.

John Meglen recalls, "Céline's show was intended to be a derivative of a Cirque production. At the time, Cirque was at its peak and *O* was considered the best show in the world. They told us, 'We're going to take the biggest female singer in the world and marry her with a creator of that show.' But we couldn't call it a Cirque show, because Franco Dragone had just left Cirque."

There was also a "math problem." When Céline first started appearing at Caesars in 1995, Las Vegas was famous for performers doing two shows a night. Linda Crane picks up the story. "We learned quickly that Céline couldn't do two shows a night. It was horrible. She was having bloody noses from the dry climate. She ended up in the hospital."

For her residency, one show a night didn't pencil out either. That was when the idea of the 4,000-seat Colosseum was born.

In November 2000, AEG met with Dion and Angélil at their home in Florida. After a few hours, Angélil told me, they shook hands on a deal for a $150 million.

The show inaugurated the $95 million Colosseum, which was built in 140 days. It seats 4,100 in a tiered theater melding into a vast thrust stage. The stage was designed to slope upward at 5.7 degrees away from the audience, to provide the view and to show lighting details, designs, and textures of the stage.

The original plan for the stage backdrop was to use a giant video projector. When the lighting designer, Yves Aucoin, pointed out that this would create shadows, Angélil went back to AEG and persuaded them to contribute an extra $10 million for the largest indoor LED screen in North America.

On January 25, 2001, Dion gave birth to a boy, René-Charles. In March 2002, *A New Day Has Come* topped the charts in more than 17 countries. Finally, on March 25, 2003, three years after seeing *O*, *Céline Dion: A New Day* opened at Caesars Palace. The show introduced a new form of theatrical entertainment, a fusion of song, performance art, innovative stage craft, and state-of-the-art technology.

Variety's review of the opening: "*Céline Dion: A New Day* abounds with acrobats floating, exotic costumes, a mixture of the earthly and the metaphysical—and all of it plays second fiddle to the armor-lunged Dion, who delivers songs in two sizes: big and bigger. Veteran Cirque du Soleil director Franco Dragone could not have found a better front person for his theatrics—her music hits the audience like an avalanche, leaving little room for musical or theatrical nuance. It allows him to provide the tasty morsels in this production, which he does, though nearly all of them have been seen before in Cirque productions."

Even without the rave reviews, John Meglen knew the residency would be big. "Man, this has got to be one plus one equals three," he calculated. "But we were wrong. It was one plus one equals *ten*."

A New Day sold out 717 consecutive shows. In March 2011, Céline launched a new show, which sold out 300-plus performances. With more than 1,000 performances and counting, she has not only shattered Elvis' old mark, she's done it in a 4,000-seat theater. As of March 2017, she has played 1,029 shows and counting. I can't imagine a string like that being beaten by any other live performer or a record as significant in either sports or entertainment.

In 2010, thanks to its dominance and annual eight-figure grosses, *Billboard* named the Colosseum "Venue of the Decade."

John Meglen says, "Céline brings 4,000 people to the property each night she performs. There's a dinner seating before and after the show for people who are attending it and a seating during the show for people who aren't. Many show-goers stay in the hotel, and not just for the night."

Jason Gastwirth, Caesars vice president of entertainment, sees the impact to the bottom line. "We had record income from our entertainment in Las Vegas in 2016. These live shows generate more room nights, increase casino traffic, and enhance the Caesars brand."

Candidates for Residencies?

Both Céline Dion and the Colosseum were breakthroughs in how shows were produced and presented in Las Vegas; they ushered in a new wrinkle in live entertainment—the residency.

When Céline opened the Colosseum, AEG Live envisioned 200 shows a year. After a couple of years, the dates started scaling down drastically. She went to 120 shows a year, then 80 shows a year, then 60. These days, the sweet spot for a superstar artist residency is 70 shows a year.

But Céline's shrinking opened up the venue for other residencies. Elton John was the first to join the rotation in 2004, performing during the weeks that Céline wasn't. Not many artists can do that level of business, but Bette Midler, Shania Twain, Rod Stewart, Mariah Carey, Reba, Brooks & Dunn, and Jerry Seinfeld have all performed at the Colosseum, doing anywhere from six to 60 shows a year. And more would like to.

The AEG team is always having conversations with artists and their management about opportunities at the Colosseum. "There's a pretty short list of artists at this point who meet the criteria for performing on a long-term basis in Las Vegas at this level and being successful," says John Nelson, senior vice president at AEG. "It's a combination of longevity, albums sold, number of hits, and history of radio airplay."

If an artist does qualify, AEG's man in Vegas, Bobby Reynolds, enumerates the advantages. "They make good money, without all the rigors of touring. They don't need tour buses or private jets. We'll give the headliner an extraordinary suite and cover all the rooms for the band and crew, the catering, the booze. It's very efficient."

An artist will gross more on a per-show basis playing arenas versus a 4,100-seat theater, but the costs will be significantly lower and the production can be customized. "So many elements in each artist's show just aren't designed to tour. You can't break it down and put it into containers and ship it places, because it's a one-of-a-kind spectacle," HC Rowe says.

Another important pitch—artists are extremely comfortable during their time in Vegas, with spaces designed to fit their needs. The Who were so thrilled with their single show at the Colosseum that they signed up for six more dates.

"So far, without exception, every artist we've produced in the Colosseum has had a great experience spending time in the city, being taken care of with great hospitality by the hotel, or finding a house on their own," he said. "Céline lives in Las Vegas. She has a home with her three sons. Others stay in great suites at the hotel or they'll rent their own homes. It's very comfortable, it's a good quality of life, and I think more managers and agents understand that it's less stress and strain on their clients than the typical touring deal that they might be working on."

Backstage at the Colosseum is actually under the stage, where the artist has a lower-level multi-room apartment to use during production, with an elevator that goes directly to the stage. The apartment includes a living room, dining room, kitchen, bedroom, and meeting space, with 24/7 security and a private entrance that allows the artist to drive directly into the apartment. The resident artists are encouraged to decorate the space to meet their own needs.

"Each artist has a different setup," Rowe says, citing Rod Stewart, who turns the bedroom into a workout room when he's playing Vegas.

Best of all, a residency doesn't negatively impact an artist's touring opportunities. "They can do both," John Nelson says. "We just need to be strategic in planning when Vegas fits in."

"As this model becomes more prevalent, it becomes easier and easier to get done," HC Rowe says. "I think that honor goes completely to Céline and her husband René. To have that vision, along with John Meglen and John Nelson, and to risk it all takes serious guts. She was at the pinnacle of her career when she did this. The whole city of Las Vegas has been able to enjoy the benefits of what those two accomplished."

And it doesn't start and stop at the Colosseum. Carlos Santana was the first residency outside the Colosseum; he performed for two years (2009-2011) at The Joint at Hard Rock, logging 70 concerts over that period. Since then, he's settled in for 30 or so dates per year at House of Blues at Mandalay Bay. Heart, Billy Idol, and Joe Walsh have also done multiple shows at HOB. George Strait is doing four two-show performances a year at T-Mobile Arena. The Venetian has had John Fogerty, Diana Ross, Willie Nelson, and Steely Dan. AEG Presents has produced residencies with Guns N' Roses, Def Leppard, KISS, and Journey. The new Park Theater in T-Mobile Plaza will host residencies, including Ricky Martin, Bruno Mars, and Cher.

Live Nation and Caesars broke other new ground, first with Britney Spears, then Jennifer Lopez—"younger artists in a broader span of genres that mirror the changing demographics of Las Vegas," says Kurt Melien with Live Nation.

Britney is doing 60 shows per year, J Lo 40, and the Backstreet Boys 26. Lionel Richie has done 20 and Pitbull up to 18.

A key to continuing the streak of residencies is tapping different genres. "Britney was the first pop residence anywhere," says Jason Gastwirth. "Pitbull was the first rap residency. Jennifer Lopez has the highest average ticket price, $200, of any tour in North America. It's because it's one of the most amazing experiences—pure fun."

"It's not Lawrence Welk or Glenn Miller coming to casinos anymore," comments Gary Bongiovanni with *Pollstar*. "These are younger people with more diverse, more current tastes. The people running the casinos are younger now, too, and they're not scared of this music."

Jason Gastwirth sees more potential, but is cautious in his optimism. "It will continue to grow, but I feel at some point there will be saturation. The artist must be truly extraordinary, the production exceptional, and there needs to be enough variety. With the opening of the Park Theater, we have three bona-fide residence theaters and that doesn't include residencies in the smaller theaters, like Penn and Teller, Mat Franco, and Donnie and Marie."

As access to music becomes ubiquitous through radio, YouTube, streaming, and websites like Spotify, new acts will develop stronger catalogs, allowing them entrée into the Las Vegas residency machine. These shows will be staged by the finest producers in the world in state-of-the-art theaters. The live-music fan can only benefit from more artists in more venues at more price points than ever before.

CHAPTER FIFTEEN

EARLY FESTIVALS—THE GOOD, THE BAD, AND THE UGLY

Since the beginning of humanity, people have been congregating for shared collective experiences. This social nature is a defining trait of our human makeup, hard-wired into our character and the driving force behind much of societal development.

The Pythian Games of ancient Greece, dating as far back at the 6th century B.C., featured competitions of musical ability in addition to the physical feats for which they're primarily remembered.

The term "festival" first showed up in the English language in the middle of the 16th century, derived from "feast" and most often centered around the harvest.

The modern evolution of festivals began with the Newport Folk Festival, launched in 1959. At the 1965 festival, Bob Dylan famously went electric amidst a chorus of boos, a moment that marked a sea-change in pop culture and further solidified the rock 'n' roll revolution. In the '60s and '70s, a small number of festivals were produced across the country. However, festivals would not begin to mushroom in America until the 21st century.

Personally, I've been to at least a dozen music festivals. I was a fan of the music at a few; the rest I went to for professional reasons, as president of Las Vegas Events, in order to know and understand each type of event we pursue.

Milwaukee's Summerfest was my first and the one I enjoyed most. I was 18 and it was 1973.

In the mid-'60s like everywhere in the country, there was a lot of racial tension in Milwaukee. The mayor at that time believed a festival of this type would help relieve the tension. The Milwaukee World Festival was created and spread out over the city. It relied on businesses and private firms to sponsor, promote, and coordinate their own events. The festival took place on an old Navy missile site, just some dirt and concrete on an empty space on the lakefront of Lake Michigan. A million people attended the first year, yet the festival lost $150,000. Admission was $1.50.

The festival's diverse music, practically free admission, cheap beer, and the liberal hands-off attitude of the police resulted in three straight years of unruly and disruptive crowds. In 1970, the late arrival of Sly and the Family Stone nearly resulted in a riot.

In 1973, the disorder peaked. Blood, Sweat & Tears and Humble Pie were on the main stage. H. Carl Mueller reported on the chaos in the *Milwaukee Journal*. "Youths from Saturday's crowd of 82,700 attacked the main stage, destroying part of the fence around it, and ripped apart beer and food stands in the area. They battled helmeted police with barrages of rocks, bottles and other debris. One officer at Summerfest said that every jail cell in the city was filled by Sunday morning. Marauding gangs of youths tore apart two bars near the main stage, destroying a tent over one and stealing more than 50 half barrels of beer."

I was there. The 75-acre downtown site was 30 minutes from my house. That was the year police did a 180-degree turn and cracked down. One of my friends was caught by a police sweep and joined the other 300 who spent the night in jail.

For the next five years, the festival's footprint changed. Guidelines were established for "family-friendly" acts, no alcohol could be brought in, and police kept a firm hand on the crowd.

Summerfest evolved into a permanent festival site with 11 permanent stages and a 23,000-seat amphitheater. Today, the festival runs 11 days and draws anywhere from 850,000 to a million people. For $20, you can see almost 700 bands from every genre of music.

In 1985, the initial Rock in Rio in Brazil drew 1.5 million fans after the city of Rio de Janeiro built a 250,000-capacity complex, the City of Rock, for stadium rock heroes Queen and AC/DC to headline. Founder Roberto Medina expanded the brand into Lisbon, Madrid, and Las Vegas.

In 1999, Paul Tollett of Golden Voice, AEG Live's far west promotion division, produced the first Coachella Music and Arts Festival at the pristine Empire Polo Club in Indio, California. The festival's origins trace back to a 1993 concert that Pearl Jam performed at the Empire

Polo Club while boycotting venues controlled by Ticketmaster. The show authenticated the site's viability for hosting large events, leading to the inaugural Coachella Festival.

In 2016, the two-day Coachella Festival sold out two weekends; nearly 200,000 tickets grossed $94 million. The newly established site at the Empire Polo Club, using much of the production from Coachella, also launched the country-themed Stagecoach Music Festival, selling 72,000 tickets and grossing $25 million in its inaugural year.

AEG Presents also added a third festival, Desert Trip, which headlined The Rolling Stones, Paul McCartney, Neil Young, Bob Dylan, and The Who. The two weekends were labeled by some as "Oldchella," as the genre was all classic rock with reserved seats and a limited lineup per day. Tickets sold for between $399 and $1,599. Both weekends sold out, grossing $162 million and shattering all festival gross records.

In the beginning of the 21st century, country music festivals, using the same formula, started to gain traction. Using their award show as a foundation, the Country Music Association is the oldest, having launched the CMA Fan Fair in 1972 in Nashville. To this day, artists perform for free with half the proceeds donated to charity and the other half earmarked by the CMA for the advancement of country music. Stars sign autographs throughout the event, now named CMA Music Festival. In 1996, Garth Brooks signed autographs for 23 hours with no breaks.

In 2016, the festival set a daily attendance record of 88,000 fans per day over the four days. In all, more than 600 artists and celebrities participated in more than 250 hours of concerts on 11 stages (seven of which are free). CMA Music Festival envelopes Nashville with a fan exhibition at the convention center, Nissan Stadium concerts, Riverfront stage concerts, as well as a more than lively Music Row.

Today, there are more than three dozen major country music festivals, two of which are held in Las Vegas.

In Europe, the live-music touring business developed much differently than in the U.S., primarily due to the proliferation of arenas subsidized by cities for the NHL and NBA. In Europe, there were neither incentives nor the political environments for the funding and construction of arenas. If you wanted to experience live music or you were an act and wanted an audience in Europe, it was either a theater, club, or festival. Roughly 500 festivals take place in Europe each year, each with a personality unique to its geography. For example, Glastonbury Festival is a five-day music festival on the Worthy Farm in Pilton Sommerset, England. Originally Pilton Pop, Blues & Folk Festival, it's the largest greenfield festival in the world, now attended by 175,000 people per day.

Europe began its spurt of festival growth in the late '60s. Why did it take the U.S. so many years to follow? Also in the late '60s, three major music festivals, one in New York and two in California, impeded their evolution for decades to come.

The Good

In 1967, the Bay Area had two back-to-back firsts in live music, one of which is mythical. Music in the world was changing; AM was slowly giving way to FM and more liberal social-conscience bands were taking hold.

On June 10 and 11 of that year, the Fantasy Fair and Magic Mountain Music Festival took place at the Cushing Amphitheater in Marin County. The festival layout looked like a smaller version of the original Greek Theater in Athens, as the rows were made up of serpentine stone installed 80 years earlier with padding compliments of the moss growing in and around the rocks—no seats, just rock.

The festival charged $2 a ticket and drew 36,000 people over the two days, spilling into the woody terrain behind the rows of stone. Among the 30 bands performing were Canned Heat, the Byrds, the Grass Roots, Jefferson Airplane, and the Doors. It went relatively unnoticed; the very next weekend, Lou Adler and John Phillips of the Mamas and Papas created the Monterey Pop Festival.

In an interview in 2007 with PBS, Lou Adler recalled its formation. "A couple of months before the festival, Paul McCartney, myself, John Phillips, Cass Elliot, and Michelle Phillips were sitting around discussing the fact that pop music wasn't considered an art form like jazz and folk. We had no real plan, other than to expose every musical genre. It [the festival] was chaotic in the sense that we had seven weeks to put it together, but what really made it work was the fact that we established the first charitable rock foundation, so that all the acts performed gratis."

The Monterey Pop Festival was held Friday-Sunday June 16-18 at the Monterey County Fairgrounds. Capacity was 7,000, but legend has it that 30,000 jammed into it for Saturday night's show. Ticket prices ranged from $3 to $6.50—adjusted for inflation, $21-$46 in today's dollars.

Ironically, it was anything but pop. Acts normally relegated to small venues like the Fillmore had breakthrough performances, playing for the first time in front of tens of thousands of music lovers. Jimi Hendrix, Janis Joplin, Santana, Jefferson Airplane, The Who, Steve Miller, Grateful Dead, Simon and Garfunkel, and 20 others played eclectic sets that set a new standard for the live-music experience.

Unlike the two other major festivals of the era, Monterey had few issues. The production was state of the art for its time. The dressing rooms were under the stage. Backstage included a 24-hour green room with a menu that included lobster, steak, crab, and champagne. Fifty thousand little orchids were flown in from Hawaii—one for every seat and plenty around the stage. The bands had no rehearsals or sound checks. They just plugged in and played.

The 7,000 reserved seats created order. Everyone in front of the stage was comfortably sitting, watching the bands. The police demeanor played a big role in the success of the festival. The day of the concert the chief of police bought a bunch of daisies. He met with his officers, had them wear the daisies in their hair and on the bikes, and told them, "We won't bust anyone unless they're out of line." There were only two arrests, redneck cowboys who were loud and bothering the hippies.

The Beatles didn't play, but McCartney recommended Jimi Hendrix, who was exploding in England.

The Beach Boys were going to perform, but pulled out. "The idea of a show with the Beach Boys and Mama and Papas is okay," said Brian Wilson. "But all those people from England that play acid rock—if the audience is coming for that, they're going to hate us."

In his book *A Perfect Haze—The Illustrated History of the Monterey International Pop Festival*, Harvey Kubernik wrote, "A homely young girl walked onto the stage with fright in her eyes ... but when the band started to play, over the twenty-odd minutes, Big Brother and the Holding Company pinned back the ears of a disbelieving audience with a volley of

12-gauge musical buckshot." The crowd had witnessed the rock 'n' roll birth of Janis Joplin.

The Byrds were feuding. Neil Young was a no-show. It would be the first of many no-shows that earned him the nickname "Shakey." Roger McGuinn at the time said, "We were a band of cut-throat pirates, stabbing each other in the back." On stage, Crosby, who had obviously ingested an assortment of hallucinogens, went into a rant about the John F. Kennedy assassination.

Soul and R&B singer-songwriter Otis Redding was starting to get a lot of respect. However, he was primarily working the "chitlin' circuit," playing to black audiences. Kubernik wrote, "Shark-skin-suited, razor-cut-groomed, and pulling four-to-the-floor, this heaving music machine assailed the facile construct of a racial-cultural chasm. As fans clustered at the stage front, Redding was crowned the king of the day-glo coalition."

Two acts scheduled to play back to back used a coin toss to decide who went first: The Who and Jimi Hendrix. Pete Townsend retold the story for the documentary *The History of Rock n' Roll*. "I couldn't deal with the fact that at this critical concert, we might go on after him." But Hendrix thought The Who didn't want *him* to go on *before* them. The Who won the toss.

"The Who didn't require the adrenaline rush of a mob to ignite," Kubernik described them. "They were combustible all on their own. And pity the poor amplifiers, they took it in the gut like Coventry during the Battle of Britain." The finale included the destruction of Pete Townsend's guitar.

Robert Christgau, one of the earliest professional rock critics, recalls Hendrix's performance. "With his back to the audience, Hendrix humped the amplifier and jacked the guitar around his mid-section, then turned and sat astride his instrument so that its neck extended like a third leg. For a few tender moments, he caressed the strings. Then, in a sacrifice that couldn't have satisfied him more than it did me, he squirted it with lighter fluid from a can he held near his crotch and set the cursed thing afire."

The Mamas and Papas closed Sunday night's show.

The festival grossed $438,955 and generated $220,129 for a Harlem-based music and instruction program. There was no Monterey Pop

Festival II. Dates were held and a deal with the county set. It went to the state for approval and then ... nothing.

Jann Wenner, who went on to create and manage *Rolling Stone* magazine, said, "Everything we cared about in music, in creating community and camaraderie and fellowship, all flowed out of Monterey."

The Bad

Woodstock, short for Woodstock Music and Art Fair, An Aquarian Festival, famously accomplished many things in folklore, but a profit was decidedly not one of them. Indeed, a combination of unsold tickets, the effect of 200,000-300,000 unexpected guests, inexperience, hasty planning, bad weather, and poor deals meant that, though history has treated it as cultural success, it was a physical and financial disaster.

"Woodstock was horrible," Pete Townsend says. "Woodstock was only horrible because it went so wrong. It could have been extraordinary. I suppose with the carefully edited view that the public got through Michael Wadleigh's film, it was a great event. But for those there, it was a terrible shamble. Full of the most naïve childlike people. We have a word for them in England—twits."

Michael Lang, described as "a sideshow barker," convinced business partners Joel Rosenman and John Roberts, along with fellow hippie Artie Kornfeld, to join in his vision of a three-day music festival that would make them a lot of money. Thus, Woodstock Ventures was born.

The Woodstock Festival was scheduled for August 15-17, but as late as March of that year, a site hadn't been selected or a single band booked. Ticket prices were set at $7 per day, $13 for two days, and $18 for all three days and camping. Based on ticket prices, budgets were built and planning began. In mid-April, the first big act committed, Creedence Clearwater Revival, followed by Canned Heat, Johnny Winters, Janis Joplin, and Jefferson Airplane. Finally, after much negotiation, a farm in Wallkill, New York, 15 miles from Woodstock, was selected as the site, at a cost of $10,000.

A poster was printed and the site was readied. But among a long laundry list of critical components, the least were staging, sound, and lights. How do you feed a crowd of close to 200,000? How will you get them in and out of a site that has only a couple of two-lane highways? Where will the water come from? How do you address drug-related medical issues? How many porta-potties would handle that many people? Each of these issues was addressed, but not without ballooning costs. It was now clear: The festival wouldn't be profitable. Then other issues started pressing in.

When the locals got wind of how big the festival was likely to be, Woodstock Ventures had to deal with an uneasy landlord and a town determined to "keep these damn hippies out." In a series of town-hall meetings, one comment summed up the local temperament. "First, we oughta shave those hippies' heads so we can tell whether they're girls or boys we are dealing with. Then we ought to rub their noses into the dirt for what they are doing to this country."

On July 15, the council voted unanimously to deny a permit for the site in Wallkill. With only a month before the gates were scheduled to open, the foursome was without a site.

If Michael Lang demonstrated anything at Woodstock, it was his incredible ability to block out the negative and focus on solutions. The next day they got a call on from Bethel, 25 minutes from Wallkill. The town wanted the festival and had the ideal site.

Max Yasgur, a dairy farmer with 600 acres carved out of the woods forming a perfect amphitheater, loved the idea of 100,000 young people having a party on his land. Yasgur cut a deal with Woodstock Ventures and guaranteed the city would fall in line. On July 22, a caravan of buses, trucks, and trailers made the trip from Wallkill to Bethel to begin the reset of Woodstock. The 165-hippie workforce took up residence at the deserted Diamond Horseshoe Hotel, which had 200 rooms.

Woodstock Ventures struck a deal with the police to provide security. The festival weeded through 1,400 applicants to find those with the right temperament.

"Tell me, Officer, what would you do if a bearded kid walked up to you carrying a lighted joint, called you a pig, and blew smoke in your face?"

"I'd bust his fuckin' head is what I'd do."

"Thank you. Next."

Woodstock Ventures also wanted security that could identify with the counterculture and one of the festival's more colorful hires was a group called the Hog Farm, an offshoot of Ken Kesey's Merry Pranksters. They arrived parading "men in dresses, top hats, and tattered pajamas and women wrapped in swatches of the American flag carrying naked babies."

The direction of traffic was turned to all lanes in, with limited access to residents and emergency vehicles. A fleet of helicopters was hired and a pad built to get bands in and out.

Dr. William Abruzzi, a local practitioner and true humanitarian, was hired to coordinate the medical tent. Abruzzi was one of the few medical practitioners in the world with experience in treating mass crowds, which he gained at civil-rights demonstrations. He put together three separate facilities for diagnosis, recovery, and bad trips to be manned by qualified nurses and doctors.

Seventy-five parking attendants, 300 food vendors, and 200 more staff were hired. Trash cans, bags, and compactors and 500 porta-potties were ordered.

At the base of the hill in the amphitheater, 23 yards of concrete supported the stage. The stage deck consisted of three layers of planks, five wood trusses, and a series of telephone poles. More telephone poles were used to build the performers' pavilion.

In the haste of putting together a movie deal, the organizers made a costly mistake when they didn't stake the producers $100,000 in exchange for more back-end points. The widely acclaimed film (one of the credited editors was Martin Scorsese) was nominated for three Academy Awards and won one, for Best Documentary Feature. Against a budget of $600,000, it grossed $50 million at the box office alone.

By early Wednesday morning, August 13, the first of many calamities that would haunt the festival took place. The fence around the site had yet to be completed, so with nothing standing in their way, 30,000 kids who showed up early nestled comfortably into the amphitheater. With all labor crews working three days without sleep, the stage not yet complete, and the challenge of trying to remove 30,000 hippies, Woodstock Ventures made the decision not to complete the fence. It was now a free festival.

The culmination of the past three months' comedy of miscalculations had come to roost. It was a crushing blow, with the losses impossible to calculate at the time, but it would be a big number.

Next, the police commissioner withdrew his consent for the police to work the festival. With 100,000 festival-goers expected within three days, this was catastrophic. Worse, the overzealous state police proceeded to bust 150 fans, ignoring what they were hired to do. Inadvertently, they blocked off entrances to the festival's two main parking lots, needlessly backing up traffic, while the lots remained empty.

By Wednesday night, 11,000 people had moved into the campgrounds. The food facilities weren't built, any rain could turn the supplies to mush, and one of the staff slugged the concessionaire in the face. So much for the availability of nourishment.

Late Thursday afternoon, the organizers got their first break. Boldly defying the commissioner's directive, 200 cops showed up. That was the good news. The bad news was their ransom was double the pay originally negotiated.

By nine o'clock Thursday night, State Route 17-B was backed up, looking like a fat 11-mile centipede with all lanes clogged. Many people simply abandoned their cars and started walking. Gail Sheehy described the scene in *New York* magazine.

"There are more beautiful, happy, healthy-faced young Americans than I remember seeing in one place. ... The road with its thousands of walking people resembles the main drag out of Delhi. No one honks. No one shouts. No one shoves. It's unnatural."

On Friday morning, cars were stalled on every road within six miles of Max Yasgur's farm. As day broke, the sight of the slowly awakening 175,000 fans brought nervous apprehension to the 150 staff still working on the stage. The Big Pink medical tent was already full.

Finally, the stage was ready, but the acts weren't. The crowd was getting restless and daring. The first scheduled act, Sweetwater, was stuck somewhere between Bethel and White Lake. Richie Havens was talked into going on first. At 5:07 p.m., Woodstock was launched.

Getting the next act to the stage wasn't as easy. Country Joe McDonald wasn't even on the bill. They found him a guitar, a strap, and a pick; just as Havens exited, Country Joe went in front of the 200,000 fans and uttered the most famous words of Woodstock: "Give me an F! Give me a U! Give me a C! Give me a K! What's that spell?"

The third act wasn't ready yet. The stage manager spotted John Sebastian. Sebastian, after writing and performing a half-dozen hits with the Lovin' Spoonful, had been out of the music scene for two years. At Woodstock to "watch some friends," he'd never performed as a solo artist. Sebastian was coaxed onto the stage to make his solo debut.

Woodstock Ventures was completely out of money. Medical problems were so bad, the Red Cross opened a satellite location at an elementary school down the road. The porta-potties were already overflowing, sewage running downhill. With no choice, staff dug an 80-foot-long eight-foot-deep trench, in which they emptied the tanks from each unit. Many opted to squat in the woods rather than get anywhere near the nauseating boxes.

The weather had been hot and muggy, with thunderstorms forecast. Until 10:30 Friday night, there was no sign of rain. Then heavy clouds concealed by darkness opened and thunderously rained on Woodstock's parade. It was only a 15-minute downpour, but it managed to soak everyone—clothes and sleeping bags drenched with mud. Still, what set Woodstock fans apart from other festivals was the attendees' spirit to make the most out of any discomfort nature put in front of them.

When the stage was ready again, Ravi Shankar, Joan Baez, Jefferson Airplane, and CSN&Y completed the night's music, which ended at 2 a.m.

As Saturday morning broke, staff handed out bags for the campers to clean their 10 square feet of Woodstock. The temperature had climbed to 92 degrees with 90% humidity when the music resumed at 2:15 p.m. After a couple of unknown bands performed, another unknown band took the stage. Santana was one of a dozen acts that rose to stardom after Woodstock. The band's searing performance took everyone by surprise and steadied organizers' nerves about the temperament of the crowd. Next up was Mountain, who infamously didn't allow their performance in the movie. Oh, what might have been.

The Grateful Dead's manager insisted they be paid or they weren't going on. Emergency money was secured and the Dead played. While Canned Heat was performing, the huge crowd was freaking out the next artist, Janis Joplin. She drowned her fear with a fifth of whiskey, performed a short set, and was gone. Sly was next, but he wasn't going on "until the spirit moved him." No one knows what finally prompted him to go on 60 minutes later. His set was billed as the best of the festival.

The Who hit the stage at 3:30 a.m. to a medley from the new rock opera *Tommy*. Their set lasted into the wee hours and ended with the traditional demolition of Pete Townsend's guitar. At 8:30 Sunday morning, the final act of the "night" took the stage. As expected, the long wait had exhausted the band, especially lead singer Grace Slick, whose voice cracked repeatedly. By 10 a.m., maybe 10% of the crowd were awake when Jefferson Airplane walked off stage.

Sunday morning, the Hog Farm women cooked up wagonloads of cold mush and were serving it on paper plates. The women's auxiliary of the Monticello Jewish Community Center prepared 30,000 meat, cheese, and peanut butter and jelly sandwiches, handed out by a dozen nuns. Dr. Abruzzi estimated they had treated as many as 3,000 people since the festival began.

Another relative unknown, Joe Cocker took the stage at 2 p.m. The festival-goers, now estimated at between 300,000 and 400,000, saw the performer arch his shoulders and contort his arms into an air-guitar performance that became legendary. During his performance, a second patch of black storm clouds rapidly covered the festival. Cocker exited the stage without a goodbye.

The winds blew in, playing havoc with the towers and speakers. Heavy thunder preceded the cloudburst, pelting the estimated 200,000 left. The stage foundation started to slide. The downpour lasted twenty minutes.

The site of the amphitheater, which just four days earlier had been pristine green, was now a mix of mud, garbage, and excrement. The concession stands were trashed. The stage was propped with stakes driven into the ground on the downhill side of the mud plates. But the biggest threat was the electricity. The dirt that had covered one of the main feeder cables to the stage had washed away and fans had worn out the rubber insulation that covered it—essentially, those cables were live. The choice was for the show to go on, risking electrocuting people in the audience, or shut down the concert while the power was rerouted to protected cables. They kept it going. For the next two hours, the organizers held their collective breath until word came that the power was rerouted safely.

Alvin Lee and Ten Years After took the stage and played two hours of progressive blues. At 10:30, The Band slipped inconspicuously behind their instruments and played an uninspired 90-minute set. By midnight, nearly two thirds of the crowd had headed back to the real world. Paul Butterfield had come to Woodstock hoping to jam; he and Johnny Winters played a drawn-out show that held the rest of the crowd until CSN&Y went on at 3:30. It was the first-time Young played with the trio and they didn't disappoint with a set that is now historic, ending with a strong ovation from the crowd. As the sun rose, the '50s band Sha Na Na took the stage. Finally, Jimi Hendrix opened with a personal version of the "Star Spangled Banner," followed by a set that lived up to his billing as an "electronic God." His set brought Woodstock to an end.

The overdraft of the event was estimated at $1.6 million. Billy Roberts, John Roberts' father, stepped up to underwrite the entire amount.

Max Yasgur encapsulated his feelings about his experience. "If a half-million people can turn such adverse conditions—filled with the possibility of disaster, riot, looting, and catastrophe—into three days of music and peace, then perhaps there's hope for a brighter and more peaceful future."

"Woodstock, oddly enough, became the beginning of all the bad places to play," says Paul Kantner of Jefferson Airplane, one of the first bands to be booked. "Once promoters saw how many people they could draw into a football stadium, and charge $50 a ticket, rock 'n' roll went down fast."

And The Ugly

While Monterey started the festival movement and Woodstock grew it, Altamont crushed it.

Between their 1966 and 1969 tours of the U.S., The Rolling Stones went through a dark period, which included the estrangement and death of founding member Brian Jones and financial mismanagement. During the latter tour, the Stones also had an image problem. Many felt that their ticket prices were too high. Answering the criticism, the Stones considered doing a free "Woodstock West" type of event at the end of the tour.

In October 1969, Rock Scully, the Grateful Dead's manager, made the 11-hour flight from San Francisco to London to meet with the Stones

and Sam Cutler with Blackhill Productions. The San Francisco movement was legendary in London; Cutler wanted to learn more about hippies, free love, and free concerts.

Scully and Emmett Grogan, who earlier had organized the Be In, a
successful free concert in January 1967 in Golden Gate Park, pitched a
plan for the Stones to play a free concert at the park. The date was set
for December 6, one day after the Stone's final tour concert.

Mick Jagger hated cops. In Europe, he watched police use tear gas,
batons, dogs, and water cannons on concert fans. He was adamant there
be no police at any Stones shows. To try to ensure it, the free-concert
plan called for the band to announce the show only 24 hours before it
would happen and for the Hell's Angels motorcycle gang to escort the
Stones through the crowd to the stage.

The Hell's Angels were part of the Haight-Ashbury street scene and
the concerts and festivals that were all part of it. Joel Selvin, in his book
Altamont, described the relationship. "In spite of the danger, the hippies
saw the Angels as fellow rebels from straight society. Musicians, hippies,
and Angels alike shared an enthusiastic interest in drugs and saw the
police as a common enemy."

Sam Cutler met with the Angels. He needed them to pick up the
Stones from the airport, take them to Golden Gate Park, and handle security. But he was naïve about the kind of people he was dealing with.

In the meantime, Jagger turned his attention to the idea of filming the
event. He asked the Maysles brothers, American documentary filmmak-
ers, to do a movie about the December 6 concert. Not completely understanding the scope of the project, the brothers signed on.

Back in San Francisco, the first cracks in the armor were appearing.
The mayor of San Francisco flatly rejected the Stones' permit applica-
tion to play Golden Gate Park. On November 28, the Stones held a press
conference in New York, announcing the concert and the movie deal, but
not the site. Less than 10 days from show time, they didn't know where
it would be held.

Rock Scully and Sam Cutler met with the manager of the Sears Point
Raceway in south Sonoma County only about 20 miles north of San
Francisco, which had everything they needed: parking for 100,000 cars,
restrooms, concession stands, security, and police nearby. The parties

came to an agreement and began the three-day blitz it would take to prepare the venue. Scaffolding was delivered, phone lines were installed, and stagehands were working when the raceway manager got wind of a crew demolishing one of the raceway's banked turns to make way for the stage. Worse, the Stones wouldn't donate to his charity as promised, and they planned to film the concert. He demanded a $100,000 fee and movie-distribution rights. Jagger said no. The deal was dead.

Another player had entered the game, Woodstock co-producer Michael Lang. Scully and Lang boarded a helicopter to look at the latest option, Altamont Speedway, 60 miles east of the Bay Area. It was hard to fathom how gloomy this site looked compared to the one they'd locked up 24 hours earlier. The track, which did just about every event possible to stay afloat, was riddled with abandoned demolition derby cars stacked on top of each other and discarded tires. But Lang liked it and they had no other choice. With 36 hours left, they started the teardown of Sears Point and the construction of Altamont.

Altamont is at the far east end of Alameda County's police jurisdiction. Only two police cars worked a substation that covered 900 square miles. On his way to his graveyard shift on Friday December 5, Deputy Sheriff Dale Smith noticed a dramatic increase in traffic on the usually dead Hwy. 50. The closer he got to Altamont, traffic was so dense, people were abandoning their cars and walking. He made his way to Patterson Pass where he could see the entire track. What he saw was chilling.

More than 50,000 fans were already setting up on the hillsides surrounding the track; 1,000 campfires burned wood from fences and barns "liberated" from nearby ranches. Inside the raceway under enormous construction lights, workers were erecting the massive stage and hoisting sound and lights.

At dawn the crowd, now 100,000 strong, broke down the scrawny fence and rushed to claim places close to the stage. By mid-morning, the first Hell's Angels showed up, assumed spots right on the stage, and started partying. But this wasn't the San Francisco chapter, whom all the Bay Area musicians knew. Because of the location of Altamont, this was the San José chapter's jurisdiction. The crowd continued to swell. At 10 a.m., the Highway Patrol estimated the crowd at 200,000, with traffic backed up for 10 miles.

The stage, fully built, had a fatal flaw. Designed for Sears Point where it would have sat on a 15-foot bank, it was only four feet off the ground, way too low for any festival, much less one expecting 200,000. The Woodstock stage, by comparison, was 15 feet high.

The show had to go on and Santana kicked off Altamont. Almost immediately, a naked fat man, obviously high, clumsily made his way toward the stage. Unfortunately, he drifted into the Angels, who began to beat him. A Grateful Dead associate jumped in and managed to ward them off. On his way back into the crowd, the fat man sucker-punched an Angel. The Angels turned on him with pool cues and beat him mercilessly, while the crowd watched in horror.

Next, a fan rushed the stage, but before he could get far, two Angels caught and beat him up, right in front of Santana.

It was on. The Angels were waging war on everyone.

The Jefferson Airplane, burned out from touring, were up next. But the stage was dangerously overcrowded with musicians, crew, Angels, and even fans when Sam Cutler went to the mic. "A number of people should not be up here. The musicians are playing with something like 200 people breathing down their necks."

Then, as they started playing, vocalist Marty Balin saw the Angels beating a black guy. He started yelling at them and threw his tambourine. Onstage, an Angel dubbed Animal punched him in the face.

Paul Kantner had seen enough. "Hey man, I'd like to mention that the Hell's Angels just smashed Marty Balin in the face." Another Angel grabbed a mic and began verbally battling Kantner.

Animal, feeling bad about the whole thing, went to apologize to Balin. "You just can't say fuck you to an Angel," he said.

"Oh yeah?" Balin said. "Fuck you!"

An enraged Animal punched him again.

Incredibly, the Airplane finished their set.

Up next were the Flying Burrito Brothers, during which the Angels seemed to calm down.

When the Grateful Dead arrived, Michael Schrieve, Santana's manager, briefed Garcia on the ordeal. The Grateful Dead wanted nothing to do with the chaos and begged off.

When Crosby, Stills, Nash, & Young landed at Tracy airport, no one was there to greet them. Road manager Leo Makota hot-wired a truck. As the group approached the raceway from the rear, they got their first peek at the venue. With Crosby and Stills on the front bumpers, they made their way through the crowd and took the stage.

By this time, the Angels had caught their breath and were pounding on the crowd again. Crosby implored them to stop. Every time Stills stepped forward to sing, a plastered Angel stabbed him with a cycle spoke, until his pants leg was soaked with blood. As soon as they finished their set, they grabbed their gear and were out of there.

The Stones arrived by helicopter and ducked into their trailer, hearing bits and pieces of what was happening outside. When it came time to play, the stage had become so packed and unruly it was impossible for them to go on. The sun was going down, the winds started to blow, and the crowd was getting restless.

One of the Angels went into the Stones trailer and didn't mince words. "You better get the fuck out there before the place blows," he told Jagger. Jagger wasn't budging. He reiterated his order, "I'm telling you, people are going to die out there. Get out there. You've been told."

For two hours, Sam Cutler had tried and failed to make room for the band. Finally, Hell's Angel Sonny Barger, one of the founding members of the Oakland Angels and revered by them all, walked up to a microphone. All he had to say was, "All right, everybody off the stage, including Hell's Angels." The stage cleared.

When the Stones took the stage, Richards ripped into "Jumpin' Jack Flash." A ripple effect of people pushing forward upended the Angels bikes they'd put at the front as a barrier.

Meredith Hunter (his friends called him Murdock) was among the crowd being pushed. He'd had a troubled past, serving three different prison terms, mainly for petty burglary. He and his 17-year-old girlfriend Patti Bredehoft headed to Altamont that morning with two friends. Murdock was in a bright lime-green suit. What Patti didn't know was he was packing a .22 in his waistband and he'd ingested LSD.

From the time they arrived, Murdock and Patti had worked their way into the middle of the lunacy in front of the stage. Murdock made a couple of attempts to jump the stage, which didn't go unnoticed by the Angels. When the Stones went on, Murdock wound up in front of the stage, where one of the Angels grabbed his afro and shook him. When Murdock glared at him, the Angel punched him and Murdock tumbled back into the crowd, five Angels following. Stumbling and hurt, he tried to scuttle away and pulled the gun out of his pants. Before he could use it, he crumbled to the ground.

One of the Angels, Al Passaro, saw Murdock fleeing, then going for his gun. Instinctively, he reached down to his boot, pulled out a hunting knife, grabbed Murdock's arm, and plunged the knife into his neck. They both fell to the ground where Passaro continued to stab him in the back.

Another Angel took the gun from Murdock. As Murdock started to get up, he was kicked in the head, while Angels continued the beating.

The Stones, noticing the beating, stopped playing in the middle of a song and begged the crowd to "be cool."

A group of fans got Murdock to the Red Cross tent where a doctor examined his battered and weak body. He needed to be airlifted, but the only helicopter available was reserved for the Stones. He died waiting for an ambulance.

The Stones were trying to bring the crowd back and broke out a song they hadn't performed live yet, "Brown Sugar." But the beatings continued. They finished their set, ironically, with "Street Fighting Man," made a quick exit stage left, jumped into the helicopter, and were gone.

In another irony, most of the crowd remained unaware of the mayhem on and in front of the stage. Many who were there raved about the event, only to find out later what had gone down.

Altamont is the perfect example of how naïve the live-music business was at the end of the '60s. In his book, Joel Selvin enumerates the missteps responsible for the music festival that put an exclamation point on the infamous decade: "The rushed preparations for the show, the absence of police presence or any form of practical security, the low stage, the scorched earth from the campfires, bad drugs and strong wine, the physical harm to members of the bands that played that day, and the very real danger that the Angels posed."

Altamont also inspired Don McLean's famous song, "The Day the Music Died."

But though the '60s ended with the counterculture coming apart at the seams, it also became the foundation of everything we listen to today.

CHAPTER SIXTEEN

FESTIVAL VEGAS

In the past 50 years, music festivals in the U.S. have gone from a handful to hundreds. Competitive pricing, a huge roster of top acts, diverse genres of music, social media, and camping have all contributed to this country's 800 festivals. According to *Billboard* magazine, 32 million people attended at least one U.S. music festival in 2014. Of that number, nearly half, 14.7 million, were Millennials. Nielsen Music reports that the average festival-goer travels an astounding 903 miles to attend a festival.

Fans travel for the music and the unique experience. *Forbes* magazine offers a reason why. "Festivals have totally redefined how we experience music. Fans can sample hundreds of bands and artists in a few days, giving them a chance to truly explore new artists and genres."

Up-and-coming bands are finding festivals a new avenue for making more money and even getting signed to a record label. The exposure to the audiences at these mass events, especially being buzzed out to millions through social media, has a major impact on their careers.

In the new digital "slice-it-up" era, music is growing an audience of Millennials looking for a unique experience that isn't primarily about music. Today's acts don't have the radio airplay of the '70s; consequently, they have smaller audiences. The 60-70 bands hosted at each festival make the total impact for bands greater than the sum of the parts. The challenges for the festival producer is blending the music with a unique social experience.

The five biggest festivals combined grossed more than $183 million in ticket sales in 2014, and more from sponsorships, merchandise, and food and alcohol sales. The big Coachella Valley Music and Arts Festival grossed an at-the-time record-breaking $78 million over two weekends in 2014. Austin City Limits made $38 million, Lollapalooza $29 million.

At the top festivals, a three-day pass costs anywhere from $185 to $450.

Compare that to the $85-$500 to see one popular act back home.

During music festivals, fans flood their social-media feeds with photos, videos, and posts highlighting festival fashion, top performances, and more. *Forbes* reported, "In just the first weekend of Coachella 2015, fans posted more than 3.5 million tweets." A survey found that "75% of the social conversations about music festivals are created by fans in the 17-34 age group. The study also found that 23% of these posts were made by fans who weren't even at the events, but were watching remotely via live streams on YouTube, TV, etc."

As for Las Vegas, though it had become one the top music markets in America, it had yet to develop a festival. In 2011, it finally crossed festivals off its "to-do" list.

Junefest—Ten Bucks, Beers, and Bands

Lael Fray grew up in Colorado—Vail, then Colorado Springs—majoring in convention and trade-show management, where he got his first shot at being a concert promoter.

"In high school, I had a friend whose stepdad was director of marketing for Casablanca Records. My friend said, 'We should do a concert in Vail.' No one had ever promoted a concert in Vail." A contact of his friend's stepdad coached the pair through their first show, Pablo Cruise. At 19, Fray sold out his first concert, 2,400 seats at $8, and netted $4,000. "We thought we hit the big time," recalls Fray.

Fray was doing three to four concerts a year when he got a call from a friend from college. "You do concerts, right?" She worked for Merrill Lynch in New York. "We want to do a concert on the beach in the Bahamas." It sounded like a great idea to Fray, who produced the concert, then a couple of radio festivals that established his business.

In 1991, KKLZ in Las Vegas called Fray, interested in doing a radio festival. "When I started putting the festival together, the agents were thrilled to hear about it, because at that time, getting a classic-rock act to play Vegas was a real problem."

Las Vegas' first music festival, Junefest, took place June 5, 1993. It cost $10 to get in and $4 for a 16-ounce beer. Those were the two critical components of financial success—tickets and beer. That year, Junefest went through 605 kegs, selling 72,600 beers. The first band went on at 1 p.m. and the show ended at 10. The stellar lineup headlined the Allman Brothers and featured Eddie Money and Stephen Stills. The Allman Brothers only played an hour, because, of all things, snow! It was the coldest June 5 on record. Junefest also included a small carnival, a couple dozen exhibitors, and a dozen food vendors.

From 1993 to 2001, Junefest was the only music festival on the Las Vegas music calendar. The daylong concerts at Silver Bowl Park featured marathon-length shows, fireworks, and a lineup of classic-rock headliners that included Joan Jett, Journey, Styx, Ted Nugent, Jethro Tull, Allman Brothers, Foreigner, Pat Benatar, and Joe Walsh, sometimes augmented by such local favorites as John Earl & The Boogieman Band, Mama Zeus, and Epstein's Mother.

After the first year, the price of tickets gradually went up as it got closer to the festival. Marketing was also unique. In addition to a month of heavy KKLZ promotion, Budweiser and Smiths supermarkets advertised $2 off 12 packs of Budweiser and no service charge on the ticket.

Looking back, Fray remembers his favorite festival, 1998. "The lineup was a great mix of bands—REO, Joan Jett, Bachman Turner Overdrive, Loverboy, Craig Norman, Kansas, and the Romantics. We ended the festival with fireworks."

Junefest had some great years, but as the century was ending, Las Vegas hotel properties began a trend of promoting some of the same acts Fray was booking. "We created our own competition," recalls Fray. "The hotels realized that classic rock attracted great audiences and started driving up the guarantees for bands. The rising cost of the bands meant we had to charge more for tickets, $19. Attendance was going down every year and it really lost what it was."

Junefest gave Las Vegas a great day of sun, music, and beer. Hotels, especially the locals casinos, targeted this audience by eventually booking classic-rock acts regularly, further melding live music into the fabric of the hotel experience.

Vegoose

Partnerships are often difficult and it usually takes three to five years to generate a profit from a festival. Put the two together and it would seem Superfly, a New York-based event company, faced an uphill battle. Not only did this partnership work, it's three for three in first-year profits from festivals they've launched. Vegoose in Las Vegas was one of those.

Rick Farman, Rich Goodstone, Jonathan Mayers, and Kerry Black spent a couple of years developing music for clubs in New Orleans for Mardi Gras and Jazzfest, which ended at 7 p.m. nightly and morphed into super jams. "We wanted to do something really cool and creative with the musicians who inspired us. It was done for all the right reasons and never about the money. One of the signature things we did was called the 'Super Jam.' We brought together artists from different bands for one-time only performances."

In 1996, they formed Superfly and started promoting concerts, but quickly discovered the math, filled with too many red-numbered nights, didn't support their passion. After a couple of trips to Europe, they had a new vision: festivals. They met Coran Capshaw through Super Jam. Capshaw's Red Light Management handles a roster of 200 artists through 60 managers in eight cities across the U.S. and UK. Some of Red Light's clients include Dave Matthews Band, Luke Bryan, Lady Antebellum, Enrique Iglesias, and Phish, all of whom Capshaw is actively involved in managing. He bought into Superfly's festival plan, funding a major portion. He also put Superfly together with Asley Capps of AC Entertainment. Capps had been promoting shows in the Southeast since the '70s.

Superfly looked at a 700-acre site their security director recommended in Manchester, Tennessee, where a festival called Itchycoo had failed. "We literally went up, knocked on the owner's door, and told him what we wanted to do. He was willing to take another shot," says Goodstone.

Things happened quickly and tickets for the festival, dubbed Bonnaroo, went on sale. "We're all standing around a computer for the on-sale. The first ticket, a $100 festival pass, sells and we all start cheering. But tickets keep selling. There was this powerful energy online. This message board was like: 'Did you hear about this? All these bands coming together. Is it real? Is it even possible?' We'd hoped to do 30,000 people.

We sold 70,000 tickets in two and a half weeks with no advertising, all word of mouth." The largest show the foursome had done previously was a 3,000-capacity theater act.

"We think of ourselves as brand builders," says Rich Goodstone. "We're building communities around shared passions. We focus on the artistic aspects. Music is the backdrop, but if people come to the event, there's this sense of discovery for everything else that's part of it. It's about people coming together and sharing a moment in time. We provide the canvas and the paint, but they create their own portraits. Bonnaroo is a commitment. If you want to go to Bonnaroo, you take off on Tuesday, you arrive on Wednesday, you leave on Monday."

Bonnaroo is now a four-day immersive experience averaging 90,000 fans a night, celebrating the best in live-music entertainment from timeless legends to emerging artists in rock, hip hop, electronic, jazz, and Americana. Since 2002, Bonnaroo has been a staple of the American music-festival scene, bringing together hundreds of thousands of attendees in a one-of-a-kind camping environment, to experience more than 125 artists and 20 comedians perform across 12 stages. It's the only large-scale festival in the country that operates around the clock and features a variety of curated experiences, including a 24-hour cinema, comedy club, beer festival, theater performers, and more.

Over the years Bonnaroo has featured Trey Anastasia with an orchestra, the Flaming Lips, Neil Young & Crazy Horse, My Morning Jacket, Radiohead, John Paul Jones, Ben Harper and Questlove playing in a Super Jam, Stevie Wonder going right into Jay Z, and Paul McCartney.

One of the first events I proposed as president of Las Vegas Events in 2001 was producing The Rolling Stones' 40th anniversary tour right on the Strip. The plan was to close about two miles of Las Vegas Blvd. South from Russell Road to Flamingo Road and offer the show for free. Though the plan started to gain traction, an executive at a major hotel property objected, questioning why a public-supported organization like Las Vegas Events would spend taxpayer dollars and compete with hotels. He was right. From then on, LVE didn't pursue events that compete with live-music tours on the Strip. It wasn't until 2005 that I figured a way around my music ban.

For three years, I'd been following Bonnaroo in hopes of finding a way to develop a festival. The acts Bonnaroo was booking weren't playing Vegas, so LVE wouldn't compete with the hotel-casinos. I got a green light to develop a festival. An ideal site would be something on or close to the Strip, but then, there was no site to accommodate what we had in mind.

In 2004, Daren Libonati and I made the trip to Bonnaroo, which is held an hour from Nashville. When we arrived, the site was drying out from a stormy opening day. We drove a mile on a narrow muddy road through woodsy terrain before the massive festival and camping grounds appeared.

We met the partners, but spent the most time with Rich Goodstone. They were intrigued about creating a festival in Las Vegas. We loved everything about the vibe at Bonnaroo, but we had four requests to differentiate our festival: We wanted it to take place over Halloween; we didn't want camping; we wanted them to create an after-festival lineup in hotel venues; and the festival needed a cooler name than Bonnaroo.

Until 2005, Las Vegas hadn't hosted a major music festival. On October 29-30, Superfly and AC Entertainment launched Vegoose at the same site the Grateful Dead made famous 10 years earlier—Sam Boyd Stadium. The festival occupied 20 acres of grass as well as 40,000 seats in the venue and featured costume contests, a wedding chapel, impersonators, and a giant pumpkin display. Upwards of 80% of the fans came from out of town. The music lineup included 30 bands, including Dave Mathews, Widespread Panic, Arcade Fire, String Cheese Incident, the Killers, Jack Johnson, and Beck.

This was a creative crowd, wearing Madam Frankenstein, Ghostbusters, and stilts, among many other Halloween costumes. The bands got into it too. Moe band members were decked out as a priest, a Red Sox player, and Elvis with angel wings. Guitarist Buckethead donned a KFC bucket on his head. "Everything is more fun in a costume. The fans fed off the energy of Halloween," says Goodstone.

That first year, Vegoose at Night, the after-shows in hotel venues, was a smashing success, selling out 10 different shows. "Vegas at Night was awesome," recalls Goodstone. "Taking over the night shows, we could do a little of everything. The hotels let us control the rooms. There was no ego involved. They just wanted to be a part of it."

Vegoose's first two-day festival sold close to 80,000 tickets, but only 15% of those were local. Superfly and AC Entertainment's first-year festival was profitable.

A major goal for year two was to increase the number of locals. The 2006 lineup had 30 bands, including Tom Petty, Phil Lesh and Trey Anastasio, Widespread Panic, the Killers, the Black Crowes, and the Roots.

Again, there were 10 Vegas at Night shows, including Dave Mathews with Tim Reynolds at MGM, Damian Marley at The Joint, Trey Anastasio with Robert Reynolds & the Family Band at Orleans, and Maceo Parker at House of Blues, with a surprise guest, Prince.

"We were never able to book Prince at one of our festivals, but in Vegas he just popped in, went on stage, played a solo, threw his guitar into the crowd, and left," says Goodstone.

However, Superfly didn't book the level of talent from the first year and attendance fell by 30%. "Every year, certain artists are touring," says Goodstone. "Some are out of the country when you're trying to book them. The second year certainly wasn't easy. When we finished, we felt like we had a good lineup. It just didn't resonate."

In 2007, Vegoose returned with an eclectic and diverse lineup, including Rage Against the Machine, Daft Punk, Iggy and the Stooges, Muse, the Shins, Cypress Hill, and Public Enemy. While attendance in 2007 increased from 2006, Superfly couldn't get the traction it needed, especially from locals, and there was no year four.

Vegoose closing was one of my biggest disappointments at Las Vegas Events. I thought we'd turned a corner on another type of event. It took four years before Las Vegas saw another music festival, but that festival paved the way for six more.

Electric Daisy Carnival (EDC)

It's impossible to understand how Pasquale Rotella balances the management of Insomniac Events with his bigger priority, family. Rotella heads a worldwide network of 12 music festivals, major club nights, a record label, a partnership with Live Nation, and 140 employees. Just as impressive, he does it with a hands-on approach. One time, Rotella and I were driving in Las Vegas and I complimented him on one of his outdoor billboards. I asked him who designed it. He said, "I did."

He beams about his family—his wife, model Holly Madison, and two children, Rainbow and Forest.

Las Vegas has Steve Wynn, Silicon Valley had Steve Jobs, and festivals have Pasquale Rotella. He has no peer. His festivals, especially EDC, are the most unique sensory experiences in the world. Sin City's Electric Daisy Carnival debuted in 2011, the first local festival since Vegoose in 2007.

When Rotella was 12, he began to absorb the culture around him, which became a big influence on his events. "My dad was extremely poor. During World War II, he lived above a stable in Italy with no roof over his head. He became proficient at stealing, all endorsed by his family. They depended on it. When he came home, he was praised by his mother and grandmother for bringing bread or a piece of food or whatever he could get his hands on."

Rotella's grandmother put his father into the hands of the Church when he was nine, bound for the U.S. When he made it here, he was placed in Boy's Town in Omaha, where he stayed until he came of age.

"My dad was very into Elvis. He wanted to be an actor. He loaded up the car in Omaha and headed to L.A.

"While I was growing up, my mom sang Italian songs, almost anything Pavarotti." Rotella's mother got a job sewing, but his father continued doing what he learned in Italy—thievery. He went to prison for five years. The rest of the family moved to a hostel in Venice Beach. That's when his journey into electronic dance music (EDM) began.

"The first music I got into was on the Venice Boardwalk," recalls Rotella. "I started going to Venice Beach when I was eight and hip hop was getting big. But it wasn't the hip hop you hear today. It was more like electric boogaloo and break dancing—Herbie Hancock, Grand Master Flash, or Talking Heads."

He learned to break dance, making money on the Boardwalk at a time when Venice Beach was crazy, with a mix of artists, gangsters, foreigners, misfits, and homeless.

"I loved Venice Beach. I ran around there as a little kid with no supervision. That's how it was in Italy when my parents grew up."

He got into skateboarding, surfing, and graffiti. One night, he was dragged by friends to his first underground party. "I walked in and my mind was blown."

In London in the late '50s, the term "rave" was used to describe the wild bohemian parties in Soho. Later, the word was adopted by the burgeoning mod youth culture to describe any wild party. Gregarious party animals were described as "ravers." Steve Marriott of Small Faces and Keith Moon of The Who were self-described ravers.

With the onslaught of British pop and the hippie era of the '60s, raves went dormant. In the mid- to late '80s, a wave of psychedelic and electronic music emerged in Chicago—acid house-music parties.

After Chicago, acid-house artists began experiencing overseas success, particularly reemerging in the UK, with clubs, warehouses, and free parties. Activities were related to the loose atmosphere of Ibiza, a Mediterranean island off the coast of Spain, frequented by British, Italian, Greek, Irish, German, and stray American youth on vacation, who held raves and dance parties.

In the late '80s, L.A. raves cost $15-$20, were held in remote locations, and were attended by as few as 500 or many as 5,000. Advertising was word of mouth; the only way of knowing when and where raves were being held depended on handouts and automated messages. The crowd was a little older. Rotella was the "kid." "I got patted on the head. I remember someone saying, 'Hey, kid, shouldn't you be home by now?'"

But the raves were shady. "They were getting busted," says Rotella. "The promoters didn't care about the crowds. They were just making money. They had a place, sold the tickets. You drove all the way out there and ... no party. By 1992, they were gone."

But Rotella defends the concept of a rave. "'Rave' isn't a bad word. It's been beaten up by the media. It has a stigma of an unorganized illegal drug party. That's not what I do, of course. But the spirit of rave is at my shows. I come from the rave scene."

Rotella's first rave didn't go very well, but he just kept doing them. "I was doing one every week, charging five bucks. I paid my people from the door."

In 1995, he gave up the weekly raves for an annual event, Nocturnal Wonderland. The first one, in east L.A., drew 4,000 people. In 1997 and '98, he sold out the first two 5,000-capacity Electric Daisy Carnivals at the Toronto Tour Auditorium. He didn't spend a lot of time coming up with the name "Electric Daisy Carnival": "I liked the way it sounded and wanted to have carnival rides. Daisies are very '60s to me and electricity, as nature, meets technology."

In 1999, EDC moved to Lake Dolores Waterpark in Newberry Springs, California. The 1999 event featured four stages by genre—trance/techno, house/breaks, drum 'n' bass/jungle, and hardcore. In 2000, Rotella moved EDC to the World Ag Expo in Tulare, California, adding another stage and booking bigger DJs like DJ Dan, BT, Freestylers, Christopher Lawrence, Bad Boy Bill, and Dieselboy. But the leftover stigma from past raves returned. "The culture was the government saying that these were terrible events," says Rotella. In 2001, the rave again moved, to Hansen Dam in Lake View Terrace, where it drew 30,000, featuring six stages complete with circus-style names.

The downsizing trend continued in 2003 with EDC's only event held in San Bernardino at the NOS Events Center. There were just four stages.

In 2006, EDC was held in L.A. at the Queen Mary Events Park in Long Beach; the lineup emphasized the time's more popular genres, trance and drum 'n' bass.

EDC 2007 was the first year at the L.A. Coliseum, where 75,000 attended to see Paul Oakenfold, Deep Dish, Kaskade, Stanton Warriors, and Pendulum headline five separate stages. The expansion continued in 2009, going to Friday and Saturday. The two-day event featured music of all genres and drew in its largest crowds, reaching 55,000 on Friday and almost 100,000 on Saturday.

The last year of EDC in L.A. was 2010, drawing 160,000. As day turned to night and Will.I.Am took the stage, the stadium floor reached capacity and was closed off to fans. On hearing the news, festies began rushing the stairwells and fences surrounding the Kinetic Field floor, causing mass chaos. After more than 60 arrests, 200 medical emergencies, the death of a 15-year-old girl who overdosed on Ecstasy, and a small scandal involving a Coliseum employee, the Coliseum would not allow the event to return.

Rotella made every effort to stay in L.A., but as time became critical, he turned east to Vegas. By then, EDM was going mainstream. The whole scene was exploding. Rotella had grown EDC from small warehouse raves to an event closing in on 200,000 fans. From lessons at the L.A. Coliseum, one site in Las Vegas stood out from the rest.

In 1996, a group of investors built the Las Vegas Motor Speedway. The 1,000-acre track hosts a NASCAR race with a second scheduled to begin in 2018, two NHRA (Drag Racing) Nationals, and a NASCAR Truck Series. Today, its capacity is 116,000, but more important, it's 10 miles north of the Las Vegas Strip and has a 100-acre infield.

Rotella was a little surprised by his welcome in Sin City. Mayor Oscar Goodman, he says, was really supportive. "When he announced his approval of EDC, he had a martini glass in his hand. That was different." Police, who had a lot of experience with big-time special events, also openly welcomed EDC. All Las Vegas' other advantages came into play, and it already had a burgeoning EDM club scene.

But there was one glaring issue. Keeping the event in June meant 100-plus-degree temperatures. Again, advantage Las Vegas: The 24-hour clock and the Speedway's remote location were a perfect combination to hold the festival at night—opening at 6 p.m., with the last act ending at 5 a.m.

The cost to produce EDC in 2016 was $50 million and included 200 DJs. It's the biggest EDC Insomniac Events, Rotella's company, produces. Others in New York, Orlando, and Mexico cost between $5 million and $7 million. Rotella amortizes the cost of the Vegas event over Insomniac's 12 other large-scale music festivals with his partner, Live Nation.

What sets Rotella apart from other producers is his priority of the experience over profits. "I don't come from money. I don't need money to be happy. I understand that there's a business side and it all has to make sense financially, but I'm a fan at heart and I love doing what I do."

Jake Berry is EDC's production manager. His iconic career includes some of the world's biggest tours, including Rolling Stones, Madonna, and U2. "I would say that we're the most expensive festival, with the most advanced production, in the world," says Berry. "Just to build the stages, we use 500 local stagehands. By the time you add security, crowd management, VIP staff, and parking, the total crew is close to 4,000."

It's so big that even the biggest DJs feel dwarfed by it. Probably more than any festival, the performers are secondary to the show. "EDC is a bigger brand than any fucking DJ who's ever played it," says Joel Zimmerman, a dance artist known as Deadmau5. "Kinda sets the tone for where your place is there."

Says DJ Joshua Steele, a.k.a. Flux Pavilion, "It's like a platform where they set up the universe. Music can just exist and be whatever it is, and people can just exist and be whoever they want to be."

Planning for EDC is year-round, but the action at the Speedway begins three weeks before the gates open. Pre-production crews remove and alter sections of the Speedway to begin the transformation; the site-ops team uses lifts to supplant the massive 10,000-pound concrete race-track barriers, which are used as ballasts for the stages. By day four, generators and portable communications are installed and the eight stage locations marked.

The pace dramatically increases; site ops goes to two shifts, 80 staff strong. With one week to go, 1,000 people are working.

The EDC experience begins with either a car, taxi, or bus trip. Considering the 140,000 that attend nightly, traffic can be confounding. There are only two main arteries from the city into the Speedway. At least 50,000 fans take buses that reduce the wait time up to two hours, thanks to a secret passage through nearby Nellis Air Force Base. Those in cars don't have your typical traffic temperament—groovin' on the deep EDM bass emanating from all the cars. The ravers make use of every minute to party and meet new friends.

Clearing security is fluid, then you get that first mind-blowing view of 100 acres of electricity. It's like stepping into another world.

Once you hit the infield, you're immersed in what's called Cosmic Meadow; the stage is fully loaded with eye-popping video and graphics. Walking the perimeter, you first encounter the Wedding Chapel, where licensed couples, including same-sex, can partake in a long Las Vegas tradition.

The NeonGARDEN stage boasts a 50-foot-high canvas ceiling and a giant disco ball.

Ground Controllers circulate through the crowd, decked out in purple shirts and fanny packs, carrying red-light sabers and with angel wings printed on their backs. They rove in packs of three, holding radios and checking for anyone getting lost in the cracks—including passing out in the porta-potties.

You weave in and out of 10-foot-high neon mushrooms, neon hula hoopers, sparkling trees, and an eight-clown team, three on stilts, all clad in wildly colored afro wigs and outfits. Longtime EDC clown boss, EZ, and her posse have clowned every EDC on the map since 2008, doing hilarious and silly things. "One time we all dog-piled this kid. I was near the bottom, so I was close to him. He started crying with joy, literally, and said, 'It's my birthday and this is the best thing that's ever happened to me.'"

In all, two dozen groups of performers work the festival from dusk 'til dawn. Throughout the night, 14 whimsical art cars weave in and out of the crowd. Around midnight, EDC collects all the performers for a parade through the festival, highlighted by a 25-foot-tall fire-throwing octopus and a 50-foot ship.

At Carnival Square, festies congregate to charge phones, hook up to free wifi, cool down under four misters, take pictures with performers, and watch live streaming of EDC.

The next stage, Circuit Grounds, used to be easily identifiable, with its domed aluminum canopy 100 feet above the crowd. But in 2016, Rotella changed things up with a 360-degree design and a structure three times larger. Wired with only the best in progressive house, big-room, and trance, Insomniac went all-in with an effusively encompassing visual experience.

Indeed, you have to look real hard to find any place that Rotella has skimped or cut a corner. The rides aren't one of them. The full-size attractions include three Ferris wheels, a gondola, bumper cars, the Super-Shot Drop Tower, and a chair swing. Around midnight, Rotella throws in a six-minute Fireworks by Grucci display that rivals Las Vegas' New Year's Eve show.

Phil Grucci describes the nightly show. "We design the performance to match the colorful high-energy dynamics of EDC, custom flower-shaped shells and other brightly colored effects—lime, lemon, aqua, magenta and lots of gold and white glitter—to match the electric energy. It's totally different than the rooftop production on New Year's Eve, as we have greater distances and a ground-based display that's much more forgiving than rubberized rooftops like the Venetian and Aria. There are more aerial shells, comets, and mines on New Year's Eve, but the shell size at

EDC is larger on average."

Basspod is a triangular mecca for low-end enthusiasts, where you're surrounded by crisscrossed streams of fire, light, and serious pyrotechnics, with water cannons balancing the elements.

Another stage, Wasteland, features a post-apocalyptic San Francisco with an immense crab destroying the Golden Gate Bridge, ships and shipping containers strewn everywhere.

In 2016 to celebrate EDC's 20-year anniversary, Rotella remade several major sets, including Kinetic Field, where he used 700 tons of scenery that includes a 90-foot-high 40-ton tree. The stage is 480 feet wide and 100 feet tall, making it the largest stage in North America; it also features custom fountains, 26 lasers, 33 flame torches, and 1,400 light features. The $3 million of scenery, sound, lights, water effects, and pyro are perfectly choreographed with each DJ, making EDC's 72 hours the most sensory stimulating musical experience in the world.

In addition to the experience at the Speedway, EDC has a full menu of official events at hotels and an industry conference, EDMBiz. This is truly an event that goes 24/7!

EDC is about peace, love, unity, and respect, preached not just at Rotella's festivals, but year-round via Insomniac's social media. Rotella himself has an unparalleled connection with his fans. Most festies don't know who produces the festival they attend. Not only is Insomniac synonymous with raves and EDM experiences, Rotella has as many friends on Facebook (500,000) as follow his festivals. He remains as committed to the culture as he is to the experience. "Because I'm a fan of the culture, I was on the dance floor and remember how much of an impression those little details impacted my life," he says. "I was snapped into the moment and I'm all about getting people into the moment. When you can live in the moment, not thinking about yesterday or tomorrow, that's happiness."

The magic of EDC is Rotella's passion for the fan experience, how he makes 140,000 fans feel like a tight-knit family and how his detailed design of your experience affects your life. "We're always pushing," says Rotella. "It's never good enough. I'll never be done. I won't accomplish in 20 years what I need to accomplish with the festivals."

Life is Beautiful

After Rehan Choudhry left his job as entertainment director at the Cosmopolitan, he was out of work. But he had an idea to create a festival. Not just any festival, but a festival that would make a difference.

"I wanted to create a festival that had a purpose," he explains. "There are two iconic festivals in my mind, Woodstock and Martin Luther King, Jr.'s 'I Have a Dream' speech. People think of festivals as just music, bands, and a field, but that speech was as much of a festival as any. Both events were representative of what was happening culturally and politically in the United States and, to a degree, globally.

"Festivals in this country and globally are creating bigger experiences that give people the opportunity to party their asses off. But most people walk out of festivals like Lollapalooza or Coachella thinking, 'I might've had a good time. I don't remember. I blacked out halfway through it.' Festivals are supposed to be points where people of common interests and perspectives come together to make a difference. I'm not suggesting you're not supposed to drink and have a good time, but you're supposed to walk out of it feeling like, 'Sure, I'm carrying something with me into the rest of my life, but I also contributed my perspective on something.'"

His idea was to create a festival for people dealing with social issues: coming out, addiction, finding a career or love, even just a fear of failure. The problem is they often don't have access to people going through the same things. He wanted to create a platform that empowered people to share their stories of resilience with people who needed to find out that their own story lines can lead to a good ending.

Choudhry knew a thing or two about food and wine festivals, but visited others, like Outside Lands in San Francisco and Coachella. "Sometimes the best things you can learn from another event is that they aren't all that! I got there and knew for a fact that it wasn't a foodie festival, because I know the chefs; I know the people who go to food and wine festivals. Coachella claims it's an arts festival, but they do six statues and a couple paintings. I know artists and art enthusiasts. They weren't there."

Choudhry had never met Tony Hseih (pronounced "Shay"). Hseih made his first $265 million selling LinkExchange to Microsoft in 1998. He spent the next couple of years investing in startups. He was down to his final company, Zappos, when he decided it was time to get back into the big game. In 2000, when Hsieh joined Zappos as CEO, it was generating $1.6 million in revenues. In 2009, revenues reached $1 billion.

In 2009, Hsieh moved Zappos' corporate headquarters from Henderson, Nevada, to downtown Las Vegas, purchasing and renovating the old vacant City Hall. Since making downtown home, Hsieh has committed to a major redevelopment and revitalization in old Las Vegas, investing close to $350 million.

When Choudhry pitched his idea, he wanted it to be held only one place. Downtown. Hseih funded LIB.

Choudhry's vision for the Life Is Beautiful Festival was to create four focal points: music, food, art, and learning. "LIB is an event that speaks to people at their passion points. The 15-year-old hardcore music fan isn't dissimilar from the 45-year-old hardcore foodie. They have equivalent passions. Now if you put them together in an environment that makes sense, that's when cool stuff starts happening."

In year one, 2013, LIB introduced culinary demonstrations, tastings, dinners, and cooking lessons with 35 celebrity chefs. The speaker series rivaled TED Talks. Monica Lewinsky appeared and spoke about being bullied as a kid; kids getting bullied at school now had a unique perspective. The linguist for "Game of Thrones," a hyper-nerd who loves languages, did a presentation; his career made languages cool and relevant. Choudhry explains, "It doesn't matter what you're passionate about, all roads can lead to this sense of popular, exciting, cutting-edge work."

The art piece also took shape. "For art, we eliminated the red velvet rope, so you could touch, feel, be a part of, and meet the people that were part of it," says Choudhry. "The art work led up to the week of the festival, so for the entire week before, anyone who wanted to walk downtown could see the art installations being created. At LIB, three days before the festival, you could walk around and meet D'Face, one of the most famous street artists on the planet, right there painting."

Another Planet, a partnership between two of Bill Graham's disciples who weren't absorbed by SFX or Clear Channel, books the festival's music stages. The first-year headliners were the Killers, Kings of Leon, and Passion Pit. 21 Pilots was on a side stage and no one knew who they were.

Most festivals need three to four years to gain traction and break even. LIB was no exception. While it was critically acclaimed and drew 40% more locals than Vegoose, it lost an estimated $10 million its first year.

Hseih was committed to a second year, but was looking for a solution for the heavy loss. He invited Justin Weiniger to a "co-working" exercise in Hawaii with the Zappos team. Weiniger proposed several ideas to boost attendance and later, Hseih asked him to run LIB. Initially, Weiniger demurred. But his company, Wendoh Media, did a lot of promotion.

In 2003, Justin Weiniger walked onto UNLV's football team. He parlayed a couple of stunt-man gigs into college tuition and started working crowd management for We Serve. In 2005, he created a business distributing flyers for Las Vegas nightclubs before he hooked up with a printer that had state-of-the-art machinery, but no clients.

"George Clooney is dating Britney Spears," Weiniger recalls. "A friend calls and says, 'I need a flyer tomorrow. It's Britney's birthday and George will pay anything to get it done.' Full Color Printing did the deed and within a week, I was doing all my printing there." In another month, he cut a lease deal with the owner to take over the print shop.

He and his partner, Ryan Dougherty, cornered the market on night-club-flyer distribution. "When the Hard Rock was being built, we did $2 million of business in a month," says Weiniger. Considering the volume they were printing and distributing for hotels, the flyers were becoming inefficient. The culmination of the nightclub-promotion business launched Las Vegas' *Seven* magazine and Wendoh Media. *Seven* became much more than a glorified flyer, focusing on UNLV, community, live music, and downtown.

A chance encounter at a Phish concert with Red Light Management's Jason Weinstock led to a deal to heavily promote the Vegoose Festival in *Seven*. They also started doing weekend festivals at the Palms and Hard Rock. But they were intrigued with what was going on downtown.

"When we heard of everything going on downtown, we wanted to get involved—not to get a part of Tony Hseih's investment, but to make our own." Weiniger opened a restaurant and bar, Commonwealth, with partners, Pasquale Rotella among them.

Justin Weiniger thoroughly evaluated LIB II. Although the festival went to three nights and attendance grew to 130,000, nearly 50,000 more than year one, there was still a big loss. He spent the next three months developing a plan.

"Tony Hseih wasn't investing in LIB to make money. The core value was how to do something special for downtown that helped create conversation everywhere."

In another brainstorm session, there were more questions. What's the long-term vision? Why do we do this? Why do you go to this festival? What's the plan to support it? The answer. Move forward.

LIB launched a new logo, changed the dates to September when hotel occupancy is lower and fans get better room rates, and invested more in the acts—Mumford and Sons, J. Cole with support from G-Easy, Empire of the Sun, and the Lumineers. Overall, LIB III drew 146,000, which helped cut its losses, but hadn't turned the corner yet.

Weiniger looks ahead. "These days, there's not a single brand, let alone a festival, that will survive with even the slightest hint of inauthenticity. The festivals left standing, that continue to grow, are authentic, transparent with messages and purpose. What I love about our festival, and what continues to grow our festival, is the way people from each of our pillars—street art, culinary, music, and the inspiration series—and most importantly the extended Life is Beautiful community of fans are equally inspired by one another. We do this because we're passionate about each of its components and the opportunity, the platform, to inspire and impact."

Rock In Rio

In 1980, when Roberto Medina convinced Frank Sinatra to come to Brazil, little did the crooner know that it would be the biggest concert—140,000—he ever performed.

Five years later, Medina produced the first Rock in Rio Festival in his home city. Rock in Rio has been hosted five times in Brazil and nine times in Spain and Portugal and has been hugely successful. Bruce Springsteen, Guns N' Roses, Prince, Metallica, and Beyoncé, among a list of other major headliners, have drawn more than seven million fans. Unfortunately for Medina and his partners, the results were not the same in Las Vegas.

The initial plan was to bring Rock in Rio USA to the Strip in alternating years. At an estimated cost of $75 million, Medina and SFX partnered with MGM Resorts, Cirque du Soleil, and investor Ronald W. Burkle to design and construct the festival site on a 35-acre vacant lot on the southwest corner of Sahara and Las Vegas Boulevard across from SLS. They put in parking lots, power, water and utilities, three permanent restrooms, 750,000 square feet of field turf, and 10 VIP suites. Rock in Rio also built 60 houses into the western side of the parcel themed for the U.S., England, and Brazil.

Rock in Rio featured six stages, a Ferris wheel, and a zip line a couple hundred feet in front of the main stage stretching across the crowd 40 feet below.

The festival took place over two weekends, May 8-9 and 15-16, 2015. The first weekend featured rock acts Metallica, No Doubt, Linkin Park, and Rise Against. The second, the pop weekend, hosted Taylor Swift, Ed Sheeran, Bruno Mars, and Sam Smith.

Rock in Rio's festival plan was dramatically different than U.S. music festivals, which spend little on traditional TV or print advertising. RIR announced its festival in Times Square, with a surprise performance from past Rock in Rio artists John Mayer and Sepultura. A media blitz, including a commercial starring Donald Sutherland and campaigns with Yahoo and Clear Channel, cost a reported $15 million.

In Rio, Madrid, and Lisbon, to support the large media campaign, Medina secured sponsorships, more comparable to U.S. professional sports teams than festivals. Sponsorship revenues for RIR international events average 51% of the total, more than triple that of major U.S. festivals.

Rock in Rio's success was dependent on two revenue sources, sponsorships and ticket sales. Though a reported 100,000 tickets were sold over the two weekends, sponsorships fell extremely short.

The shortfalls of the first year can be attributed to several drawbacks, which might or might not be correctable. While the brand was well-established internationally, it had no history in the U.S. Expenses were massive—$25 million alone for infrastructure. VIP tents were too far from the main stage. Rock in Rio also competed for both fans and bands with Coachella, which took place only a few weeks earlier in April.

Rock in Rio had the biggest headliners of any other Las Vegas music festival. A successful return would mean adjusting the media budget and plan, expectations on sponsorship, and scale of production. Las Vegas benefited from one of the most iconic festivals in the world, but will there be a Rock in Rio II? Stay tuned.

Route 91 Harvest Festival

In 2013 before developing the Rock in Rio site, MGM built Las Vegas Village on a 15-acre parking lot across from Luxor on the south Strip. The Village has a stage and 12,000 square feet of field turf in front of it; on each side stage are eight triple-decker VIP suites seating 125. It annually hosts a one-day outdoor spinoff of iHeart's music festival held at T-Mobile Arena, plus some beer and wine festivals. But the site's major event is Route 91 Harvest Country Music Festival, named for the original US highway that ran between Las Vegas and Los Angeles. It launched on October 3-5, 2014, featuring Jason Aldean, Miranda Lambert, Blake Shelton, Dierks Bentley, and another 35 other country acts.

Chris Baldizan is the senior vice president of entertainment at MGM Resorts and responsible for developing festivals. Brian O'Connell runs a division of the entertainment production and booking company Live Nation that stages country music concerts. O'Connell pitched Baldizan on staging shows in the parking lot.

O'Connell has been producing 12-14 country tours annually for more than a decade and has launched six country-music festivals in the past four years. Like Bill Graham and Pasquale Rotella, he's obsessed with his fans' experience, to the extent that Live Nation offices copy him on every email that has to do with his acts. That often amounts to 3,000-4,000 a day and he addresses every one of them, if only forwarding to someone else to answer. "Not only do I pay attention to the email, I also go on the Facebook page and answer questions, so the fans know that it's not a nameless, faceless, one-sided mirror with nobody on the other side."

O'Connell also created the Megaticket for Live Nation amphitheaters. This "season pass" allows fans to purchase the same seat to every country show that comes to a Live Nation amphitheater. Live Nation's 34 amphitheaters sell about 1.5 million Megatickets annually to country shows.

"You try to curate the festival in such a way that it has variety. You look at the playing field and say, 'Here are all the artists that are eligible. Let's take out all the artists that played last year, so it's probably too soon to bring them back. What's hot? What's not? What's no one thinking of?'"

O'Connell continues, "For me, that provides the festival atmosphere where you can have some discovery. I really like programming the second stage with bands that no one has heard of, watching them play at four in the afternoon and then boom, a few years later they're headlining."

The festival runs 10 hours a day. There are a lot of cover songs, tanned skin, plaid shirts, boots and hats, and beer. Fans sit in the stands, on the turf, or on portable camping chairs.

In its first year, the festival drew 15,000 a day. Year two, 2015, Route 91 returned with Florida Georgia Line, Tim McGraw, and Keith Urban headlining with another 30 acts. It sold out its capacity of 25,000 per night.

In 2016, Luke Bryan, Toby Keith, and Brad Paisley headlined another sold-out festival.

Live Nation and MGM have managed to raise the price of tickets gradually, insuring continued growth on the Village festival site.

"We've outkicked our coverage," O'Connell says. "When we started Route 91, it was all very fast in developing, in like 100 days. But now, it's very popular, a big success, and that location feels right. It's known as the only spot you can see Route 91, and fans are becoming used to that as a destination."

ACM Party for a Cause

The Academy of Country Awards was first held in 1966, honoring the industry's country-music accomplishments. The awards were first televised in 1972. In 2003, the awards show left Los Angeles and moved to the Mandalay Bay Events Center in Las Vegas. In 2006, the show again relocated, but only across the Strip to MGM Grand Garden.

There are two major country awards shows. The CMA's (Country Music Association) and the ACM's (Academy of Country Music). What distinguishes the two is the development of the fan experience around the awards.

Beginning as Fan Fair, the inaugural event was held on April 12–15, 1972, and drew 5,000 fans to Nashville's Municipal Auditorium. The 2016 CMA Music Festival sold out months in advance with a daily attendance of 88,500 fans, including four-day ticket packages. In all, more than 600 artists and celebrities participated in more than 250 hours of concerts on 11 stages (seven of which were free), plus events, panels, and meet and greets inside Fan Fair X.

Las Vegas hosted the ACM Awards show, but didn't have a festival. In 2012, I flew to Nashville to experience CMA Fan Fest. I came away with a plan I shared with ACM CEO, Bob Romeo. On April 5-6, 2013, ACM launched Party for a Cause at the Orleans Hotel. The outdoor event was headlined by the Band Perry and Dierks Bentley, as well as Brantley Gilbert, Justin Moore, Florida Georgia Line, Lee Brice, Kix Brooks, Hunter Hayes, and the Eli Young Band. ACM integrated sponsors into the festival and a second stage. The awards show was held April 7. The first-year festival drew close to 15,000 fans per day.

The following year on April 4-5, the festival was produced at the newly opened LINQ on the Strip with headliners Rascal Flatts and Keith Urban, as well as Florida Georgia Line, Lee Brice, Brett Elderidge, Justin Moore, Danielle Bradley, and 10 other acts. Attendance per day was just shy of 18,000.

In 2015, the ACM Awards moved to Dallas and AT&T Stadium to celebrate its 50th anniversary. The difference between Las Vegas and Dallas was the capacity of the stadium and the ability to package tickets for the awards show with Party for a Cause. Most of the fans who went to the awards show and festival were from the Dallas area, whereas 95% of those attending in Las Vegas were out of market. Party for a Cause was held April 17-18, 2015, at Globe Life Park in Arlington, Texas, which included multiple stages, interactive experiences, and a country marketplace. The ACM Awards broke the Guinness world record for the highest attendance at an awards show, a total of 70,252 fans.

In 2016, the awards show and Party for a Cause returned to Las Vegas. The festival, held April 1-3, expanded by a day and was held on the 35-acre Las Vegas Festival grounds, developed for Rock in Rio in 2015. ACM pulled out all the stops, headlining Carrie Underwood, Dierks Bentley, and Kenny Chesney, with Stapleton, Martina McBride, Sam Hunt, and another 20 country artists. Of the four festivals ACM produced, 2016 was their best, drawing 54,000 over the three days. The Las Vegas Festival site provided a much better footprint for the caliber of talent and festivities.

In 2017, ACM Party for a Cause created a festival integrated into the pools, theaters, and clubs. The four-day event included an All-Star Guitar pull, very popular in Nashville. Six to seven guitarists and singers formed a simple half-circle and played with one another. In all, 18 separate official ACM events included five ACM Awards after parties, Songwriter Showcases, pool parties, tailgates, and a bash at Mandalay Beach.

Big Blues Bender—Land Cruising

Amir "AJ" Gross was born in Israel and at a year and a half came to America. He grew up in New Jersey, but his parents divorced. He ended up living with his dad in L.A. until he decided living on his own was the best option. At 16, he got his first job at 7-Eleven. "I spent my teenage years on the streets of L.A., where punk was happening and I got into music like U2."

At 20, his mother and youngest brother moved to Las Vegas, so he made the jump too. He started as a dealer at the Golden Nugget and Gold Coast, then moved up to be a floorman at the Mirage. He dealt at the World Series of Poker.

One night, he went to the Sand Dollar Lounge to see a band. Sand Dollar opened in 1976 and has a history almost as turbulent as the Aladdin Theater.

"I hadn't seen live music in ages. It just connected for me," recalls Gross. "I spent the next two weeks going to see the Rough Necks. Rob, the bass player, said to me, 'Hey man, if you help us move our gear, we'll give you three beers and 20 bucks a night.' And that was my first job in the music business."

Gross was done with dealing. He toured with the Rough Necks before taking a job buying talent for the Fremont Street Reggae and Blues bar and doing everything he could to help keep it open. Though it closed, Gross came out of it with contacts and experience.

Between 1996 and 2006, Gross was booking as many as 200 shows a year in Vegas venues large and small. "I'm a blues guy, but I couldn't figure a way to make blues events pencil," says Gross. He was experiencing the same competition as independent promoters across the country. "I couldn't compete. The hotels were giving bands 115% of the door. Crazy deals.

"I was the first promoter to book Papa Roach, when 12 people came to see them. Then they blew up and went straight to The Joint. I didn't even get a call. I was hurt. I called CAA. 'Really? I've been doing these shows to help you grow the band and when they're finally ready, I can't make a dollar.' I became disenfranchised with the business not having my back. Competing with Live Nation, AEG, Golden Voice, hotels, and then, the nail in the coffin, the live-entertainment tax [9% of every ticket]—there had to be a better way to make a living." He wouldn't find it for another five years.

In 2013, Terry O'Halloran, whom Gross had worked for at Fremont Street Reggae, launched Sin City Soul and Blues Revival. The festival featured BB King, the Dirty Tricks, Robert Cray, and Los Lonely Boys. Gross had to step in to "save the event," which was mostly a success, but O'Halloran burned too many bridges to do a second year. Gross picked up the pieces, customizing the concept and rebranding it as the Big Blues Bender. In 2015, he launched the festival at downtown's Plaza with Buddy Guy, Robert Randolph, Bobby Rush, and Walter Trout.

The Big Blues Bender is a "land cruise." Live-music ship cruises have become popular. You can cruise for a week, practically anywhere in the world, and be entertained nightly by a diverse genre of bands. Just some of these are: The KISS Cruise, Ship Rocked with Breaking Benjamin, Papa Roach, and others, Rock Legends Cruise, Smooth Jazz Cruise, Country Cruise. Gross's cruise is on land, but comes with everything you'd get on a ship: an up-close-and-personal experience, but with a hotel as the festival grounds. It's comfortable and unique, and the festival is the focus of the weekend for the hotel. It's also affordable. "When fans are spending 18 hours a day listening to music and drinking, you can't charge them $12-$15 for a drink."

The allure of BBB is the connection that takes place among people who love the same music and the price point. "There's a family feeling," says Gross. "The fans return each year and take ownership in the event. When we started, I was out there hard with social media. Now I've got tons of people telling the stories. They're excited to share and it has become an annual vacation."

In 2016, Gross sold out BBB in advance, with headliners Keb Mo', Beth Hart, Delbert McClinton, and Samantha Fish. He's back at the Plaza in 2017 with headliners David Bromberg, Mavis Staples, Dr. John, and Doyle Bramhall.

Festival passes start at $499 and include access, artist panels, autographs, and late-night jams. More expensive packages come with VIP seats, laminates, and pool cabanas. Ninety-five percent of BBB is from out of state, so the customer probably hits the higher end of the Veganomics scale.

Gross is onto something. He has 30 land-cruise monikers registered—Electric Bender, Big Country Bender, and Jazz Bender among them.

What's Next?

Las Vegas is now a vibrant festival market. But an explosion of festivals to match the creation of new clubs, theaters, and arenas isn't expected. Even with four festival sites, the city can't produce a festival a month. While Route 91 continues to grow, ACM Party for a Cause switched to a format where the acts in town for the awards show will collaborate with one another in theaters and clubs.

One festival in each genre may be what the market will support. Electric Daisy Carnival, Life Is Beautiful, and Route 91 all have solid foundations. A new hard-rock festival, Las Rageous, could fill in that genre. Live Nation is producing the festival with Godsmack and Avenged Sevenfold headlining. The two-day hard-rock fest is being held at the Downtown

Events Center as this book goes to press, Friday and Saturday, April 21-22, 2017.

A festival must evolve a strong brand with opportunities to connect with and build unique communities. Bonnaroo in Tennessee, for example, requires a week-long commitment to camping out. "It's an attitude of 'we're all in this together,'" says Rich Goodstone. "You must persevere at Bonnaroo. You wake up in a tent. It can be hot. It can rain. It's like a runner's high."

Vegas festivals will never, most likely, include camping. It must be a special three- to four-day experience that targets a customer who wants and can afford a room.

In the past 10 years, music festivals have steadily grown, but can they continue to grow?

Goodstone is cautiously optimistic. "I don't think we've reached the tipping point, but I do believe the bar continues to be raised. We must continue to be on the leading edge of culture, of where culture is headed."

For a music festival to be successful, regardless of the genre, it must stand out. It must be an immersive experience integrated into the fabric of what's offered by its location. That's a tall order in Las Vegas—a "festival" 24/7-365 and the Strip its midway.

CHAPTER SEVENTEEN

THE FUTURE OF LIVE MUSIC

In 2020, Clark County is projected to have a population of 2.3 million. By then, close to $4 billion will have been invested in opening T-Mobile Arena, renovating and expanding the Convention Center, and building a new stadium and the first large music-only concert hall.

In 1993, Las Vegas sold less than 200,000 tickets for live music. In 2016? More than three million tickets, a 15-fold increase. And it wasn't until recently that Las Vegas became home to two of the biggest bands in the world (and growing), The Killers and Imagine Dragons. Both have headlined LIB. Both are deeply entrenched in the community. Despite their quick rise to stardom, Imagine Dragons maintain a culture of humility, relatability, and creativity. The Killers second album was titled *Sam's Town*. "It brought so much attention to this town," says Zoe Thrall, the Palms' studio manager. "We weren't known as a music-centric town. We've had our share of other bands who've emerged from here since. It was a big deal for this city."

Hotels are looking for a bigger and bigger piece of the live-music pie. Live Nation and AEG are further aligning with hotels and venues. Madison Square Garden and others want to move into this market. Las Vegas' investment in live music is paying dividends, but to compete for the acts across a broader spectrum, the city has to continue scaling up.

Las Vegas is at the epicenter of entertainment, but a revolution is brewing. No shots will be fired, no one will get hurt, but the access to and promotion of music will explode.

We live in an on-demand world, with technology supporting cheap distribution and data allowing new artists a bigger audience. Streaming is starting to arrive. A mere $10 a month provides access to all music and it's more organized and portable than any record or CD collection could ever be. And with every song that's played, algorithms curate playlists recommending new artists. Right now, Spotify is king of the hill, but the biggest play-ers—Facebook, Amazon, Microsoft, Apple, and Google—will jump into making music even more accessible and affordable. Google alone is re-viewing its business models for Google Play and YouTube to create ser-vices for 1.6 billion Android phones.

Mark Geiger is global head of music for William Morris, a talent agen-cy with 100-plus music agents. Geiger is one of the most respected and influential people in the music industry. Over his 30 years in the busi-ness, he's seen a diverse cycle of live music. For the future, his prognosis is bullish.

"In 2016, William Morris did 35,000 shows. We just launched Lol-lapalooza in Paris. Berlin is off to the races. South America is way up. It's the best it's ever been. Everything in live music is selling."

Geiger continues, "This dramatic growth is fueled by the transition to streaming. In the first six months of 2016, a trillion tracks were streamed. Music is being streamed all over the world, from the Middle East and Africa to India, China, and deep Siberia. We're in a Golden Age of music. The access to music fuels ticket buying. The recording industry will grow 10%, 20%, 30% per year to $100 billion-$200 billion in revenue. The live-music touring industry, now at $26 billion, will probably grow to $40 billion annually over the next few years. It's a bull growth market."

Research conducted by PSA Management projects streaming services to lift industry revenues more than 80% by 2020. Streaming current-ly reaches only 8% of smartphones; it's estimated that the number of phones worldwide will double from 2.5 billion to 5 billion by 2020. Paid subscriptions to streaming services will grow from 450 million to 2.62 billion by the turn of the decade.

Whether it's Top 40 terrestrial radio or Top 40 Spotify playlists, people are still listening to hits. They're the lifeblood of live music. Every gener-ation identifies with music attributable to their formative years. Music will always take people back to moments in their lives; music creates an emotional timeline. But there will always be new music, and soon the introduction to new music will be unlimited, creating pathways to more artists breaking through and making their way onto radios and playlists.

The social aspect will also benefit from the bundling and integration of social-media platforms. "Alexa" of Amazon Echo, the hottest voice-recognition platform, is one of those. Scott Perry, author of *Snapchat 101,* gives an example: "When you hear a band playing on a streaming service, you will be able to say, 'Alexa, buy me two tickets.' Two tickets show up on your phone that can be scanned at the door."

The battle for market share means that Facebook, Snapchat, Instagram, and Twitter will constantly refine the services in which we digest and share information. We've only seen the tip of the iceberg when it comes to understanding and using social media. We're still in the infancy of how people connect to one another and music.

What does this all mean for the live experience? The new model doesn't proportionally reward artists, as the album, CD, and MP3 formats did. To maximize earnings, they must tour and look for unique engagements, such as residencies. More people listening to more music means more concerts and festivals around the world.

Especially in Las Vegas.

In addition to efficiently operating their venues, Las Vegas hotel-casinos can take advantage of new media technology and their enormous databanks to market music to millions. A customer is no longer just a name in a gigantic database. Like Amazon and Spotify, hotels with rich data can better target customers with customized campaigns directly connected to people's interests. In addition, Ticketmaster and AXS ticketing, MGM's M life database, along with the databases of all the casino companies large and small, all provide opportunities to reach customers.

"Vegas is a wonderful place to experience live music," says Jason Gastwirth, senior vice president of marketing and entertainment at Caesars Entertainment. "Entertainment will continue to evolve in this market. We must be innovative and decisive. But when you get it right, the results happen very quickly and in a large scale and that makes this business very exciting."

"We'll continue, as a city, state, and company, to embrace, in a responsible fashion, and grow the market," says Mark Prows, now MGM's senior vice president of entertainment operations. "Las Vegas is the epicenter of entertainment. It's a matter of how quickly we can scale the market so it's a must play."

By 2020, Las Vegas will have 11 live-music theaters and clubs ranging from 1,800 to 17,000 seats. Las Vegas already has five arenas with capacities between 8,000 and 18,000 and four proven festival sites, and a 65,000-seat stadium. More and more venues opening means more competition, which will create more inventory, especially residencies. And it won't just be today's hit-makers. Another generation of artists is dreaming of "playing Vegas" and the audience is getting younger and younger all the time.

Michael Rapino, CEO of Live Nation, addresses this issue. "Who's the next Rolling Stones? Who's the next U2? We see the new Taylor Swifts out of the blue, the Justin Biebers, the Luke Bryans selling out stadiums, the Nicki Minaj, the Rihannas. We've always seen this regeneration of superstars."

In the meantime, however, the business of live music had its best year ever. On February 19, 2017, Michael Rapino reported Live Nation's earnings: "Our three core divisions, concerts, ticketing and advertising, each delivered their strongest results in the history of the company. We believe the live business will continue to have strong growth for years to come as fans drive demand, artists are motivated to tour, and technology drives conversion. Live Nation added 7 million fans in 2016 for a total of over 71 million fans, driving revenue up 20% and more than doubling concerts' [return on investment]."

The ticket-distribution system will have to undergo its own revolution. As it stands today, the system is surreptitious and unfair. Will the industry be willing to jeopardize a multi-billion-dollar revenue stream? Yield-management ticketing systems have worked for the airlines and hotels. Why not for live music?

Another explosion about to take place is immersive theater. Shows that make the audience part of the performance are among the most popular in Las Vegas. It's only a matter of time before they discover how to carve out a live-music niche.

Finally, what about the future of music itself?

Until recently, technology and music were viewed as two separate industries. As they slowly become intertwined, it's clear that there can and will be no separation if either wants to survive. While some still see technology as an enemy that cannibalized album and CD sales, it's actually the music-industry's strongest ally. Neither clinging to the old model by finding ways to increase album sales nor creating the next streaming platform has any long-term potential. The industry must understand exactly what it means to completely embrace technology. To survive in tomorrow's music industry, companies will need to not only work with technology, but become technology companies themselves.

More music. More experiences. More shared realities. Life *is* beautiful.

But don't stop here. Turn the page for the ...

AFTERWORD

I tend to get a bit carried away.

The publishing goal for the first draft was 80,000 words, or 320 pages. I delivered 120,000, on 480 pages. You would have hated that book. The Huntington Press editorial staff skillfully cut the clutter, added some cool stuff (they're big rock fans, too), and put it all in an order that made for a good story. But it's April 26, 2017, and I'm not done. Since it's well past deadline, this is the only way I'm going to sneak in one more concert.

Tonight, I went to see Steely Dan (for about the 12th time—all in different venues). What I love about live music is the opportunity to witness, live and in person, masters of the craft and their commitment to providing a unique show. You get that every time you see Steely Dan—the most sumptuous sound and music experience in live music.

I'm one of those fans who prefer to focus on the show and not the recording. However, tonight I wanted to exemplify my taste in rock 'n' roll for my daughters Nicole and Danielle and my wife Vicki and there seemed to be no better band than Steely Dan and their song "Kid Charlemagne." I sent them the iPhone recorded version, with instructions to either put on good headphones or crank up the home theater system.

In the previous pages, I didn't say anything about the Venetian Theater. I hadn't been there. It's an intimate venue, with 2,000 seats, great sightlines, and fantastic sound. Best of all, for Steely Dan, there were no video screens, automatically making it totally live and perfect.

In the middle of the show, I had a revelation. Vegas offers such an incredible diversity of live music choices and quality venues that I couldn't let the story end here.

In conjunction with the book launch, I've established a *Rock Vegas* Facebook page and Twitter account. However, not everyone is being friend-ed. It isn't about numbers. I have two requirements: you be a fanatic live-music fan and/or an expert in the live-music business. I'm recruit-ing the experts, so if you make a compelling enough case that you're a worthy fan, you're in the loop.

The experience continues ...

ABOUT THE AUTHOR

For nearly 35 years, Pat Christenson has participated in the evolution of live-music events in Las Vegas—more than 500 concerts. From 1983 through 2001, he managed the major arena (Thomas and Mack Center) and stadium (Sam Boyd Stadium) in Las Vegas. Since then, as president of Las Vegas Events, he has been involved in the development of five major music festivals.